# Listen, Here Is a Story

...........................

D1057544

ISSUES OF GLOBALIZATION
Case Studies in Contemporary Anthropology

*Labor and Legality:*
*An Ethnography of a Mexican Immigrant Network*
Ruth Gomberg-Muñoz

*Listen, Here Is a Story:*
*Ethnographic Life Narratives from Aka and Ngandu Women of the*
*Congo Basin*
Bonnie L. Hewlett

*Cuban Color in Tourism and La Lucha:*
*An Ethnography of Racial Meanings*
L. Kaifa Roland

*Our Blood Does Not Agree:*
*An Ethnography of HIV/AIDS Prevention Programs in Botswana*
Rebecca Upton

*Gangsters Without Borders:*
*An Ethnography of a Salvadoran Street Gang*
T. W. Ward

# Listen,
# Here Is a Story

...........................

*Ethnographic Life Narratives
from Aka and Ngandu Women
of the Congo Basin*

## Bonnie L. Hewlett
*Washington State University*

New York    Oxford
OXFORD UNIVERSITY PRESS

*This book is dedicated
to the women of* CENTRAL AFRICAN REPUBLIC *who so
generously shared their lives, and to my husband Barry and
our children. They are all precious to me.*

Oxford University Press, Inc., publishes works that further Oxford University's
objective of excellence in research, scholarship, and education.

Oxford  New York
Auckland  Cape Town  Dar es Salaam  Hong Kong  Karachi
Kuala Lumpur  Madrid  Melbourne  Mexico City  Nairobi
New Delhi  Shanghai  Taipei  Toronto

With offices in
Argentina  Austria  Brazil  Chile  Czech Republic  France  Greece
Guatemala  Hungary  Italy  Japan  Poland  Portugal  Singapore
South Korea  Switzerland  Thailand  Turkey  Ukraine  Vietnam

Copyright © 2013 by Oxford University Press, Inc.

For titles covered by Section 112 of the US Higher Education
Opportunity Act, please visit www.oup.com/us/he for the
latest information about pricing and alternate formats.

Published by Oxford University Press, Inc.
198 Madison Avenue, New York, New York 10016
http://www.oup.com

Oxford is a registered trademark of Oxford University Press

All rights reserved.  No part of this publication may be reproduced,
stored in a retrieval system, or transmitted, in any form or by any means,
electronic, mechanical, photocopying, recording, or otherwise,
without the prior permission of Oxford University Press.

**Library of Congress Cataloging-in-Publication Data**
Hewlett, Bonnie L. (Bonnie Lynn), 1961-
Listen, here is a story : ethnographic life narratives from Aka and Ngandu women of the Congo
Basin / Bonnie Hewlett.
    p. cm.
Includes bibliographical references and index.
ISBN 978-0-19-976423-5 (pbk)
1.  Aka (African people)—Central African Republic.   2.  Ngandu (African people)—
Central African Republic.   3.  Women—Central African Republic.   I.  Title.
DT650.A38H48 2012
305.4096741—dc23                                              2011051374

# CONTENTS

# PREFACE

This book is due in large part to a group of Ngandu women who knocked on my door one hot afternoon and asked me to listen to their stories. Hearing of my work with the Ngandu women, and not wanting to be left out, a group of my Aka women friends told me they too wanted me to "listen to their lives." So I did. The women and I worked side by side in the fields, river, and household, taking care of children, preparing food, washing clothes, fetching water, buying and selling at the market place, both in the village of Nambélé and in Aka camps where we lived together in the forest. I also talked to their husbands, fathers, mothers, friends, and children. The women spoke not only about their lives, but as a way of teaching me what it meant "to be" an Aka or Ngandu woman, they shared folk tales, songs, drawings, dances, and childhood games.

Taken together, this collection forms the foundation of an in-depth portrait of their lives. Their narratives address contemporary issues and perspectives placed within key theoretical literature and debates, challenging critical gaps in our understanding and analysis of women's lives and the limiting generalizations and theoretical assumptions concerning the "universal" ways in which women behave, think, and learn. As too few studies have explored the subjective experience of women from small-scale societies (one of the last ethnographic texts highlighting the voice of hunting-gathering women was Marjorie Shostak's *Nisa: The Life and Words of a !Kung Woman*, written in 1983), in addition to evaluating Western theoretical frameworks, a further purpose is to provide an understanding of the life histories and experiences as recounted by the Aka and Ngandu women themselves. This comparison between the Aka forager women's and Ngandu farming women's inter- and intracultural experiences is important: although they live in similar natural ecologies, have similar mortality and fertility rates, and have frequent social, economic, and religious interactions, they also have very distinct modes of production and social relationships. As a result, Aka-Ngandu comparisons may provide insights into how social structures and relationships influence gender roles, status, perceptions, and experiences of sub-Saharan African women.

At the heart of this book are the voices of the women of the Congo Basin, recounting their lives, past and present. This work spans ten years of fieldwork among the Aka and Ngandu and brings together cross-disciplinary and cross-cultural perspectives on key issues throughout the life course, making use of anthropological and developmental theories to contribute to an integrative analysis and view of the lives of Central African women. The text begins with a general introduction of the women and my first experiences in the field as an anthropologist. Chapter One continues with a general cultural and historical introduction, highlighting the history of Central African Republic and its people. Each additional chapter is divided by themes based upon the women's narratives, and places these data within theoretical debates and literature. I include theory because as much as the women themselves guided this research, different theories as well prompted and directed the questions I asked, helping me to understand better what they were telling me. Chapters conclude with a brief summary, excerpts from my personal field notes and questions to promote reflection of the material.

Comparing Aka and Ngandu women offers two different sources of information about both contemporary and historic life in Central Africa. The interviews with older women from these two communities focus on the impact of economic and political change, and perspectives on gender and familial relationships over the course of their lifetimes. Particularly evident is the great potential that life-story narratives have for understanding the very diverse, and at times similar, experiences of women from two cultures who differentially subsist in a similar ecology. In the conclusion, I examine marginalization at the microlevel of community relationships, the intermediate level, and the macrosocial level of global political-economic systems. The goal is to understand how existing social structures influence the relationships among the participants in the systems, leading to human rights abuses for the Aka and Ngandu women.

Throughout the book I have included field notes from my personal journal, as I wanted to acknowledge that I was never a benign presence in this process. The field notes also guided my research, at times causing me to look again at events, words, or behaviors that were important. Students have often asked me what it's "really like" in the field. My personal journal notes, I hope, help provide a glimpse into what, at least in my experience, fieldwork is like: fascinating, difficult, boring, exacerbating, and wonderful. I have also interwoven folk tales into the text, as this is one method the women used to teach me particular values and beliefs, much as they taught their children, usually at night around the fire. Surely, a full and complete portrayal of these women is no doubt impossible; the primary reason for writing this book is to highlight and give preeminent status to Aka and Ngandu women's life experiences, perceptions, and interpretations. We can continue to learn much about, and from, hunter-gatherer and small-scale cultures. It is these cultures that enrich our understanding of human diversity and potential. At a time when the foraging and subsistence farming lifestyles are being threatened by a variety of influences and cultural changes, it is my hope that the stories of these women will draw attention to the lives and challenges of diverse peoples and thus potentially aid in creating a more equitable world for Aka and Ngandu women.

# ACKNOWLEDGMENTS

Many people have been involved in the birth and life of this book, and the time and research it represents. I am deeply indebted to Janet Beatty, Sherith Pankratz, and Cari Heicklen, the talented editors at Oxford University Press who have been key in guiding me through this process. To the reviewers who provided detailed comments, I extend my appreciation for their careful reading and insight provided:

Kate Centellas, University of Mississippi
Robin M. Hicks, Ball State University
Gina Louise Hunter, Illinois State University
Paul James, Western Washington University
James Stanlaw, Illinois State University
Robert J. Gordon, University of Vermont
Alexander Rodlach, Creighton University
Richard L. Warms, Texas State University–San Marcos

I am forever indebted to the women of Nambélé who so generously shared their stories, friendship, trust, and many long moments of their lives. I want to express my deep gratitude to Edouard I. who kept me well fed and safe, and whose friendship and guidance I highly value and appreciate. I am grateful to Tim Tikouzou and his wife Sylvie, whom I cannot thank enough for their kindnesses through the years. I am highly appreciative of the various research assistants that have worked with me during my trips to the field—in particular, Aubin M. and Priscilla M., whose patience should be rewarded with a medal. Papa J. S. Mongosso for his friendship and help with translations. I am thankful for the laughter (and hard work) Courtney Meehan and I shared when we would meet up in the field.

I wrote much of this in Ethiopia while on a Fulbright scholarship teaching at Hawassa University, and would also like to send a note of gratitude to our dear friend Samuel Jilo, Head of the Behavioral Science Department, for his support, understanding, and friendship. My thanks also to the faculty and students of anthropology and our other good friends in Hawassa, who showed such friendship and graciousness during our time there. My thanks to Judith Brown for her encouraging comments. Robert Moïse offered extensive and useful suggestions. I deeply appreciate his thorough and thoughtful reading. I thank Wendy Belcher for her brilliant title suggestion. Much of Chapter One is based upon the work of Serge Bahuchet; his contribution to anthropology illuminates our understanding of the crucial role history has played in the lives of the people of Central Africa. I am grateful for the positive comments of Jared Diamond, Jerome Lewis, and when this book was just a thought, the encouraging words of Mel Konner. I am indebted to, and in awe of, the life work of my husband, Barry Hewlett, who laid the foundation for my own passion and love for anthropology, research, and the people of Central Africa. His love, support, and encouragement helped make this work possible.

Many heartfelt thanks go to Jessica Bentz, our oldest daughter, who patiently and generously agreed to read through the drafts (even the theory parts!) and without hesitation told me, "I read somewhere a good piece of writing advise you need to learn: kill your little darlings"—although I think it might have been closer to "slaughter the bastards," meaning, get rid of long poetic digressions (which I love and am too often guilty of writing). Her ideas and opinions were extremely insightful and helped me to think more deeply about the issues. I would also like to acknowledge the support of our other children; Forrest, David, Jordan, Allison, Erika, and Lindsey, as well as our grandbabies and sons- and daughters-in-law, all of whom somehow understood and encouraged my desire to go into the field, even as it came at the cost of our time together. Among the many who deserve special acknowledgement are my father Don, who passed away while I was in the field, and my mother Margie. I am grateful for their encouragement and support throughout the years. My continued love and thanks to my family and friends, the most important part of my own life story.

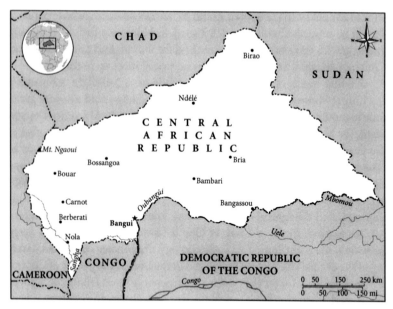

Source: *Central African Republic, at http://www.lib.utexas.edu/maps/cia11/
central_african_republic_sm_2011.gif (accessed December 2011).*

# Women's Lives at the Crossroads

I will tell you of my day. When I wake in the morning I brush my teeth and wash my face. After this, I make a fire and put water on to boil and I wash the faces and brush the teeth of all the children in the house and my grandchildren. I wash the plates, I sweep the house and yard. I take my basket and walk to the field, when I am there I pray to God to take care of me and I begin to take up the manioc. After this I carry the roots to the river to soak and I come back to the field and cut firewood, manioc leaves, and bananas. When I arrive at the house I make a fire and cook gozo. I share this on each plate and give this food to all in the house, the children and grandchildren and we eat. Every night after the meal, when all this work is finished, when everyone is full, I ask them to be quiet. I tell them, "Listen, here is a story that I want to tell." This is the life of me, a woman who lives here in Nambélé. This is the life of women and how the life for women here has been going for many, many years.

—BLONDINE

This story begins one hot afternoon with a knock on my door. Standing in my yard was a group of about eight Ngandu women and Adoxi, my research assistant. "They want to talk to you," she said to me, "They want you to stop talking to the children and start talking to them." The women crowded around her, nodding in agreement. "They want you to hear about their lives. They want to tell you their stories." Not wanting to be left out, when Aka friends of mine heard about my work with the Ngandu women, they too wanted to work with me, to teach me. So I began listening as they told me what it means to be women of the forest and village, women of the Congo Basin.

Deciding to work with these Aka and Ngandu women was an easy choice, primarily because women from both populations came and asked me to. This work also addresses the problem, as I see it, that so much of anthropological research in sub-Saharan Africa focuses systematically and quantitatively on men, women in dyadic partnering with infants and young children, and only infrequently on the women themselves. Where are the individual women? What are their subjective experiences? What do women have to say about their lives? Their life stories, embedded within the larger narrative of the vast African continent itself, tell of the dramatic immediacy of life and death, where each day can unfold in both tragic and joyful ways, of experiences much deeper, harsher, and more delightful than one small book can tell. More than half a century ago Simone de Beauvoir posed the question, "What is a woman?" Although "what is a woman" and "what it means to be a woman" vary across time and place, their lives provide an enriched understanding of womanhood.[1]

The everyday lives of the Aka, known as "pygmies," and their Bantu neighbors, the Ngandu, illustrate how women from diverse cultures within similar ecologies and intertwining histories, encounter and respond to a changing world in unique ways. Women who have carried on with dynamism and creativity, surviving, coping with, and taking advantage of new opportunities, transforming their lives by connecting tradition and modernity, the past and present in distinct and dynamic ways. Globalization, disparate access to education, healthcare, human rights abuses, and sociopolitical power are realities interwoven within the social fabric of their lives. Their narratives capture the strength and resiliency of the Aka and Ngandu women of the Congo Basin as they confront challenging issues within their diverse and shared cultural worlds.

It is from these women, as well as many others, that I learned about "field methods" and what it means to be an "anthropologist." Nali, for example, taught me about the difficulties of speaking of one's culture and the dynamics of power relations. She politely declined each time I ended our interview sessions by asking her, "Do you have any questions you'd like to ask me?" One day I said to her, "Do you want to be the anthropologist today and ask all the questions?" She did, and asked if I had a pen and pad of paper. I handed her a small notebook and pen. Sitting for a moment, she suddenly looked up, frustrated, "But I can't write." As she herself had so often taught me, taking my clumsy fingers in hers and directing me in how properly to do whatever task we were working on, I took her hand in mine and together we wrote her name, *Nali*. Satisfied, she turned to me and began asking questions. For hours. Apparently emboldened by the growing crowd, the questions became very intimate and detailed. What are "European" women really like? "What work do you do when you are far away?" "Do you and your husband walk together in the forest?" "Do you work for your husband and children?" "What do you teach your children?" "How often do you menstruate?" "Do you have pain when you give birth?" "Have any of your children died?" "Do your husbands bring home other wives, and do you fight with them?" Often others would tell her to ask me this or that, things they had apparently been wondering about. (See Figure 0.1.)

By the end of our interview, exhausted, I dragged myself back to my hut and collapsed on my bed of twigs. When I came back the next day, and many days following, at the end of our interviews, she would ask for pen and paper, and armed with more questions, ask another round. Half the time I would be embarrassed by the questions she'd ask—"What do you do at night on the bed with your husband?" "What do your breasts look like?"—and at times laughing at her shocked responses to my answers. Mainly her role as an anthropologist and mine as an informant made me realize how hard this business of being

FIGURE 0.1 | *"What it means to be a woman."*

FIGURE 0.2 | *Ngandu woman preparing to go work in the fields.*

an informant of ones culture really is. It is one thing to live a culture, quite another to speak of it. Additionally, what did this event speak to, in terms of power relations and dynamics? Did it take my handing her a pen and writing her name before she felt she could ask me questions? I'd known her for years. Did this mean nothing, or speak to many things? I realized in a way I had never before that I could not step over, or go around, my position as an educated, healthy, vaccinated, and very foreign white woman. Privilege and power, like something in the way, to be avoided, could in fact never be avoided and were there whether acknowledged or not. Nali, Konga, Therese, Blondine, and many others taught me how to be a better friend, parent, and person and importantly, what it means to be Aka and Ngandu women. (See Figure 0.2.)

On the lighter side, I also learned that you can go days without brushing your teeth or bathing, and wear dirty clothes, and not only do your teeth not rot, hair not fall out, or the earth stop revolving, but nobody cares! I learned that no matter how many chickens you eat, you will never manage to eat the noisy one crowing in the still-dark morning and preventing you from sleeping in. That the forest buzzes like an electrical current, and the animal noises change in sound, tone, and frequency as the day shifts into night, and again when the night eases into day. That goat babies sound like human babies (especially when you desperately miss your own children). And speaking of goats, that their turds look like coffee beans, and when they are mixed together, make for an interesting-tasting morning cup of coffee. That *embacko* (moonshine) is very strong and can make you very sick.

I learned that praying mantis make good pets when you're lonely, and that they like liquor (I had one named Pastis after a French aperitif I am particularly fond of). That ants from the forest form long endless lines, rapidly moving eggs and food underneath the watchful guard of what I call the huge "box head" ants, and that if you blow on them they rear up, waving their razor-sharp mandibles in threat (which hurt, a lot, when they bite). I learned new meanings of the words "Explosive!" and "Projectile!" (as related to drinking Blondine's moonshine); and that sometimes no matter how culturally sensitive you want to be, it's okay to refuse hospitality offered in good faith (as related to drinking moonshine). That sometimes, eating in the dark can be a good thing, especially when what you're eating is staring balefully, unblinkingly, back up at you with glassy round eyes precariously perched on a big whiskered snout. That snakes are icky and need to stay on the ground where they belong. And that the pride and dignity of others in their life and life accomplishments (". . . Twenty years, twenty years!!!! as a taxi driver in the capital [Bangui] and not once, Not Once!!! did I ever hit a chicken!"), no matter how funny, sad, or peculiar they may seem, demand and deserve respect. I am still learning.

## INTO THE FIELD

**(Note from my journal entry as I went, for the first time, to the field.)**

*—On the first leg of my flight to Africa, from west to east coast. What was I thinking, to leave the kids, to come alone? I've been bawling my way across the U.S. Right now my heart just hurts. Saying goodbye to the kids last night was tough. They cried and told me not to go, and L. asked if I'd get fired if I didn't go. They all had such lost and sad looks on their faces, or maybe I imagined that. The kids slept in our bedroom and we all talked, laughed, and bawled. Stayed up most of the night. It might have been a good idea to have waited and come with the other students. Too late now. And what kind of mother leaves her kids to go halfway across the world to Africa? A rotten one, I'm thinking . . . I already miss them a lot and have doubts about this.*

After working for ten years as an RN in a Family Birth Center, I was ready for a change and went back to Washington State University. To fulfill a course requirement, I took an anthropology class. I had no idea what anthropology was, other than "the study of" something. In class, I was absolutely intrigued by how incredibly diverse our world's cultures were. The ethnographies of the people of Africa in particular were so fascinating, so different from anything I had ever known. I read an article about father-infant relations among the Aka, foragers in Central Africa, who lived in small intimate family groups in the rainforest, and I was hooked, thoroughly seduced with the possibility of learning not only about, but *from*, other cultures.

I grew up in Alaska and spent my summers living next to a small village of Yupik people who had taught me about tracking animals, picking ripe tundra berries, and fishing for salmon. They told me stories of people who had whistled at the Northern Lights, calling down the ancestor spirits who took them away forever, stories about little people who lived in the tundra, kidnapping people out at night alone, enslaving the unfortunate victims in their small underground homes. But this was normal to me, a part of my culture, a culture different from the Aka and other people I had read about. A culture transmitted by my parents and peers, speaking of lifeways within a broad social history, symbolic, and integrated into the very fabric of our lives. To this day, whenever I go back for a visit, I am still not brave enough to whistle at the Northern Lights, for as I learned, culture influences our perception and classification of reality. But there is also a strong emotional component to culture.

I reflected on this the first time I was in the field in Africa, sitting in a mud and thatch-roof house eating dinner with my hosts—a dinner, by the way, of what looked like spinach on top of which lay several large, grubbish-looking caterpillars. In my culture, bugs are not classified as a food item, but I was a student of anthropology! And anthropologists are open-minded! I also did not want to offend my hosts. I put a spoonful of the spinach stuff, and a caterpillar, into my mouth as everyone leaned in, waiting to see my reaction. I knew I would have to swallow it whole. *Chewing* a bug was more than I could do, I did not want the innards squishing out in my mouth. I willed it down. I drank glasses of water. I tried to pretend it was yummy! Just like eating a harmless shrimp! Not a caterpillar growing exponentially as it sat there on my tongue. But years of cultural learning—bugs are not food—and my body was not fooled. All ports of entry slammed shut. I couldn't swallow. The caterpillar would *not* go down my throat. Finally, after a few very, very long and awkward moments, I took another big gulp of water, closed my eyes, crossed my fingers and somehow wrangled it down. I think everyone sat back and breathed a sigh of relief. I learned that day that it is not merely that we feel differently, or do things differently, but that we feel strongly about our cultural ideas, beliefs, behaviors, classifications, and worldviews; there is a strong emotional component to culture. (I now can enjoy *smoked*—that is, small, hard, and crunchy—caterpillars.)

Three days into my first time in the field, in the farming village of Nambélé, I woke up to the sounds of furious knocking on the tired door of the red-brick mud home I had rented just the day before. The house was small, with two tiny windows opening from lopsided wooden frames. A rusty tin roof amplified the sound of lizards tap-dancing across it in the heat of the day, and during the frequent downpours, the sound of the torrential rainfall on the tin was deafening. The packed-dirt floor needed daily sweeping as the walls tended to crumble, leaving piles of red dirt and dust everywhere. Mice ran rampant from room to room, and spider webs crisscrossed the ceilings. The home was set off from the main red dirt road running through the village and afforded me a chance to be both observed and an observer of the daily life passing a few feet from my front door: colorfully clad women balancing huge loads on their heads and, often, heavy baskets of manioc or babies strapped to their backs; little bare-bottomed, barefooted toddlers walking hand and hand down the street, their mother urging them on to a relative's care as she left to work in the fields; the evening news delivered (almost daily) via the town crier blowing on his whistle every few feet then hollering the headlines; young boys calling out "Petrol, petrol!" as they sold kerosene for evening lamps; men and women stopping to visit as they made their way to the market, water pump, "coffee house," or fields; random groups of goats and sheep eating, running, *maaa*-ing, and pooping up and down the street, and in the coffee beans laid out to dry on the concrete slab next to my house. In the front yard, a huge old tree offered shade and a home for what seemed to be hundreds of noisy birds, and people often stopped to rest under its huge branches, staring in at me, a foreigner, the village cultural-idiot. I liked this view of village life passing by the little mud red house, my refuge and for a while, my home.

But on this day, I opened a wobbly wooden shutter and found my newly hired research assistant, Sato, urgently whispering, "Stay inside your house all day today." He motioned across the street to where a hundred or so people were gathered in the yard of my tall neighbor, the village mayor. I could see him in his flowing white robe, reserved and dignified, moving amongst the crowd, occasionally stopping to listen to people who would jump up and start shouting, airing their grievances to him. "What's going on?" I whispered back. "He has taken *mbengue* (a poison oracle made of strychnine) and named the sorcerer who is causing so many problems in Nambélé. So now the sorcerer will be taken to the edge of the village and buried," Sato replied, all the while keeping his eyes on the growing crowd. "Buried?" I squeaked. "Yes," Sato said, "Sometime today they will take him and he will be buried alive." I did as I was told and stayed indoors for the rest of the morning. Fortunately, as it turned out, there was to be no burial that day, as the accused man's family had successfully pleaded for his life, and at the last minute, he had been granted a reprieve and hurriedly left. The village however, remained tense, hostility and suspicion hanging in the dense humid air. I gathered a small group to lead me into the forest, and we set out as soon as we could. Like so many before, we fled to the tranquility of the forest.

Setting out from Nambélé, we walked along narrow trails in the cool of the forest, the canopy of ancient trees sheltering us from the harsh sunlight. For hours we carefully picked our way over fallen trees, lines of ants, and swath-cut branches, roots rising like sharp stakes from the forest floor. We crossed several small streams winding through the dense underbrush before arriving at a small camp of Aka foragers. Four small leafy domed huts stood grouped closely together in a circle, doors facing toward the center. Three men came to greet us, their wives pausing for a moment from chopping small bundles of leaves, while children of various ages shyly hid behind them. Sato asked the *kombeti* (a male of the Aka camp, who has somewhat more influence in that he is the one looked to for advice) if we could stay overnight, and while the men chatted, the women and children gathered around me and made room for us all to sit thigh to bare thigh on a nearby log. The Aka men quickly made us beds of poking twigs, (small branches laced together over a frame of larger branches set off the ground), we ate a quick meal, duiker meat, given to us by one of the women, and *koko* leaves (Gnetum species, a spinach-like forest plant). [2] After eating we collapsed on the new beds and fell asleep to the hushed night sounds of the forest.

The next morning as we sat around the campfire eating a breakfast of bananas and coffee, Justin sat down, motioning in his articulate sign language that he had a headache. Deaf and mute from a childhood fever that had destroyed his hearing, he and another deaf boy had created a form of sign language, which nearly everyone in the village could understand. He was actually quite chatty and expressive enough even for me to follow. We struck up a quick and easy friendship, albeit based upon a unique system of exchange. Every evening precisely at 8:00 PM, when darkness had settled over the village, he appeared at my door, pineapple in hand. We silently completed the nightly transaction: a Powerbar for a pineapple. (I worried, unnecessarily as it turned out, that I might not "adapt" well to the local food, so brought over a small supply of Powerbars to hold me over until my gastrointestinal system adjusted.) He came only at night because, I later found out, on the way over to my house, he would stop off in someone's garden and steal the pineapples. But at that time, blissfully ignorant of the source of my purloined pineapples, we enjoyed our barter system. I knew something was up when he knocked on my door in the early morning of the day of my departure into the forest and asked if he could have a job as a porter, helping to carry supplies into the forest. He was after all, as he explained to me, very strong as he had been eating Powerbars. I was glad to have him, and when the rest of our small group arrived, we set off.

Justin ate a small banana then, complaining of a headache, went to lie down. Two hours passed and he rose from sleep, stumbling, falling to the ground where he began rocking back and forth on his knees, silently howling. Within a short time he was lying still on the ground, burning with fever, his huge body working to burn away the disease. He was totally nonresponsive, taking labored breaths as he exhaled and struggled to inhale. Standing next to me was a friend of his, a village farmer as well, singing loudly about the walls of Jericho tumbling down, redemption and salvation, his hands raised skyward. "He is sick because he ate the rat-mole, so we have to pray for him and then kill the animal," Sato explained to me. We waited anxiously for the men we had sent for to return and carry him into town, and finally the Aka hunters came running into camp and hurriedly, and very gently, lifted Justin onto the back of the strongest. His huge body draped over the frame of the man who carried him, and with two other hunters running alongside to take over for each other as they tired, the group disappeared into the forest. He was dead within just a few short hours. "I know death. Many people die and I see this and do not fear it," a young Aka adolescent girl told me as she watched them depart, "Death is for all the world. With death all is finished."

I watched them leave and turning back to a surprisingly empty camp, saw only a few remaining Aka men sitting quietly near their huts and occasionally looking anxiously across the camp to the forest. A small girl came running to me and, taking my hand, led me quickly across the clearing, urging me to hurry. At the edge of the forest, in the middle of a circle of children, a very pregnant young woman in the pangs of birth labor, gripped a tree and moaned as the other women of the camp massaged her back, held her, murmuring encouragement. Squatting down, she gave a final moan, and pushed her newborn child into the waiting hands of an older woman. Quickly assessing the health and wellbeing of the new life, the Aka midwife laid the baby girl down onto a bed of leaves, the arms of the forest—a forest that would become for her, as for other Aka foragers, a giving, nurturing presence throughout her life. The baby lustily cried for the first time, forcing life and forest air into her tiny lungs, as kicking and squirming, she was wiped down with leaves and water, her umbilical cord cut with a sharp, spiny leaf, then tied closed with a vine. Still gripping the tree, the new mother pushed out the placenta, and the lumpy bloody organ was planted, cord up, into the dark red earth. In this way, I was told later, the young mother would have more children, as planting the placenta cord down would serve to prevent further pregnancies. The newborn was handed to another older woman, and together with the new mother, the small group slowly made their way back to the camp clearing, where the father saw his baby daughter for the first time. The baby was given my name, a generous gesture I was to find so typical of the Aka. The new family disappeared into their leafy domed home as night settled completely on the forest world. Death and life. The intertwining lives of the Aka and Ngandu. This was a lot to take in as a student, my first time in the field.

## Anthropological Methods: Collecting the Data

Following Justin's death, we packed up, leaving in the early morning mist, walking deeper into the forest. Sato had insisted there was nothing more I could do for Justin, as he was already dead and therefore we needed to leave the camp where his death had occurred, as it was "not good to stay in a place of sickness and death." We were all upset and unsettled by his death. Justin had been young and strong just the day before.

Several days into our walk from the camp, we crossed a huge bog. The swamp was hot and muggy. Moss hung down from the water-burdened trees and I swatted it away, first looking for snakes that might be up in the trees, waiting to swing down and have a bite. Finally, we stepped out onto a small trail leading to dry red dirt, and bending down to put on my shoes and socks, I let out a howl. All over my legs were little balls of grey snot. I pointed down, horrified because I had a hunch as to what the little globs were. Eloko, a young Aka man I had hired to lead me deeper into the forest, simply shrugged and confirmed my suspicions: "Leeches." I think I might have let out another stream of expletives as I tried to scrape them from my skin. He laughed and bent over to help me pick them off one by one, before attending to the snot-like balls clinging to his own legs. Finally he straightened up and, nodding in my direction, said to me with a note of approval, "You are brave." I'm what? Brave? I had just screeched and cursed for three hours. He solemnly nodded again: "To cross that place like you did, you're very brave. I once worked with a French woman, and she made me carry her on my back the whole way. But not you, you carried yourself." I didn't tell him then, but had I known a piggyback ride across the swamp was an option, I'd have happily climbed aboard at the start.

That first year, in spite of snakes, leeches, and tragically too many deaths, or perhaps because of all these things, I knew I had to go back to Africa, to experience again the tranquility and haunting beauty of the rainforest, the hot, dusty business of the village, and the kindness and generosity of the people I had come to know. Having a house full of my own teenagers at home and noticing a void in ethnographic work on adolescents, I began my research in Africa by working with Aka and Ngandu youths. They readily shared their experiences of life in and at the edge of the forest, detailing their social-emotional development, family, and friend relations, issues of gender, and male and female adolescent's views of their lives. I wanted to have this research generated from existing frameworks of analysis based upon indigenous concepts of this stage of life, so I worked with eighty or so "teenagers" varying in ages from approximately 10 to 20-some years of age. Working with the adolescents, I noticed that very often they spoke of the frequent deaths of their parents, relatives, siblings, and friends. My next field study arose from these tragic accounts of loss, and I began a comparative research study examining responses to death and loss among these two culturally distinct adolescent groups. I hypothesized that grief is a cry for survival, a time in which corollary social networks of kin and other caregivers are established as a reorganization of attachment figures takes place. I reasoned that grief is a human universal although the experience and manifestation may vary greatly cross-culturally and individually, particularly among children.

I next looked at adolescent health, as I wondered what rendered these youths so vulnerable, what exactly caused 45 percent of all children from both populations to die before reaching their fifteenth birthday? During the next couple of field seasons, I examined the relationship between indicators of health (such as body mass index, parasite loads) of Aka and Ngandu adolescents and demographic variables that may enhance the adolescents' continued survival. More precisely, I studied patterns and variability of health, growth, and nutritional status both intra- and interculturally; how kinship, family composition, wealth, behavioral profiles, and social networks are linked to child health; and the emic perspectives (insider's view or interpretation, as opposed to etic or outsider's view) of health and disease among the Aka and Ngandu adolescents. This research represented one of the few studies to examine, thoroughly and systematically, the health of foraging adolescents, and it helped me to better understand the life of adolescents in Nambélé, Central Africa.

I would have been happy to continue my research with the "teenagers" as it was amazingly interesting, very informative, and usually fun. But my work shifted abruptly with the knock on my door that one hot afternoon, when the group of about eight Ngandu women, and later Aka women, asked me to listen to their stories. My research with the adolescents, their families and these women eventually covered a ten-year span. I began by working with sixteen women, eight from each community, and later included another twenty Aka and twenty Ngandu women to check reliability and validity of the data. I eventually narrowed the focus to four women, two from each community. My hope is to present a balance of stories. Nigerian novelist Chimamanda Adichie eloquently explains the importance of polyvocality:

> The single story creates stereotypes. And the problem with stereotypes is not that they are untrue, but that they are incomplete. They make one story become the only story. I've always felt that it is impossible to engage

properly with a place or a person without engaging with all of the stories of that place and that person. The consequence of the single story is this: It robs people of dignity. It makes our recognition of our equal humanity difficult. It emphasizes how we are different rather than how we are similar.[3]

To understand these women's lives, as Adichie illustrates, multiple life stories are important and make up the foundation of this book. The Aka and Ngandu live, and make a living from, a similar environment. They have a long shared history. Both populations are increasingly affected by the far-reaching arms of a global political economy. They have similar fertility and infant mortality rates. Yet they have adapted to their environment in very distinct and striking ways. They have very different kinship and political systems, modes of production, gender roles, husband-wife relations, and patterns of childcare. And as their lives are so intertwined and intimately connected, how could I understand one group without listening to the stories of the other? This work is cross-culturally comparative. But my hope is that this book is a *comparative*, not *oppositional*, look at the lives of Aka and Ngandu women. This is an important distinction. Comparatively, one culture, or cultural belief or practice, is not better than the other. Euro-Westerners tend to have a romantic view of foragers, and this is often evident in research, in human rights advocacy, in conservation efforts, and occurs at the expensive of neighboring groups, many times populations of horticulturalists. Hunter-gatherers have cultural beliefs and practices that Euro-Westerners value highly (including egalitarianism, near constant and intensive infant care, high father [and other's] care of infants, a close connection to the natural environment). Consequently, in comparative studies, these cultural traits are oppositionally emphasized in various ways: by the communities we choose to focus research on, the type of research questions we ask, and the descriptive language we as researchers use.

There are, of course, biases, ethical issues, and problems in the use of oral histories to understand how Aka and Ngandu women explain and make sense of their individual lives. How much did age, ethnicity, class, and gender impact how the women recalled their past? How much did my age, ethnicity, class, and gender direct the narratives they shared? Other issues I needed to address included concerns about the ethics of confidentiality (I use pseudonyms for the village and people I write about), and I obtained informed consent from each woman.

Listening to the women, how they spoke to me of their lives, the behaviors I observed, and what others said about the same topics, provided insight into cultural frameworks within which they lived and remembered their lives. The life history method of research (not to be confused with life history theory[4]) serves to identify patterns of individuals, allowing me to explore each person's individual life experiences within culturally specific contexts. Taken together and coupled with theory, these insights helped direct the questions I asked and the overall research flow. I told them that I hoped they could teach me what it meant for them to be an Aka or Ngandu woman. As a novice of their culture and lives, I think they were more explicit in what they said and often would show me, so I could get it right. For example, when Blondine was telling me about her early childhood, how she fought with her playmates or danced *gbagba*, she would get up and punch and kick at her imaginary friend, or grab the nearest woman and start dancing a childhood game. Nali would usually show me what she was talking about too—how she carried around a stick baby when she was a little girl, or how she taught her children to dig for yams. All the women were patient and excellent teachers.

The women began their life narratives by telling me of their first memories. I initially did not want to prompt them to speak of life stages or specific events, but instead tried to remain focused on how, what, and when they remembered what was important to them. What I may think of as a major life event, they may not, and vice versa. At times I might say, "Tell me about your life when . . . ," or I would point to a child of a certain age and ask, "What do you remember when you were that size (or age)?" There were times, however, especially toward the end, when I would ask very specific questions, such as "How do you teach your children to share?" These direct queries arose from themes (which I had coded in my field and journal notes) that ran throughout their narratives, as well as behaviors I had observed, that I found conceptually and theoretically interesting. Fortunately, the women did not need much prompting, and described their life histories revealing of the crucial role culture plays in the narration of memories. Transitioning from informal interviewing as we walked to the fields or in the forest, to more structured interviewing was accomplished without difficulty. As they had come to me first, wanting to tell me of their lives, the stories seemed to come naturally and easily from the women.

The anthropological tools of participant observation, informal interviews (discussion and questions as you participate in and observe the diverse contexts of daily life), semi-structured interviews (easy flowing interviews with specific topics, particially coded questions, plan and direction), structured formal interviews (specific questions presented in the same sequence), demographic data, reproductive histories, life history narratives (recounted life stories of individuals), and anthropometric data (body measurements), gathered while I lived in their village and forest communities, including the dozens of informal conversations I had had previously with them, taught me what it meant to be, in their eyes, an Aka or Ngandu woman.[5] Perceptions of these women further an understanding of the previous, quantitative data I have collected. I was fortunate too in that by the time I began this more "formal" research with the Aka and Ngandu women, I had been coming to Nambélé for a number of years. I had worked with some of their children. I had been in their homes, in the fields and forest. We had seen one another on the trails and in the market. We have (although recently the roof was blown off in a severe windstorm) a home in the village. We generally come back every year, all of which helps in building and maintaining rapport, the bond, established upon a foundation of trust, so vital between a researcher and people of the study area.

Of key importance to me has always been the need to gain proficiency in, or at the very least some working knowledge of, the languages the woman spoke. I am still learning. Several local Ngandu research assistants, male and female, were invaluable (and very patient) in translating and clarifying fine points. As I was learning, for interviews with the women of the village who did not speak French (and following the example of a colleague, Hillary Fouts), I would pose a question to my research assistant (in French), who would repeat the question in their language. I would listen to the response, recording the reply in English and then listen again to the translation provided by my assistant. I have since returned and again spoke with each of the women, to better understand what they had previously told me and to find out how their lives may have changed since I'd last spent time with them.

My field and personal journal notes proved to be an invaluable reference both while I was in the field, recording and reading through the written pages every evening, and when I returned to the United States. As cultural and very expressive beings, we tell a story of ourselves and our culture through behaviors and language, both spoken and unspoken. The observations of both helped me to understand better these two populations and, as well, my own cultural biases influencing the research. Cultural patterns and themes are woven throughout the women's narratives. But interwoven within the pages of notes I kept throughout ten years of field research were critical relationships and perspectives that in the daily experience of field research, I might have missed, misunderstood, or needed to explore further. The notes provided a record of behavior, observations, and interpretations (theirs and mine) that directed further study and analysis, informed my methodologies, and provided a form of triangulation. My first time in the field, for example, I wrote the following:

*—I am always amazed at watching the women balance the huge loads on their heads....Not sure yet what the men do except drink palm wine and visit.* This caused me to question the gendered roles and tasks of the Ngandu men and women. How and why are they different from the Aka? How do individuals form an understanding of their gendered identity, and how is this related to gender and work, gender and power? I found it interesting to see how the differing adaptations of the Aka and Ngandu within similar ecologies led to very strikingly different modes of subsistence, which in turn had a direct bearing on gendered tasks, patterns of kinship, male-female relations, and childcare patterns.

*—We came upon a camp here, like a hospital in the forest, as G., a traditional healer, lives here....He treats many, many people.* I became interested in what illnesses were most prevalent, and if there were differences in health between the Aka and Ngandu, men and women, young and old, and what subtleties of egalitarianism and hierarchy this might speak to. I was fascinated with the indigenous forms of theory, diagnosis, and treatments used (ethnomedical systems), and wondered if both men and women could become healers and how they learned.

*—It is so interesting here, especially in the forest camps, how close everyone sits together. Also in camp there was this little toddler who kept walking over to his dad and snuggling up, then going over to someone else in camp and snuggling up to them.* This entry made me pay attention to allomaternal care, attachment behaviors, and the importance of physical and emotional

proximity, which I later researched and wrote about in a study on death and loss among Aka and Ngandu adolescents.

Embedded within these few, simple observations are key cross-cultural issues and themes running through the narratives in this book: gender roles and tasks, hierarchy, egalitarianism, autonomy, attachment, and resilience. But I also include things that may seem irrelevant, because although my notes clarified and distilled what I was trying to understand, at other times, they are simply a reflection of my idiosyncrasies and struggles, illustrating how the anthropologist is never a benign presence in the field. Our personalities, our age, gender, ethnicity, and personal quirks, all serve to inform and have a bearing on our research.

Anthropological research is a science of discovery and failure, misunderstandings and clarification; imperfect, messy, and at the same time, systematic and directed. The empirical data gathered from a representative sample of these two populations of women brings together cross-disciplinary perspectives on key issues throughout the life span, making use of anthropological and developmental theories. Theory frames research, directing the research questions you ask and making you pay attention to particular things. Theory educates us, provokes us, and helps us to think more deeply about what we are trying to understand. It can also be boring to read. There are a handful of people who can write about theory in ways that educate and entertain. I am not one of them, so I include a discussion of theory (generally) at the *end* of each chapter. I was influenced in the field by recent evolutionary theoretical contributions and methodologically this caused me to pay particular attention to individuals within these cultures because throughout the life course, individual choices and interests within different social and natural environments may vary. Human biology and culture both have their own properties and need to be understood in detail, but they also interact to pattern human behaviors.

Developmental, cultural, psychological, biological, and ecological factors contribute to an integrative view of the lives of these Central African women. Human development, gender, sex, love, grief, and life changes such as childbirth, menstruation, and menopause, can only be understood as interactions between biology, ecology, and culture. This integrated theoretical model acts as a heuristic tool for thinking about these interactions, leading to an integrative analysis.[6] My primary analytic strategy included content analysis of the interviews, daily observations, field and journal notes. I began analysis of the interviews by simply coding the emerging themes, assessing the reoccurrence of general patterns, and forming data-driven categorizations from their narratives. In this way, I could see differences between individuals and the frequencies of thematic content.[7]

## The Women

The women I originally spoke to varied in age from 15 to 70-plus years and thus were both living and or recalling specific events and memories of their lives that centered upon the themes emerging from previous research and during our interviews. As a participant-observer, I made numerous visits to each household and worked with them in their fields and homes. I also learned that as an anthropological method, "participant observation" often means you participate in activities and the people observe *you*. I was a source of great entertainment, the "exotic other" they would happily watch on and off for hours.

I chose to focus on these particular four women for several reasons. Some I had worked with before and therefore had data that I could validate for accuracy; others fit the demographic profile in terms of age, life stage, and number of children. They were also the most articulate, expressing an interest and energy in speaking of their lives. I obtained data according to the perspectives and interpretations of these women, who served as both participants of their cultures and fellow researchers. The four women who shared so much of their time and friendship with me are as varied in their ages as in their life experiences, and are introduced in the following paragraphs.

### BLONDINE
### a Ngandu Woman

Blondine is plump. Where most other women in the village are thin from the constant and demanding hard labor, work in the fields, caring for numerous children, and dealing with parasitic and infectious diseases on a regular basis, Blondine is round, muscular, and at 43, full of energy. She walks with a bounce. Other women walk elegantly, sedately, straight-backed, balancing heavy loads on their heads, but not Blondine. She bounces. Watching her walk down the street, Therese observed, "She walks like she is dancing." She is an exuberant, hilarious woman. Whenever she would say something funny, she'd grab my hand and shake it. She likes sharing laughter. She also likes to swear loudly and emphatically, often entering the room, stomping her foot and saying "Merde!" She enjoys making, selling, and drinking moonshine, especially "première," the best of the brew. She likes a good argument, a good drink, a good laugh, purple fingernail polish, pants, and takes an enormous amount of pride in being a single, hard-working woman able to support herself and her children. Blondine lives in a red-brick mud house with two other women. The inside of the house is large and somewhat dark, with three rooms separated by woven reed walls. In the back of the house is a smaller "work" house, a drum for making moonshine and a clothesline. Various children, grandchildren, and neighborhood kids are often running through the house or playing in the back. Their home is a bustling, busy place.

................................................................................

### THERESE
### a Ngandu Woman

................................................................................

Therese is small, angular, and tough. She is somewhere between 70 and 75 years of age, maybe older, she is not sure exactly. Upon receiving her wages for the weekly interview work, she would tell me each time, "I hide my money so my daughters won't take it from me," and shaking her head looking perplexed, "but I can never remember where I put it." Once holding my hand to her small sunken chest, she said to me, "You are the daughter of my heart. I have so much I want to teach you." When we talk, she tips her lean-bone face toward mine and listens quietly, her eyes dark and kind in a sun-weathered face. She wears shapeless dresses for work, but generally dresses up in her best clothes for our times together. Therese's daughters always hover nearby, helping her memories along, adding forgotten words to the stories she tells, stories and histories they have no doubt heard many times before. "It is good," she said to me, "that you are talking to an old woman like me. Many thanks to you for talking to this old woman." Therese married when her "breasts were still small, and I stayed with him, just him for all these years until he died. I never married again. One husband was enough." She gave birth to six children and only three are still alive. She lives in a home built for her by her son, and at times, her two adult daughters, their husbands and children who come to visit her.

Therese is one of the strongest women I have ever known. I hired her 50-year-old son Basil to guard our house, and he built a small lean-to nearby where he lived during his employment as our "sentinel." One day when I came home, he and two other young men were wrestling with a big log, trying to half drag it, half carry it to the fire smoldering inside. I asked him where he had found such a nice big log to use; it would last him a couple days and save him the trouble of searching for small branches to keep the fire going. He looked up rather sheepishly, "My mother found this in the field and when she was done working she carried it here for me." I gasped, his mother, this tiny old woman? The log was huge. "Your mother carried that alone from the fields to here?" He looked over at the two men who had helped him lift the log and gave a small shrug. "Yes. She is very strong."

## NALI

### an Aka Woman

Nali is sturdy and taller than most Aka women. She is smart and kind and funny. She is also always busy with some task, always working hard to take care of her family, often leaving early in the morning to search for food, water, and wood in the forest or her field. She smiles a lot and laughs in a quiet way when I ask her something, but always graciously answers, no matter how silly the questions might seem to her. She has rows of small scars running along her temples, treatments, she told me, for the many headaches she suffered as a young girl. She has a gentle, dignified air about her. When I asked if she would teach me what it means to be an Aka woman, she took my request very seriously, spending hours showing me different plants, nuts, and mushrooms, where to find clean water, how to prepare food. I would watch and listen and she would repeat the lesson (and make me repeat it) until satisfied I understood.

One time in the field, we began making a small carrying basket together. She started by showing me which vines to use and how to strip the outer bark from them. She made the square bottom of the basket, then ripped out what she had just done and handed the vines over to me to give it a try. Day after day she sat by my side, sometimes even taking my clumsy fingers in hers, helping me with the complicated weaving. Often a crowd would gather, watching and laughing as I worked on the little basket. She would shoo them away, saying, "This is a serious business." Once the weaving was completed, Nali took a red piece of bark and ground it into a powder, mixing in water until it became a thick red paste. She smeared it on the basket and left it to dry in the sun. The next day, she knocked the dried paste off the basket, and underneath the fibers were stained a brilliant red. She held the basket up for all to see and declared it beautiful.

She taught me about so much more than how to weave a basket. She taught me about being patient, about being generous with one's time, and she taught me about friendship. Two weeks after I left, she gave birth to a baby boy, named after me. I always wished I could have done the same for her. Nali lives with her family in a grouping of ten domed huts spread out on either side a trail, close to the village of Nambélé. People, Ngandu and Aka alike, daily pass through their camp on the way to the fields or nearby river. They have been settled there for about three years. Nali and her family go into the forest only occasionally now.

......

## KONGA

### an Aka Woman

......

Konga is a sweet old Aka woman, as small as a child. She wears only a small piece of cloth, looped between her legs and held in place by a liana cord, covering the essential but leaving her backside bare. She is wrinkled from head to foot, the skin on her belly and thighs hanging in small vertical drapes on her little bird skeleton. She must be 70 years old, maybe older. She has kids around her constantly. I can't think of a time when there wasn't at least one child on her lap, or standing next to her with their arm draped over her skinny shoulders. Often her 3-year-old granddaughter could be found nursing from her shriveled and drooping breasts, so flat and long they hang down to her lap when she sits. She is toothless and mostly quiet, but once she starts in, she tells stories for long, long stretches of time. She has a wonderful sense of humor, and others often gather round her, laughing at what she would say.

Konga is a great teacher, too. She told me once of how in her day, the people did not have clothes to wear, but instead made their clothes from softened bark. I asked how this was accomplished. She called to some older kids nearby, sending them scampering into the forest to get the leaves of a certain tree. They each brought back armfuls of several varieties, she picked among them until she found what she was looking for and, finally satisfied, stripped the tough stringy part off the leaf. She rolled the leaves against her wrinkled old leg until the fibers loosened and became a softened piece of "cloth." She then took a liana cord and, looping it around her big toe, tied the other end around the leaf bunch and cut the leaves to even the edges. Reaching for the nearest child, she fastened the fiber cloth around his waist, the leaves covering his front and backsides. She then looked up, telling me with a toothless smile, "It is important you arrange the leaves very carefully or parts fall out when you sit down."

Confronting the challenges of their changing lives and cultural worlds, these narratives capture the strength and resiliency of the Aka and Ngandu women of the Congo Basin. Stories matter, and as Adichie expresses, "Many stories matter. Stories have been used to dispossess and to malign. But stories can also be used to empower, and to humanize. Stories can break the dignity of a people. But stories can also repair that broken dignity."[8]

This ethnography is about listening to the many deep, harsh, and delightful life stories of the women of the Congo Basin. Their stories matter.

## NOTES FROM THE FIELD
### Fall 2000

—*We went to the market today. It has little stalls filled with cookies, oil, flashlights, cigarettes, hair-gel, and surprisingly, Adidas shorts and shirts. There were also women who just spread their "for sale" stuff on a plastic tarp on the ground. There were pots of dark orange palm oil cooking in a tin with a flame floating on top, a lady selling raw peanuts wrapped in a banana leaf, and another lady sitting behind a small mountain of peanut butter. There were mounds of onions, beans, peppers, and other things I am not sure what they were. There is such a rhythm to life here in the village. In the mornings roosters crow to begin the day promptly at 6:00 AM, and then the birds, bugs, and goats start in, women and girls sweep their yards, babies bawl, kids laugh and play, and then you can hear the pounding of manioc* begin, "thunk, thunk, thunk." Also I am always amazed at watching the women balance the huge loads on their heads—they walk so straight and gracefully. Not sure yet what the men do except drink palm wine and visit.

—Thick description of the day: Blahhh. *This morning my temperature went up to 103° or so and I felt really, really horrid. I was sure I was going to die in the little room in E.'s house. Without seeing my kids again. So I told E. I probably should go back to Bangui and rest for a week, get better, then come back. And he explained that no, I would get better if I just stayed there and rested. So I said, well that would be fine, but if I go to Bangui I can get medicine and get better faster. He and A. discussed this and came back and told me there were no cars going to Bangui anyway due to the gas shortage. By then I thought to take my malaria medicine and sure enough, not long after I broke out in a sweat, and then poof! I felt better.*

—I am terrified of falling into the toilets here, a huge, deep hole in the ground overlaid with rain-soaked rotting boards and kept private by a "wall" of branches and leaves latticed together. And when you look down, you see maggots crawling around. I learned a good lesson (not found in anthropology method books), as I have been having problems with the toilet issue here, that is, which one to use. I was using the one across the street (as I was asked to), but then I accidentally walked in on someone, a Horrible! faux pas. I switched to the one behind this house, but I never could figure out how you know if someone is in it or not. So I asked P. and he says to clap as you approach! So problem solved! But I feel like an idiot clapping as I approach the latrine—"Way to go toilet! Woo-hoo!" Clap, clap, clap . . .

—As we sat together last evening I learned G., an Aka traditional healer, "sees" into the future. With great ceremony he pulled out two light bulbs from a plastic blue bag, a small (to see the present) and big one (to see the future), and told me that my "team" was assembled by Komba (God) who is watching over us, keeping us safe, and that he is waiting for us in the other camp we are going to, and when we get there we will eat lots of honey. G. also told me my research would be successful, all my family was well, and their thoughts were focused on me. Glad to hear that. Now we are in this new camp, and here is what is amazing: I have never been to this camp, or met these people, so I show up and they pull up a log for me. I sit down and my skin feels itchy and crawly so I scratch for a while, then it gets worse so I look down and my arms are covered in little red dots. I look into a mirror and my whole face is red dotted, like someone cut loose on me with a red marker. So here I sit, and no one seems to mind or give it much notice, as though it is an everyday thing to have a red polka-dotted, damp, dirty, smelly, strange woman in camp. But the point is that you are accepted and welcomed, no matter who you are, or what you look like, I guess. And that is an amazing feeling.

—Made it to another camp for the night. You can really tell the difference between old and new camps, old camps are brown and messy. In this camp there are seven kids, three babies, two men, three women, and this old, old woman all wrinkles, bones, sinew, and muscle. They made a bed for me in about five minutes, four sticks stuck into the ground with branches lined up and tied to the end, looks good to me. This young woman is now making a hut. She tore down the old one, swept the ground and then laid down four branches. Now she is taking the twigs, and each twig is shoved into the ground and then bent over, shoved into the ground, and all these small twigs are intricately intertwined and form a small dome-shaped hut. When the whole structure is in place, she put new green leaves overlapping each other, and there you go, a home is made. Now the lady next door is tearing her old home down. The kids spent the day playing, either on the vine swing or just romping around, it's like the whole forest is a playground. It is so interesting here, especially in the forest camps, how close everyone sits together. When I want to talk to an adolescent, a whole group of them will pull up a log (stick, mat, or leaf) and lean on each other, giggling and laughing. They even sit thigh to thigh to me. I love this physical closeness, it is comforting somehow.

—I left the camp just for a little walk and when I came back the camp had grown in size—not sure who all the people are. But I sat down with the women and C. said she had a story to tell me. First the women started singing and oh the singing is so beautiful! The harmonizing and counterharmonizing, rich tones and clapping, simply amazing. First the story begins by clapping a rhythm, then C. chants some line, then the last line is repeated by others, a call-response form. Every story they tell me is accompanied with a song. The men sing well, a deep, low tone, but it is the women who I think sing so beautifully. The camp is in a clearing surrounded by huge umbrella trees with birds singing and flitting around and insects buzzing and this little camp of five leaf-domed huts, all these Aka women

FIGURE 0.3 | *A woman, drawn by an Aka child, and a pregnant woman, drawn by a Ngandu child.*

*with their shy sweet smiles and the men off a little ways, laughing, and the babies! Fat, darling babies and adolescent girls holding them, passing them from girl to girl. As I was sitting here writing in my journal, I handed the kids paper and pens and they drew a few pictures (as with the Ngandu kids, they love to do this). It is fun to sit together "writing." (See Figure 0.3.) I like to watch as the evening comes and it begins to get dark, a slow descent of darkness from the canopy to forest floor. What a terrific day—I love being here in the forest camps!*

### QUESTIONS FOR REFLECTION

1. How might one's own culture, gender, and age shape the focus of the research and questions asked? What ethical issues might one face in eliciting life stories from people?
2. How might conducting anthropological fieldwork challenge your personal perspective on any number of key issues, such as gender roles and power, childcare practices, or husband-wife relations?

3. Why might these two populations occupying the same environment have such different cultural behaviors, beliefs, and values?
4. What do you imagine would be the most difficult aspect of conducting anthropological research in an unfamiliar place?

## NOTES

1. de Beauvior 1976, in Elfmann 2005, xv.
2. Bahuchet 1990.
3. Adichie 2010.
4. "Life history theory grew out of the recognition that all organisms face two fundamental reproductive tradeoffs. The first tradeoff is between current and future reproduction. The second is between quantity and quality of offspring." (Kaplan et al. 2003, 153.)
5. See Bernard 1994 for a detailed description of research methods in anthropology.
6. B. S. Hewlett and Lamb 2002a.
7. Elfman 2005.
8. Adichie 2010.

.................................

# CHAPTER 1

# The Forest and Village Worlds

With colonization the white people came to Africa. They came to show the Africans their God because we had many gods before, the sun god, the river god. The white people came to change Africans. They brought coffee and hospitals, big roads, they came to develop the country. Boganda did not invite them. They came for the riches of Africa.

—THERESE

In southern Central African Republic and northern Congo, between the Oubangui and Sangha Rivers, is a region that is considered home, occupied as it is by "forest foragers" and their Bantu-speaking neighbors, descended from Bantu farmers who began migrating from western Africa several thousand years ago, eventually spreading across the continent. And in the rural southern region, lies the dusty red, green and vibrant village of Nambélé, where the Aka and Ngandu make a living from the same dense tropical rainforest. Their lives are intertwined within the shadow of this rainforest and as well within the shadow of the complex and troubled history of Central African Republic. Placing the narratives of the Aka and Ngandu women within the broader economic, political, and historical background underscores the effect this history has had upon these two groups.

The slave trade, Aka and Ngandu coexistence with one another, European colonization, globalization, and the encroachment of multinational economic pursuits has challenged, and changed, their history, culture, relationships, and lives. This chapter begins with a broad historic outline of the Central African Republic, illustrating how national, political, and social change has been shaped by dynamics of global power. The focus then shifts to local histories where the consequences of globalization were, and continue to be, acutely felt: population growth in urban, and due to HIV/AIDS, decline in rural areas, increased participation in market economies, unsustainable practices of forest and land use that force people to adopt more intensive agricultural practices, increasing exploitation of the Aka, civil unrest, political instability, and transformed socio-cultural relations between the Aka and Ngandu. An overview of the two populations illustrates how these women from diverse cultures, living within similar ecologies and intertwining histories, respond to the particularities of globalization in unique and nuanced ways.

Lastly, we hear in their accounts how the two groups are economically and socially interdependent; their lives interconnecting in complex alliances of clan membership, lifelong friendship (at times), mutual aid, and dependency. The collection of ethnographic narratives by the Aka and Ngandu speak of the myriad ways in which external forces change their everyday lives and relationships.

## Socio-Economic and Historic Context of Central African Republic

Africa for Europeans was not only the "Dark Continent," a vast and dangerous place, but one that was ripe for plundering, not only providing economic gain but also appealing to the European aim to enslave and, for centuries, dominate those viewed as the "other."[1] Africa was seen as a raw commodity, overflowing with natural resources to be exploited for Europe's imperialistic objectives. Africans themselves were part of the resources to be exploited as well: the entire Oubangui region became a "slave reservoir," with people being traded north over the Sahara to West Africa for "export by European traders."[2] During the nineteenth century, Central African Republic (CAR) and its people were governed by an Egyptian sultan (in 1875) and eyed by the French, German, and Belgians.[3] By 1887, a convention with Congo Free State "granted possession of the right bank of the Oubangui River to the French," who began the process of establishing their legal claim to the area.[4] In 1894, Oubangui-Shari became a French territory partitioned among commercial concessionaries, although their control over the area was not consolidated until 1903. Four years after unification with the Chad colony in 1910, Oubangui-Shari became one of the four territories (Chad, Congo-Brazza, and Gabon were the others) making up the Federation of French Equatorial Africa.[5]

During the Second World War, General Charles de Gaulle appealed to these French territories to fight for "Free France," and their response helped set the climate at the end of WWII for a series of reforms, eventually leading to a shrinking of French rule in western and central Africa.[6] French citizenship was granted to some of the inhabitants of the four territories of the Federation, and with this newfound citizenship came the right to establish local assemblies. Shortly, all the African colonies in the Assemblée Nationale in France had political representatives. A Catholic priest by the name of Barthelemy Boganda led the CAR assembly, calling for African emancipation. In 1958, the French dissolved the Federation of the four territories and, within a few months, declared Boganda as head of the government of the new country of Central African Republic.[7]

Barthelemy Boganda, viewed by the people of CAR as their beloved "Father," was appointed prime minister of the country, but died before he might have become president. Therese explained to me (perhaps confusing the dates of Boganda's death and the date of CAR independence),

Boganda told the people, "There should be no working like this and no fighting with my people. You white people leave my population in peace. I like peace in my country. I don't like this fight between the white and black people." White people heard this and respected the laws of Boganda. On December 1, 1960, the Declaration of Independence happened, and all of Central Africa made a party! People said, "Now we are free! In Central Africa we are free!" Everyone, students, children, old people, we walked in the streets. When Boganda said to the white people, "Today we are free!," Boganda had the white people give him the state flag, and he said, "I want my flag and also I need to sing my national song for my country." He took this flag and brought it to many villages to show this new liberation. He said to all the populations, "Soon I am going to die and my blood will clean my country." He got on a plane and the plane crashed and he died. He was the founder of the country. Every year the new president has to come to the cemetery in the Lobaye to respect our President Boganda.

The citizens of Central African Republic grieved over the loss of their first president:

> When Boganda died, people were sad because Boganda was the president of development and peace. He made the population. He had good ideas to develop the country, and when he died many Central African people were so sad and said, "Boganda our president is dead!" They sang a special song for him, a song of sadness. They fell to the ground and cried in grief. Everywhere, people said, "Our president, why did you die? We loved you and now what we will we do? Oh Boganda, oh Boganda! You said to the white people to live in peace with us. Now you are dead. What will we do?" Boganda had said, "Zo kwe zo—I am a person, everybody is a person. You are white but you are a person. We are black but we are a person."
>
> —Therese

Boganda was soon replaced by his cousin, David Dacko. Dacko remained president for five years, during which time the country declared its independence from France on August 13, 1960, ending thirty years of small-scale revolts against French rule.[8] A coup in 1966, the first of many coups or coup attempts to follow, installed Colonel Bokassa as the new president. Bokassa promptly declared himself president for life, abolished the constitution, disbanded the assembly, and declared that all legislative and executive power lay in the hands of the president.[9] Then in 1976, Bokassa, a big fan of Napolean Bonaparte, proclaimed himself "Emperor" of the Central African Empire, invited the Pope to his coronation, brought six white horses and a carriage from Europe, and crowned himself and his "Empress" ruler of the land. Following riots in the capital city over the many human rights atrocities occurring during his regime, for which he was later sentenced to death for "murder and embezzlement," he ended up dying in exile in France in 1996. Dacko once again, and this time backed by the French, took over in a successful coup.[10]

President Dacko was followed in rapid succession by General Andre Kolingba, who drafted a new constitution calling for a multiparty system. Kolingba was defeated by Ange Felix Patasse in 1993.

Patasse held his post until 2002 amid "economic difficulties caused by the looting and destruction during the 1996 and 1997 mutinies, energy crises, and government mismanagement."[11] As Therese explains, "The last president Patasse was a bad work, a bad man. When Felix Patasse was president, many people died, many people fled out of the country, many people were homeless, and they abandoned their wives and children." In 2001, Andre Kolingba led a failed coup. In 2002–2003, Bozizé launched a successful coup attempt that overthrew President Patasse, declared himself President, suspended the constitution, and dissolved the National Assembly.[12] Bozizé, by Therese's account, was and continues to be, following elections in 2011, a good leader:

> What I think now of the President Bozizé is that he is the president of peace, the president of development, the president of all the people, for all the people. Now I see many young people getting work because of President Bozizé. It is a good thing, this peace. Bozizé leads the state well. He has brought many projects to this country. This is what I know of the past and the presidents.

Coups, failed coups and mutinies, riots, unrest, corruption, mismanagement, and human rights abuses have plagued the history of the impoverished country of Central African Republic.[13] From 2005 onward, rebel activity in the northwestern and northeastern part of the country intensified, 300,000 citizens were displaced by fighting between government and rebel troops (for example, Ugandan Lord's Resistance Army, Popular Army for the Restoration of Democracy, the Union of Democratic Forces for Unity, and rebels from neighboring Sudan).[14] Various peace agreements had been brokered, disavowed, and entered into, by 2008 most rebel groups had declared a cease-fire or signed a peace accord. However, although peace dealings and international interventions were intended to help end instability in CAR, by 2009, the United Nations reported that "over a million people had been affected by the civil unrest."[15] Currently, displaced Chadians and refugees from Sudan's Darfur, coupled with occasional rebel attacks, contribute to the continued volatility of one of the least developed countries in the world.[16]

## The Impact of Colonialism on Nambélé, Central African Republic

Lying in the heart of the vast continent of Africa, Nambélé, the small but vibrant village in Central African Republic, was not isolated from colonialist ambitions. The region and its people bore witness to terrific hardship, exploitation, and cultural transformation, as Therese describes:

> When the white people came, many people fled into the forest. Because when the white people came, they hit Africans for the work. The black people did not refuse because if they refused they would go to jail. The white people took a village chief, and each chief knew the populations and knew the names of the people. This chief would oversee the populations and this work: "You have to work hard! You have to work and even when the sun is hot you have to work." The black people did not refuse.

With the arrival of the colonizers and the subsequent division of areas of CAR into concessionary companies, allowing the foreign companies the right to exploit natural forest products and "granting them commercial monopoly," the colonial period became a time of dramatic change for the Aka and Ngandu.[17] "We live," said one Ngandu man, "thanks to the wealth of the forest." But it was the wealth of the forest that attracted the colonizers as well. Ivory was in demand, and during the period from 1899 to 1910, the trading of ivory began in earnest with the "whole of French Equatorial Africa" exporting more than a hundred tons of ivory tusks per year.[18] The Ngandu were compelled to fill the market need, but in actuality it was the Aka hunters who were the principle suppliers of the elephant tusks. This resulted in the promotion of Aka *tumas* (great elephant hunters) to an elevated social status in a society known for egalitarianism amongst its members. The extraction of wealth from the forest had the transformative effect of both increasing the connections and types of exchange among farmers, company agents, and the Aka as well as increasing the quantity of exchanged goods.[19]

The creation of a commercial market, the European demand for forest and plantation products, and an imposed trade (and later taxes) upon the sedentary villagers compelled them in turn to constrain the Aka to participate, supplying meat, ivory, and pelts via their relations of exchange.[20] As the colonial trade intensified, the demand for these natural products with "commercial appeal" increased among the American and European companies and profoundly changed the way of life of the foraging Aka and their sedentary neighbors, the Ngandu.[21] For Aka, colonial trading in the Nambélé area increased hunting (supplying Bantu rubber-gatherers with meat, hunting elephants for ivory) and some gathering (of copal, among other things), but did not involve them directly in labor as such; however, "the rise of cash-crop production certainly meant increased farm labor for Aka."[22] Foragers principally supplied forest products, and the farmers became chief traders of products from the village, as the local economies became merged into global networks of trade, "intensifying contacts" between the two populations as well as the amount of goods exchanged.[23]

As thousands of elephants were slaughtered for their ivory tusks, the elephant population plummeted, and the colonizers turned their eye to other sources of wealth to extract from the land. From 1910 to 1940, concessionary companies began exporting wild rubber. Eleven companies merged to form the Compagnie Forestiere Saghna-Oubangui on a 17-million-hectacre concession surrounding the whole of Aka territory.[24] In the wake of this merger, compulsory labor was not the only burden for the conquered people; the villagers were taxed, government taxes payable "only in rubber."[25] To avoid the compulsory toil needed to collect rubber to pay their taxes, villagers often fled into the remote forest where the Aka foraged. Therese explains, "When the colonizers came, they took the villagers for hard work and the Aka fled into the forest. They knew the forest well. But the villagers did not know the forest as well. So we came and lived with the Aka." As a young child Therese further recalls the hardship of this time:

> During the time I was young, my mother and father went to work for this white man. He and his wife told my mother and father to work. They hit my parents. When I was little I saw this with my own eyes. The white people told them to help make a road, to cut with the machete and make a road. You see the big road to Bangui? That was made by black people with machetes working under the hot sun. White people made the black people work for gold, too, and there was a big hole in the earth where they had dug for gold. The white people came and pushed the black people into the hole. Many people died. This was something I saw when I was a small child.

The men of the village were forced to work in the forest, and the women were forced to work on the manioc plantations in the villages "in order to feed the porters."[26] It was also at this time that Aka increasingly began the use of net hunting to fill the European demand for duiker skins. The Aka as well were relied upon to meet the subsistence demands of the villagers living in work camps. However, this did not change the view the colonial administrators had of the Aka. They perceived the foragers as uncivilized, not quite human, and sought to liberate them, to "civilize" their "primitiveness."[27] The Aka were not the only ones the colonists attempted to change: "With this colonization, the white people came to Africa . . . the white people came to change Africans" (Therese). The colonial government attempted a "taming policy" aiming to "free" the Aka from the authority of their Nganda neighbors.[28] As Therese explains,

> From the past, the villagers saw the pygmies like subjects, like animals. I saw bad things many times. The villagers told the Aka to carry them a long way, to run with him on their backs. And when the Aka man was tired and fell down, the villager hit him. The villagers bartered away their pygmies. When I was 14 years old, I saw an Aka boy killed by the villagers. After he was killed, many Aka fled into the forest because of fear of the villagers. The villager killed him for no reason. Now the Ngandu respect the Aka because of the law and church that the white people brought. God says that white people and black people are all created by God, and he doesn't like the hate and fighting. We are all people.

The real aim of the colonialists, however, was to "transfer the mantle of domination" from the village "masters" to the colonists, creating a dependency upon the colonial administration.[29] The colonial "masters" justified by their "prudent" and "humanitarian" motives, ensuring the foragers participation in the colonists primary interest, "productive work," carrying on the "development of the colony" and colonial economic interests.[30] Few Aka complied, and being mobile hunter-gatherers who knew the forest well, they fled to the refuge it provided. The policy's influence was limited, and the program had only minor influence on the Aka of the Lobaye district. The imposition of colonial rule and policy did however, have the effect in some areas of increasing Aka dependency upon their village neighbors.[31]

A market for duiker pelts developed in France, with the market peaking in the 1950s, which the Aka supplied by net-hunting. As elephants (and their ivory tusks) were hunted out, the demand for the services of the *tuma* (great hunter) fell, and that of the *nganga* (healer) rose as traditional healers practice divination on the net-hunt and directed hunting rituals.[32] Net-hunting had a profound impact on Aka social organization, as the Aka continued to use the "family" net-hunting technique in which men, women, and older children all participated. Aka camps gradually became larger and more permanent.[33] The Ngandu's lives changed as well, becoming centered around the village because of new economic and political structures and opportunities introduced by the colonists. With the development of coffee plantations, logging, gold, and diamond mines, the population of Nambélé increased further.[34]

Through forced labor, taxation, the taming policy, and the integration of the local cash markets into global trade economies, the colonial period drastically changed the political and economic lives of the Ngandu. Although the lives of the Aka remained centered around the forest, their farming neighbors acquired "access to a variety of resources" that the Aka did not have.[35] During the colonial period there was always a "social asymmetry" created by their differing modes of subsistence, cultural values, and the ways in which they were put to use and exploited for Europe's imperialistic objectives. Post-colonially, Aka-Ngandu relations continued transforming as the Ngandu increasingly relied upon the Aka as a labor force following an expansion in agriculture and coffee production, and less upon them as suppliers of forest products. Additionally as the Ngandu took on the role as "intermediators" between the Aka and the outside world, the dominant position of the Ngandu was solidified, and the inequality between the two intensified.[36]

The distinct division of identities between the two groups sharpened this asymmetry as Aka were "associated with the forest, traditional peoples, not fully recognized as being a part of the citizenry," whereas the Ngandu were "associated with the village and modernization."[37] The equation of inequality and identity introduced during the colonial era has since continued to permeate the structure and intensity of the nature of social-political relations between the Aka and Ngandu.[38] Increase in abuse and exploitation are deeply related to increases in the rise of cash economy in which the Aka supply cheap labor for the hard toil necessary for cash crop production. "New social orders" may arise as the Aka respond to various forces impacting their lives (for example, recent conservation efforts, development, new understandings of capitalistic relations of production, new political and social opportunities, employment, advocacy by missionary and NGO groups) and the new opportunities available to them.[39] Additionally, as they enter into agricultural production for themselves and their dependency upon the Ngandu decreases, it remains to be seen how this may transform the intimate, complex, and at times conflictual nature of their social relations, identities, and alliances.[40]

The Central African Republic has had a turbulent political history. The country's present and future lie not only in its resourceful people, but also in its enormous potential for wealth.[41] Although relatively undeveloped, its natural resources, found as well within the Nambélé area, include diamonds, uranium, iron ore, gold, lime, zinc, copper, tin, and hardwoods. Cultivated resources such as coffee, cotton, tobacco, manioc, yams, millet, corn, and bananas, established in the plantation economy during colonial times, continue to be a source of revenue, generating more than half of GDP (timber accounts for 16 percent, diamonds, 40 percent).[42] CAR is the zone of Africa's best humid savannas, suitable for cultivation, with numerous ore and mineral deposits. But despite its great potential, the country remains dependent upon foreign aid, with grants from the international community unable to meet humanitarian needs. Following a mission visit of the International Monetary Fund (IMF), the organization issued following statement:

> Despite a recovery of forestry and diamond exports, the external current account position weakened, reflecting a deterioration in the terms of trade due to high world oil prices. Owing to a weakening in the control of budget execution due to the prolonged general elections process, significant fiscal slippages led to the accumulation of domestic and external payments arrears.[43]

In the face of structural imbalance of public finances, the burden of national debt, political instability, labor strikes, and unrest, the country remains one of the poorest in the world, ranking 168th out of 175 countries listed in the 2003 United Nations Development Program Human Index.[44] There has been an almost total disregard for the long-term needs of the people, "despite receiving larger amounts of foreign aid";

life expectancy at birth (currently set at 43 years) has been declining since 1990, and currently is among the lowest in sub-Saharan Africa. Seventy percent of the people live on less than a $1 per day, and 86 percent live on less than $2 per day.[45]

The inhabitants of the country are young: the median age of the population of 4,950,027 is 18.8 years for males and 19.6 for females. Total fertility rate is 4.63 children born over the lifetime of a woman. The adult prevalence of HIV/AIDS is 4.7 percent, 37th in the world.[46] The degree of risk from infectious and parasitic diseases is very high, and the people of CAR contend on a regular basis with food and water-borne diseases, bacterial and protozoal diarrhea, hepatitis A, typhoid fever, malaria, meningococcal meningitis, and schistosomiasis. The probability that a person will die between 15 and 60 years of age is 471/1,000 for males and 466/1,000 for females. With a total expenditure on health care of only 3.9 percent of GDP—certainly not adequate to fulfill the basic human right to health care—this mortality rate is hardly unexpected.[47] A lack of long-term planning, neglect, mismanagement, and exploitation began even prior to colonization continues today, to the detriment of the people of Central African Republic.

Within these shifting balances of population dynamics and economic, historic, and political forces, the unstoppable complexities of globalization challenge, and often forever transform, traditional life-ways. Globalization is creating opportunities and change in traditional life-ways even as it creates an ever-widening gap in wealth, prospects, health, education, and human rights between and within these two populations. For the Ngandu, globalization has brought substantial benefits, as well as a reliance upon a global economy with variable markets for coffee, agricultural goods, hardwoods, and minerals.[48] Lifestyles based upon subsistence farming in rural economies are becoming increasingly difficult to sustain. Economic globalization and the expansion of world trade challenges the lifestyles of the Aka, as one of the few remaining hunter-gatherer people on earth. The lure of opportunity and employment and the desire for material items, medicine, and money bind Aka closer to the cash economy, and Ngandu are increasingly migrating to the capital city.

The CAR government, concessionary companies, missionaries, and various nongovernmental organizations (NGOs), for differing reasons, have tried to encourage (or force) Aka to become sedentary as a means of addressing human rights violations. The goal "via integration and assimilation" is to have the Aka represented in and a part of main-stream society.[49] As in the past, these organizations seek to intervene and improve the life situation of indigenous cultures, to provide better access to legal, health, educational, and social systems, to give them voice and agency. Acting with "humanitarian aims to combat margin-alization," these organizations very often actually "reinforce it in what would appear to be a more benign, but is in fact an equally destructive way."[50] This aid instead becomes a form of the past "colonial civilizing mission to lift up indigenous populations into the dominant society," undermining and devaluing their very particular cultural systems.[51] National and international aid and intervention, often mismanaged and disconnected from the people they seek to help, become as a form of structural violence, destructive of indigenous societies, amplifying inequalities, and changing traditional subsistence, social, and cultural patterns.[52]

From this foundation, Aka and Ngandu women continue to expe-rience disproportionate economic, social, and political marginaliza-tion in relation to the powerful forces of globalization. This collection of ethnographic narratives by the Aka and Ngandu reveal the myriad ways in which external forces change their everyday lives, illustrating how these women from diverse cultures, within similar ecologies and intertwining histories, encounter and respond to the particularities of globalization in unique and nuanced ways.[53]

## Overview of the Aka and Ngandu Peoples

The country the Aka and Ngandu live in is a basin, a collective water-shed for Lake Chad and the Shari River to the north and the Congo River basin to the south. Streams originating in southeastern CAR empty into the Ubangi, the "great river" joining the Congo River at the headwaters of Mbomu and Uele, whereas waters springing from northwest in the country empty into the Lobaye River, with this great flow of rivers outlining the modern borders of the Congo and CAR.[54] But it is the rainforest that borders and defines the lives of the Aka and Ngandu. For the Ngandu, the forest has been a refuge from warring villages, slave traders, and colonists, a relatively dependable source of wealth providing edible and marketable products, including meat, cat-erpillars, medicine, and wild vegetables. The forest is also a frightful place filled with the wailing, revengeful spirits of the dead, cast down by the Creator, mourning their separation from family and friends, banished forever to "cry in the forest."

For the Aka, as Turnbull described of the Mbuti, the forest is a mother, father, provider, and friend.[55] Aka sing and dance to *djengi*, the spirit of the forest, to show their appreciation at what the forest, *ndima*, provides. They dance for joy. They dance in grief. They dance to express themselves, to communicate to each other and to the forest. The forest spirit often has an entrance into camps: A doorway through which the spirit calls the *tuma* or *kombeti*, the camp elders and great hunters, to the bounty of the forest. A doorway leading into the lives of the Aka and Ngandu, where the forest is a joyous place, a tranquil and at times frightening place, an environment where the rhythm of life and death are experienced, and social meaning is intertwined within and from the landscape.

Within the small camps of leafy domed huts, Aka consider themselves the first people of the forest, this tropical environment they share with their village neighbors, the Ngandu. At one time foragers living off the abundance of the forest, many Aka now farm at least part of the year. The Ngandu are sedentary farmers who often go into the forest to hunt, gather, and trade. About three hundred Aka live in association with approximately five hundred farmers in the neighborhood of Lokoka.[56]

A trail winds from the village of Nambélé to forest camps, connecting the three Aka bands associated with this Lokoka "neighborhood." The population density is low, one person per square kilometer. Aka and Ngandu have similar demographic patterns: many children are born and many children die (Mortality rates for children under the age of 15 for both populations are 35–45 percent, with high fertility, at about 4–6 live births per woman.)[57] There are basically two seasons. It's hot and dry—"dry" is a relative term here, as what constitutes "dry," as in the "dry" season, really translates into hot, always damp, and very humid (although it does not rain every day!)—or hot, humid, and (very, very) wet. Torrential downpours during the "wet" season find Aka often living near the village, working on a villager's or their own farms. (See Figure 1.1.) When the skies dry up, Aka are in forest camps, spending their time net-hunting, trapping, gathering wild fruits and vegetables, and generally enjoying the tranquility of forest life, away from the "hotness" of the village. Aka trade forest game, wild starch,

FIGURE 1.1 | *Aka village camp.*

mushrooms, forest vines and leaves, vegetables (*koko*), and manual labor for cultivated foods, pots, cigarettes, and clothes from their farming neighbors. Ngandu have family gardens, small coffee plantations as cash crops, or farms that produce an ample assortment of foods: manioc, maize, yams, sweet potatoes, plantains, peanuts, papayas, bananas, and pineapples. Aka and Ngandu lives are bound together and bound to the forest. Sharing social, economic, and religious interactions, they maintain distinct patterns of settlement, modes of production, male-female relations, childcare practices, values, and beliefs.[58]

## The Aka

Aka (*BiAka* is plural, *MoAka* is singular) have minimal political hierarchy (there are those such as the *kombeti* with very limited authority, but no "big man," or person who holds absolute power over others) and relatively high gender and intergenerational egalitarianism (no one among the men, women, children, and elderly are given more respect simply for their age or gender). Patriclan association is weak: membership to

clan is through male lines (*dikàndá*), but female lines (*mobila*) are recognized as well. Aka kinship terms reflect a generational "Hawaiian"
kinship classification system; *tao* is the word for father but also refers to
the father's older brother and the husband of the mother's sister. *Ngue* is
the term used for mother and refers to both the mother and the mother's sister. All grandparents are called *koko*, and all grandchildren are
*ndala*. Brothers, sisters, and cousins are called *kadi*. Known historically
as "pygmies," Aka are among the shortest people in the world, although
their height varies considerably.[59] Reasons for this "pygmy phenotype,"
a well-described phenomenon, remain unknown, (although recent
research suggest it is genetic). Perhaps it is a thermoregulatory adaptation to the climate or density of the equatorial rainforest (an evolutionary hypothesis), or perhaps it results from limited edible forest foods or
of marital preferences (ethnology) or of high adult mortality rates due
to the intensity of infectious and parasitic diseases (life history theory);
many alternative hypothesis have been proposed.[60]

Great diversity exists among the 350,000 foragers who occupy Congo
Basin forests. With at least thirteen distinct ethnolinguistic groups, the
"pygmies" are not a unified culture or singular ethnic group.[61] However,
some commonalities also exist between the many Congo Basin foragers:
many farm at least part-time, live in association with farmers, exhibit
extensive sharing, have a profound respect for autonomy, maintain a
strong identity with and knowledge of the "giving" forest (although
some may live in savanna or mixed savanna-forest environments), and
have pronounced allomaternal ("other than mother") care.[62]

Aka believe in *Komba*, the creator of all living things who retired
after creating the world and its people. *Dzengi*, the spirit of the forest,
is the most widely recognized and regularly interacted with of spirits.
*Dzengi* likes singing, vigorous dancing, and play and when represented
in ceremonies, stops dancing when the enthusiasm of the singers,
dancers, and drummers diminishes. The expression of these beliefs are
notable in the forest. (See Figure 1.2.)

Aka trust in the generosity of the "giving" forest. They do not, however, have a "completely romantic view of their life in the rainforest;
accidents, food shortages and malevolent spirits can cause problems."[63]
This view of the socio-natural environment has many impacts on their
behavior. Aka share about 50–80 percent of what food is brought into
camp, generally cooked and portioned out by the women, who in turn
often give the plates or pieces of food to their children to deliver to

FIGURE 1.2 | *Dancing Djengi.*

other members in camp.⁶⁴ Aka "demand share," which means that when someone comes asking for something, one is obliged to give. Aka do not accumulate wealth or goods, or until fairly recently, plant a garden or field (that is, they do not have long term subsistence plans), as they trust the future will take care of itself. Their social relationships, including their relationship with the natural environment, are based upon key values of trust, generosity, and cooperation.

Their culture of music and dance is striking. Every story told is accompanied by a chorus of song, often created by the storyteller and echoed by those sitting around, attesting to the spontaneous creativity and autonomy of individuals. Babies are often lulled to sleep by song and rhythmic patting on their back. Hunting trips include yodeling in various registers, indicating the position of particular individuals in the dense forest. Trips to the river to bathe, wash clothes, soak manioc, or collect water are occasionally turned into playful musical performances, with the "rhythmic percussion of rivers' water with various body parts."⁶⁵ This complex "musical game . . . one of the most original expression of their musical culture" is an activity enjoyed and performed by many peoples, foragers and farmers alike, of the Central African rainforest. There are special songs and dances for specific events: for funerals, to attract the attention of a potential mate, for love, seduction, sexuality, and learning of one's role and place within camp life.[66]

The polyphonic singing in particular communicates culture—the values, beliefs, desires, actions, locations, and objects important to the Aka people. As a form of cultural transmission, the language of music and sound communicates more than the surface meaning of the words. Discourses of sound and song representing cultural realities become a web of meanings, whereby the Aka speak of themselves, cultural beliefs and values, autonomy, sharing, social organization, of love, life, and death—all expressed through the shared language of music and song. Furthermore, this musical "language" carries action, the action of meaning, of social learning, gendered discourses, cultural practice, of political and cultural representations, and ideological subtext. Metaphorical song, dance, and storytelling serve to bind together, inform, and define the lives of the Aka.[67]

In the small intimate camps in the forest or village, the number of people varies day to day, as people travel off to visit other camps, or relatives and friends come over. The camp is a busy place, with little kids playing and people chatting, cooking, and working. Although the Aka are multilocal (married couples live with the wife's or husband's family, their residence pattern is very flexible), newly married Aka couples often live matrilocally (the new couple moves to the wife's family home). During this time, the new husband conducts brideservice (service by the groom for the bride's family), and his activities are dictated by the demands of his in-laws. This work continues until the couple's first child is born and begins walking. Once the groom is "released" from his service, the new family chooses which relatives to live with. (However it cannot be said that camps are always comprised of close biological kin, often they are not; there is diversity in the camp compositions.)[68] There are also many smaller camps of only one family, but they are close to the other Aka camps.

Camps are encircled by the forest, a mosaic of green arising from the dense undergrowth with lianas embracing the tall semi-deciduous trees forming the canopy, and rising to the vast expanse of African sky. Their homes are made of branches shaped into a conical dome and covered with overlapping layers of large leaves. The homes are small, at most three meters in diameter and two meters high. Inside is a bed of interwoven twigs where the family sleeps together (which, with enough rearranging of poking twigs, can be almost comfortable) and a small fire, with a few possessions (collected roots and plants, a pot or necklace) hanging from the branch walls. The huts built by the *ngondo*, young adolescent females, are smaller and have room enough for one, or at most two, inhabitants. The bachelor lean-to, built by the *bokala* or young adolescent males, are usually leaky, precarious rectangular structures. An Aka woman named Djaba explained to me, "This is how the Aka were created, building a hut is only for woman. The women choose where to stay. They build the homes because the men go and hunt in the morning to look for food for the children. When they go, the women do the building."

This may be, in part, the reason for the flexibility of residence patterns. If the wife wants to visit her parents or live elsewhere for a while, and her husband does not, she simply leaves. In a few weeks the family home begins to leak, then falls apart, and soon the reluctant husband goes to live with his wife. The opening of each home faces a cleared center area, and all living takes place out in the open. Cooking, cleaning, making nets and baskets, caring for children, arguments, conversations, and activities are shared by those within the camp setting. Privacy is another matter. The placing of the huts is "not left to chance" as the woman constructing her family's home is well aware of her "social position" relative to those with whom she lives in the camp.[69] By the strategic placement of the family home, she limits conflict in the camp. The women assess and take into account the "nature of the relation which unites each resident [family, friends] to others and the current quality of affective relations, meaning who at the time she shares friendship and love, rivalry, or simple lack of interest."[70] The implications of where the Aka woman positions the family home is significant. Konga described it this way: "You choose to live by those you love a lot, you choose who to live closest to. If you have a dispute with a neighbor or a friend, you stay away and do not talk to each other."

Today, some camps in the Nambélé area have large numbers of people, (over 50 in a single camp) especially along the Congo road, where "villager" homes are found alongside the more traditional leaf-and-branch homes.[71] Within the forest, a few Aka have also built village-type homes, perhaps one in a camp, with five or six leaf-and-branch designed homes, located near small gardens of plantains, cassava, and maize. Forest camps are often abandoned if there is a death or when hunting is bad.[72] Today, Aka spend less time in forest camps and more time in large camps closer to logging roads, their village farms, schools, and missions.

In addition to the contemporary practice of "forest gardening" and increasingly farming near village fields, the Aka have a bounteous selection of forest food: hundreds of forest plants and animals, although game meat is decreasing as areas are being hunted out. However, they prefer to subsist on "sixty-three plant species, thirty-two insect species (twelve species of caterpillar), honey (a favorite, from eight species of bees), twenty species of game, roots from six species of plants, leaves from eleven species, and fruits from seventeen species."[23] They collect mushrooms, termites, grubs, and caterpillars. They net-hunt for several species of duiker, use a crossbow for monkeys, set small snare and net traps for forest rats, armadillos, and porcupines. Hunting and foraging are seasonal, and the amount of time spent in these activities varies. During the dry season from January to March, most of the time is spent net-hunting, whereas during the wet season from August to September, the time is spent gathering food, like caterpillars, and working on the villager farms. Aka have "immediate return" values and social organization: their activities are oriented directly to the present, in which they labor to obtain food and other resources consumed on the spot or perhaps over the next few days. There is a minimum of investment in accumulating, in long-term debts or obligations, or in binding commitments to specific kin.[74]

The Aka family generally lives in camps along the same trail for generations, where members hunt and gather together. This trail is associated with a Nganda village *konza*, a "patron" and clan associate (Aka and Ngandu often share clan names) with whom the family has a multistranded and generally cooperative, albeit frequently unequal, relationship. The members of one clan trade with the Ngandu family of the same-named clan.[75]

## The Ngandu

Ngandu is an ethnic group originating from a set of clans that came from an area approximately 85 km from the present village of Nambélé in which they now live.[76] They were most likely forced to move north to escape ethnic wars and slave traders working along the Oubangui River and pushed deeper into the forest, intertwining their lives with the lives of the Aka.[77] According to one myth of origin, all villagers are believed to have descended from a common founding ancestor. This is in sharp contrast to the myth the Aka recount in which they founded the first village, but lost their claim when a woman asked her husband to go with her into the forest, following the sound of bees to honey, and upon returning found the village taken over by the "usurping" Bantu farmers.[78]

European colonization impacted the ethnic composition of Nambélé, as colonial agents tried to create a homogenous "Nambélé Tribe" with a designated chief, without considering the heterogeneity of the villagers.[79] The "deliberate policy" enacted by the colonial power in French Equatorial Africa sought to concentrate village populations in order to control and "force" labor needed, for example, to exploit wild rubber for European companies. Certainly the "Nambélé villagers" constitute several diverse ethnic groups. The local language of the village is from the Bantu linguistic family, and "[r]emains strongly related to the original branch; they use their ethnic name to identify it, Dingandu."[80] Sango was imposed as the national language in the 1960s, and is the language of instruction in primary schools. The Ngandu, men in particular, also speak French, the language of their colonial past.

As slash-and-burn horticulturalists, the Ngandu live alongside roads in sedentary villages of anywhere from 100 to 400 people. In the Nambélé community, the "neighborhoods" are divided based upon patrilineal (descent raced through the male line) associations, and clan solidarity is strong. Ngandu kinship terms reflect a version of the "Iroquois" kinship classification system. Political hierarchy begins with the elected mayor who oversees the community, followed by chiefs of each village-neighborhood, then the patriarchs of the individual families.[81] Their fields, land, and homes are communally managed and can be bought, sold, or traded whenever the need arises by individuals within the family, but the family-clan is consulted before the transactions can occur. The son (or an older clan male) may inherit the land from his father; daughters inherit material household items (pots, pans, and the like) from their mothers and grandmothers. The men build one- to three-room dried-brick homes, and once married—as polygyny is relatively frequent; although declining, more than 35 percent of all marriages are polygynous—the husband may add on an addition so that each wife has her own room or separate house within the larger compound.[82] The married couple share a room (or rooms if there is more than one wife and the compound is small), and once children are weaned, if there is room in the house, the children occupy a separate bed and/or room, shared with their siblings.

The main room is used as a gathering place when friends or family visit, or a workplace for the women if it is raining. The homes open to the street, but daily living, cooking, socializing, and family life generally occurs in the yard behind the house. Ngandu often have small gardens near their homes, where they may grow medicinal plants, herbs, and some fruits and vegetables. Many families also keep chickens, pigs, goats, or sheep, allowed to roam freely through the village. Women are active in the informal market economy, selling their excess produce or game meat, manioc, moonshine, peanuts or peanut butter, and palm oil at the local market. A few women will sell their harvest of manioc, caterpillars, or other produce to buyers in Bangui. Other women have set up small restaurants, bars, coffee shops, or teashops catering to a local and fairly consistent clientele. There is marked gender and intergenerational inequality. The Ngandu share food on a daily basis, usually with immediate members of the household, although they will occasionally share food and labor with neighbors and clan members through "cooperative exchanges" a few times a year. Men's work tends to be seasonal. During the dry season from January to March, Ngandu men clear the fields for planting, although it is the women who continue the work, planting, weeding, and harvesting the fields throughout the year. If the family has coffee fields, particularly if they are large, it is the men who are responsible for the planting and production of the coffee.[83]

Ngandu men and women take pride and find satisfaction in the hard work they do. Their lives are devoted to their families, friends, crops, and fields. A high value is placed upon meeting the needs of the family, including clan members of their extended family, over the needs of the individual (communalism). They connect the feelings of love and closeness to others with economic or material items; these dimensions are intertwined within the social and emotional aspects of relationships. Economic activity, social continuity, delayed production, and consumption, long-term planning and concern for the future, a "delayed system of return," are bound in the sense of the patrilineage, social commitments, and the importance of remembering those to whom you are bound and committed, even beyond the grave. Ancestor spirits are shown continued respect and retain an active place in the lives of the living. Extensive kinship bonds, clan alliances, and the maintenance of long-term social ties provide security against economic and social misfortune.[84]

The Ngandu concentrate on maintaining good social relations, but because of the close proximity of a potentially large extended family, egalitarianism and sharing between households is less frequent and not extensive, as sharing could end up being amongst a very large family network. However, individuals who do not share with their families and accumulate material items, status, or wealth are suspected of being sorcerers or the targets of sorcery, which is believed to cause illness or death. Sorcery as a form of ideology is remembered and transmitted, and is strongly conserved as a cultural trait. Sorcery acts as leveling mechanism, helps to maintain household equality, and is a deterrent to accumulation. Sorcery decreases family differentials and maintains egalitarian relations. No one person can accumulate without extensively sharing with family, as those who accumulate wealth, land, power, and prestige are accused of using sorcery to gain at the expense of others. If one accumulates, others go without, and there can be profound implications in this, especially for women and children. Aka and Ngandu take *mbengue* (strychnine), a poison oracle, which speaks through them and provides the information about who is a sorcerer, that is, who is causing death, misfortune, or illness within the community. The person identified by *mbengue* can be put in jail if convicted within the court system. Sorcerers have an extra organ called *gundu*, it is small, pale, round, and has many "mouths." As the sorcerer child grows and "eats" the life force of others, the organ becomes larger, and redder with more mouths. Sorcerers can change their human form and fly at night to eat the life force of others, which gives them power and advantage. Generally, the victims are biological kin or in-laws not helping or giving to others.

Among the Ngandu farmers, sorcery functions in much the same way as the extensive and daily sharing among the Aka, acting as a leveling mechanism; a means of maintaining a relatively egalitarian society. Sorcery is also a way of governing behavior, as sorcery is not only governed and controlled by the law, it is itself a form of law and social control. Additionally, sorcery for both the Aka and Ngandu explains death, misfortune, and uncontrollable events, and functions as a way of exerting control over uncontrollable events and circumstances.[85]

# The Nature of Relations Between the Aka and Ngandu

The two groups are economically and socially interdependent; their lives intertwine in complex alliances of clan membership, lifelong friendship (at times), exchange, and dependency. It is difficult, if not impossible, to speak of one without speaking of the other. The nature, extent, and structure of these relationships have undergone profound changes over time and have been alternately analyzed. The ecological and economic approach emphasizes the complementary domination of the Ngandu vis-à-vis the Aka, the ideological and "social-political alliance model emphasizes the relations of subordinations and its causes."[86] Suffice to say, their relationships are multifaceted and have been variously portrayed as being based upon a combination of clan alliance, obligation, partner-trade exchange, friendship, solidarity, subordination, and domination, depending upon the language and approached used, the discipline and interpretation of data, and the level of relations (national, regional, community, personal) being explored.[87]

Gene flow between the two groups resulted from the long history and nature of these relations, linguistic borrowing, and interwoven systems of trade, social organization, cooperation, and alliance.[88] What remains distinct is that in spite of this long history of contact, these relations have not resulted in the "assimilation of forager into farming populations."[89] The Aka and Ngandu have strongly conserved their own foundational schemata, beliefs, practices, ideologies, and values. Though bound, as some would suggest, for generations, the Aka and Ngandu have retained their own cultural forms. Each gains access to "needed resources without surrendering their own values."[90] Each has preserved a very unique culture, "not by isolation, but by learning to negotiate and adapt to one another and the larger world."[91]

# In Their Words: Relations Among the Women

## NGANDU WOMEN
### Blondine

When I was younger, I bought meat from the pygmies along the trail. The pygmies would hunt, and I would exchange manioc, cigarettes, or palm oil for the meat. I was so happy when I could go into the forest and buy meat and then sell it and make a lot of money. I could buy shoes and clothes for the children. I'd always go down the same trail. After the exchange of merchandise, certain pygmy women would treat me like family and walk back down the trail with me and pass the night in my home. The villagers think that the pygmies do not have homes because they live in their huts. When they sleep here in our houses they are like children.

Many times when I was in the village, I'd give them manioc, and for one or two hours they would work for me. Then the pygmies went back to the forest. But now they have abandoned us. Before they were like family. I had three or four pygmies who would work with me. They depended on my family and me. I depended upon them, because they helped us. The change is that now the missionaries built a school and taught the pygmies in school. Before they did not understand anything, but now they know the church and other things of civilization. The pygmy children go to school, but the adults do not, so some pygmies still work in the fields for us. This is good, working together.

We share the same clan names, the villagers and the pygmies. When you marry, you depend upon the clan of your husband and usually you live with them for a long time. If a pygmy is sick I will give money for medicine, clothes, or food to help them. I love the pygmies on this trail like family. I am sad when they are sick, and if they die I go to the funeral and cry. I give them respect. Life for pygmies in the forest is very difficult.

I have many good pygmy women friends, and when we speak together we compare our ways of life. We have very different ways of life. Here we have nice clean clothes, and we wash our feet good and our clothes. The pygmy women do not. There are certain pygmy women who are clean like women in the village, but others are dirty and they smell. In the past pygmies would just wore loincloths and their butts were open to the air. But now the women wear clothes, and they wash them sometimes too.

They do teach their children the same lessons of respect and obedience. Some children of the villagers and pygmies show respect and obedience, and some do not. The pygmies may hit their children, if they have a lot, but most never do. The villagers hit their children a lot more because the village children have hard heads and do not respect their parents. Village children go to school, and if they do not show respect the teacher hits them. But most pygmy children do not go to school, so the parents do not teach them to show respect. The village women here, we will say, "Son, go get water and brush your teeth before you eat." The pygmy mothers do not say, "Wash yourself, wash your clothes, brush your teeth." They go days without washing! Another difference is the relationship between the men and women. The pygmy women make decisions. If the husband says, "Tonight I want to sleep with you," and asks her for sex and the woman says "No," that is the decision, they do not. If a man wants to go on a hunt and the woman says "No," they do not go. A pygmy woman loves her husband very much. They work together, they hunt together, they go together to find food. They walk together in the forest. Some villagers also love each other like this and help each other. But not as much as the pygmies.

Before when the old grandparents died, they would give their pygmies to their son, but now because of the missionaries and the school there is independence. The missionaries gave us these instructions, "If you hit a pygmy, we will take you to the police and you will have to go before a judge, and the COOPI Italians too." But in the past it is true, if they did not respect villagers they'd get hit. But now if you do, you go to the police. This is a problem because now there is no respect. If you hit them, they'd respect you. When I see my children and they do not show respect to others, I hit them! The pygmies are not children, it is different, but even if a villager does not respect me, I will speak to them and then hit them also! Now they work with who ever they want, and they do not just work for me. But this is good, learning civilization. I think it would be fine if the pygmies lived here in the village, and pygmy children and village children went to school together. In the missionary schools both pygmy and village children go to school together. It would be fine if they lived close, but pygmies do not like the sun in the village. They are used to the forest with trees and shade. Here in the village it is open to the sun, and they do not like the sun. So they live in the forest, shaded by the trees.

................................................................

## NGANDU WOMEN
### Therese

................................................................

I remember the pygmies of my father. They brought us many animals, meat to eat from the forest. They were like family to me. I went into the forest during the caterpillar season with my parents. We lived together with the pygmies, and if my parents wanted caterpillars or meat, they bought it with oil or salt. My parents and grandparents and great-grandparents have seen the pygmies like animals to work for them. But now if a pygmy gets meat or caterpillars, you have to buy it. You don't take your things in force because the pygmies are people like you. They have knowledge. They have blood. They are people. But pygmies have power too. They can make themselves invisible and take the shape of animals, so they can steal more easily from our fields. We villagers put fetishes in the fields to frighten them, but they replace it with their own and this casts a spell on the villager who sometimes dies. They also have power for curing illnesses. Some illnesses can't be cured with modern medicine, but pygmy healers are very successful.

There is a great difference, a great change from now and before in the pygmies. Aka were divided into groups between the Ngandu, each Ngandu had his own Aka. They were given lots of work and if they refused this work, the Ngandu hit them. Aka and Ngandu did not eat together or walk together. Ngandu protected their Aka from the other Ngandu. The Aka killed meat for the Ngandu, and if the Ngandu went on a long trip, the Aka would maybe carry him on his back. Ngandu bought and sold Aka between them. But now Aka are free, they do what they want. Aka now hunt with a gun, snare, spear, and net-hunt. Before they didn't wear clothes, now they have radios, shoes, glasses, and pants. If they hunt and have meat, they demand a radio and payment for it. I think nothing of it because today the pygmies go to school, and now the village children and pygmy children are more alike. Before the pygmies loved their proprietors, but now with the sensibilities of the white you are not the owner. You need to give money for their work, but before in my time we were the proprietors. Now if you do not give money to them, they do not work. That is the big difference.

Before when the pygmies would come to Nambélé and if there were problems or war in the village, they said to the villagers, "Come to us in the forest. Come and live with us in the forest." We would follow the pygmies and work together. In my time, the relationship with the pygmies was good. I thought of them as my sons and daughters, and they thought of me as their momma. All the pygmies I knew, I loved a lot and they called me momma. When they had children, a baby, I gave them a name so they all called me momma because of that. There is no change in this because they still call me momma and I still call them daughter, father, cousin, brother, and sister. I love them all very much. Many pygmies came to my house for work. When I was in the forest with my husband, I prepared food and gave it to them to eat because they did not have very much to eat. They said, "Oh mama! You are so nice to give us this food." They gave to me also, honey, meat, and many things. I had many good pygmy women friends and we walked together.

## AKA WOMEN
### Nali

When I was little I saw a villager for the first time, and I was afraid because I had the mind of a child. I fled because I thought the villager would kill me. I called them, "Bilo, ya sou nai." The villager was like our chief. My parents said to me, "Don't be afraid. The villagers will not kill you, they are people just like you." They taught me not to fear the villagers. When I heard that advice of my parents, that the villagers gave things to us, I began to take into my head to find food for them, to be good to them, but I never played with villager children, because I was always afraid of their parents. When I was small, I had no villager friends.

Sometimes I work for the villagers. The villagers are very difficult. They love problems. They have a bad character, if you have a debt with a village woman, she comes into the camp and takes all your things to her house. If you work for a village woman and you are sick and you say, "No I can't work," the village woman will say, "You have to work anyway!" They are bad people. They say, "You are a thief. You steal all the time!" They speak badly to us. They are mean. They do not respect us. They insult us. They shout too much. If there is debt, they hit us. If they give us money for work and we do not work, they hit us. We have lived together for a long time, but they are not like family. They want you for the work. We are their workers. We work for them, they pay us and that is all. There are no relations with them. I do not consider them family. It is only the cooperation of work. I do not love them.

I fear the village women, but now there are limits. If you work for the villagers and they hit you, then you do not work again for them. You do not take money from them. You have a choice. You wait for a villager who is nice to work for. We work for villagers because we do not have many things, money, machetes, cups, pots, clothes, and so we work for them, because maybe they will give us these things.

There is a great difference between the village women and me. Village women wear nice clothes, they are clean, and they use crème. They prepare food good for health. The village women sleep in a good bed in their houses. The food I prepare is different. The house is different. We do not hit our children. We do not yell a lot. There they do not respect their children. If village children refuse their mother or father, they are hit. If they do not obey their parents, they are not fed. The children fear their parents. But here, Aka children do not fear their parents. Aka children respect their parents but not like the village children. The difference is the children of the village, if they do something and the parents yell "Stop!," they will stop and listen to their parents. But here if we say "Stop!," the children do not stop because we do not hit our children and they do not fear us. If children are bad and you yell, the children will cry. In the village, if children are yelled at, they obey.

In the past Aka were in the forest, and they found meat and honey, and the Ngandu were in Congo. There was a war and the Ngandu fled into the forest because of the fighting. When the Ngandu saw the Aka there in the forest, they began to take them in force to live beside them in the village. They made a vine and put it around each Aka and led them to the village. The villagers told the Aka to stay in the village to work and to not go into the forest to live any more. The Ngandu built houses and villages. This is how Aka and Ngandu first came together. The contact between Aka and Ngandu was bad because Ngandu used Aka like animals. The Ngandu did not pay the Aka, and they fought when the Aka did not want to work. But *Komba* created Aka first. *Komba* created the big forest and set Aka in the forest and gave them yams, meat, and honey of the forest. In the forest there is the season of caterpillars and the season of honey. All of this *Komba* made for the Aka. After this *Komba* created the villages and the white people. That is why we respect the laws of *Komba*: "You Aka are created first and I gave you a big forest. You stay in the forest, I gave you everything you need in the forest." That is why you see white people and villagers in the villages.

*Komba* gave Aka the forest he created. I want to always live near the forest, life is more peaceful in the forest. Even when we live close to the village and have farms, we will never become Ngandu. We will always stay Aka. I am not like the village women. I am Aka in my heart.

## Konga

When I was young, I saw a person with clothes on, a villager, and I thought, "Now this is a different person." I kept my distance. My parents said to me, "When you see a villager, you respect them. Show the respect, they live differently then we do. But do not go too close to them." I began to build a relationship when I was a young girl, and I started to work with a Ngandu woman in the fields and caterpillar camps. I worked for her and I began to know her better. But I had fear then because I was little. I thought the villagers were no good, they were like chimpanzees.

In this chapter we have seen the effect history has had upon the Aka and Ngandu. The threat of slave trade, enforced labor, colonialism, their coexistence with one another, globalization, and the encroachment of multinational economic pursuits has challenged, and changed, their cultures, relationships, and lives. Beginning with the women's first childhood memories, Chapter Two builds upon this shared history, illustrating how two different cultural lifeways arise from differential exploitation of the same ecology. As neighbors in the rural southern regions of Central African Republic, the Aka and Ngandu maintain frequent social, economic, and long-term interactive relationships, yet live in very different physical and social settings, with distinct modes of production, male-female relations, and patterns of infant care that affect childhood development and social learning.

## NOTES FROM THE FIELD
**Fall 2002**

*—A day ago the town crier went through the village early! in the am tooting his whistle to inform all the women that the mayor wanted them to meet at his palace—yes that's right, palace—tomorrow. Not sure how long it takes him to make the whole route, but sure is more interesting than email messaging. It seems like the more deaths here, the more accusations of sorcery,*

the more tense the village is and the more the mayor meets with the people, which makes sense. I was also asked by the mayor to help with "tea" money, meaning, "It would be very nice of you if you could pay the boys clearing the road with some money for tea." Not sure what road he is talking about, where it is or where it goes, but oh well. Now I am sitting at my little house writing and outside the window are three goats watching me, very seriously, as they chew their cud. Wonder if they have to go to the meeting too. Probably working up the nerve to ask for some tea money too.

### Winter 2003

—E. dresses up every morning and often wears the hat I got for him, which he really likes. Only problem is everyone wants his hat and asks him for it so while he loves wearing it, he can't. As he told me, "Here if someone is jealous they can look evil on you," which causes harm or illness or some such thing, so now he only wears it when he is visiting in the house. I'd forgotten how noisy the night is here in the village. First you hear the kids shouting and playing and people chatting, then the little boys yelling "Petrol, petrol" as the evening starts, then thunder in the distance, Aka drumming, and wind in the trees. But it's the constant hum I'd forgotten, like an electrical current, countless bugs, crickets, night animals, and one lone lizard, or maybe hydrax?, that honk-barks all night long. So I am lying here (not able to get to sleep) and I've counted two-three honks per each of my breaths. That's a lot of honk-barking.

—Someone came to our house the other day and told us that the Polish priests wanted to use our sat phone, and if we could bring it by at around 7:00. "Sure," we say, smiling and nodding (we smile and nod when we don't understand what someone is saying), so we went to dinner at E.'s, to the market and then over to the priests. We walk in and this huge table is set and we are invited to sit down and eat! Apparently the priests did not in fact need our phone. There was just one lonely priest who apparently wanted someone to eat with, so he had invited us over. So we sat down and ate dinner for a second time, a 5-course meal. We had mushroom soup, Italian noodles, meat, vegetables, wine, salad and cheese!! And the Polish priest talked and talked and talked! Mostly in Polish. C. turns to me and asks if I understand what he is saying, "Nope, not a word. Just smile and nod." So we spent the evening keeping a lonely Polish priest company. It was several days before we were hungry again. Maybe the smiling/nodding routine is not such a good idea. And speaking of priests, pastors, ect., there are many different religious denominations here all *trying to "save" the Aka and Ngandu populations. I am not sure from what. What is "wrong" with what the local people believe?*

<hr/>

## QUESTIONS FOR REFLECTION

1. How might have colonialism, forced labor, and the introduction of a market economy changed the relationship between the foraging Aka and their sedentary neighbors, the Ngandu?
2. Colonialism is a form of structural violence, an economic exploitation destructive of indigenous cultures, changing traditional subsistence patterns, forcing people into market economies, influencing social relations, and amplifying inequalities. Colonialism was also a major component in the development and formation of the modern world as we know it. How do you think the colonialism of Africa influenced the modern western world?[92]
3. Therese's ethnohistoric account describes how she experienced and explained events as they happened in her life. Why might an understanding of historic Africa be important in understanding these women's lives in contemporary Africa?

<hr/>

## NOTES

1. Pakenham 1991.
2. U.S. Department of State 2010; Kalck 1993; Moïse 2010.
3. U.S. Department of State 2010.
4. U.S. Department of State 2010.
5. U.S. Department of State 2010.
6. U.S. Department of State 2010.
7. U.S. Department of State 2010.
8. U.S. Department of State 2010.
9. U.S. Department of State 2010.
10. U.S. Department of State 2010.
11. U.S. Department of State 2010.
12. BBC Monitoring 2001.
13. U.S. Department of State 2010.
14. BBC Monitoring 2001.
15. BBC Monitoring 2001.
16. CIA 2011.
17. Bahuchet and Guillaime 1982, 199.
18. Bahuchet and Guillaime 1982, 200.
19. Bahuchet and Guillaime 1982, 199–201; Moïse 2010.
20. Bahuchet and Guillaime 1982, 200–204.

21. Moïse 2010; Bahuchet and Guillaime 1982, 200–204.
22. Moïse 2010; Bahuchet and Guillaime 1982, 200–1.
23. Moïse 2010; Bahuchet and Guillaime 1982, 200.
24. Bahuchet and Guillaume 1982; Moïse 2010.
25. Bahuchet and Guillaume 1982, 201; Moïse 2010.
26. Bahuchet and Guillaume 1982, 201.
27. Bahuchet and Guillaime 1982, 202–204.
28. Bahuchet and Guillaume 1982, 203.
29. Bahuchet and Guillaume 1982, 203; Moïse 2010; Delobeau 1989.
30. Bahuchet and Guillaume 1982, 203; Delobeau 1989; Moïse 2010.
31. Bahuchet and Guillaume 1982, 204–5; Delobeau 1989; Moïse 2010.
32. B. S. Hewlett 1992, 16; Bahuchet and Guillaume 1982, 202.
33. Bahuchet and Guillaume 1982, 202; B. S. Hewlett 1992.
34. Bahuchet and Guillaume 1982, 202; B. S. Hewlett 1992.
35. Bahuchet and Guillaume 1982, 205–06; Moïse 2010.
36. Moïse 2010; Bahuchet 1985; Bahuchet and Guillaume 1982, 205–6; Delobeau 1989.
37. Moïse 2010; Kisluik 1991.
38. Moïse 2010; Bahuchet and Guillaume 1982, 206–9.
39. Bahuchet and Guillaume 1979, 124, 133–36; Joiris 2003, 72; Delobeau 1989; Moïse 2010.
40. Bahuchet and Guillaume 1982, 206–9; Delobeau 1989; Moïse 2010.
41. Appiah and Gates 1999, 396–400; CIA 2011.
42. Appiah and Gates 1999, 396–400; CIA 2011; CIA n.d.
43. IMF 2011.
44. Ghura and Mercereau 2004, 3.
45. Ghura and Mercereau 2004, 6.
46. CIA 2011.
47. CIA 2011.
48. B. S. Hewlett 1992.
49. Kenrick 2005, 107.
50. Kenrick 2005, 107.
51. Kenrick 2005, 107.
52. Kenrick 2005, 107; Farmer 2004.
53. Kenrick 2005, 107. For a more detailed analysis of Central African history, see also: Moïse 2010; Giles-Vernick 2002; Vansina 1990; Delobeau 1989; Bahuchet 1985; Bahuchet and Giullaume 1982; Kazadi 1981; Harms 1981; Demesse 1978; Arom and Thomas 1974; Bruel 1911; Parke 1891; Schweinfurth 1874.
54. O'Toole 1986, 2–4; Shannon 1996.
55. Turnbull 1962, 4.
56. B. S. Hewlett 1992.
57. B.S. Hewlett 1992.
58. B. S. Hewlett 1992, Hewlett et al. 2000b.
59. Becker et al. 2010.

60. Becker et al. 2010.
61. B. S. Hewlett and Fancher 2011.
62. B. S. Hewlett and Fancher 2011; B. S. Hewlett 1992; Meehan 2005; Woodburn 1982, 205; Bird-David 1990.
63. B. S. Hewlett et al. 2000b, 295; Ichikawa and Kimura 1992, 40–41.
64. Kitanishi 1998, 18.
65. Devin 2010; Fürniss 2008.
66. Devin 2010; le Bomin 2010; Fürniss and Joiris 2010; Arom et al. 2008.
67. Fürniss and Joiris 2010; Lewis 2010; le Bomin 2010; Arom et al. 2008.
68. B. S. Hewlett 1992; Meehan 2005. Often described residence patterns of the Aka and other hunter-gatherers around the world have focused on the biological relatedness of camp inhabitants in trying to understand why it is that foragers share so extensively. (Of course! They are all somehow related!) However, this may not be so, as in a recent study of over five thousand individuals, it was found most were not in fact genetically related. Their common residential patterns do, however, mean they interact with large numbers of people (Hill et al. 2011).
69. Berry and van de Koppel 1986, 38.
70. Berry and van de Koppel 1986, 38.
71. Berry and van de Koppel 1986, 38; Shannon 1996.
72. B. S. Hewlett 1992; Shannon 1996.
73. Bahuchet 1982 cited in B. S. Hewlett 1992, 24.
74. B. S. Hewlett 1992. 24; Woodburn 1982, 205.
75. B. S. Hewlett 1992, 45.
76. Bahuchet and Guillaume 1982, 194.
77. B. S. Hewlett 1992, 15.
78. Bahuchet 1979, 191; Bahuchet and Guillaume 1982, 194; Shannon 1996.
79. Bahuchet 1979, 191.
80. Bahuchet 1979, 191.
81. B. S. Hewlett et al. 2000b; B. L. Hewlett 2005; Meehan 2008.
82. B. S. Hewlett et al. 2000b; Meehan 2008, 214.
83. B. S. Hewlett et al. 2000b, in Meehan 2008, 214.
84. B. S. Hewlett 1992, 24; Woodburn 1982, 205.
85. B. L. Hewlett and B. S. Hewlett 2008, 71.
86. Joiris 2003, 73; Moïse 2010; Grinker 1994.
87. Joiris 2003, 73; Rupp 2003, 2011; Bahuchet and Guillaume 1982; Takeuchi 1998.
88. B.S. Hewlett and Fancher 2011; B. S. Hewlett et al. 2002b; Cavalli-Sforza 1986, 406–11; Bahuchet 1993, 2010; Moïse 2010; Rupp 2003; Joiris and Bahuchet 1994.
89. Moïse 2010.
90. Moïse 2010.
91. Moïse 2010.
92. Pakenham 1991; Brown 2001, 16.

...............................

# CHAPTER 2

# Children of the Forest and Village

All the world sang with the joy of us girls, because we'd play and sing so
much in the forest.

—Konga

The work of childhood when I was very little was to play, to amuse ourselves. When you are small, you just live. The most important and good
memory was the playing. I was free.

—Blondine

The basic research question explored in this chapter is: What
is it like to grow up as an Aka or Ngandu child? This initial
query is built upon a foundation of key issues in development: How and from whom do children learn social beliefs and values, subsistence skills, and knowledge? Children everywhere must
learn particular cultural values, beliefs, and practices, and this "work
of childhood" is accomplished through a variety of mechanisms and
means. Children are learning in a multiplicity of ways, "observation,
emulation, imitation, teaching, and from a variety of people—fathers,
grandmothers, siblings, and other children."[1] Social learning also occurs through play, as playing is one way children learn social and subsistence related skills.

The ethnographic overview described in the Introduction is
expanded upon in this chapter, highlighting parental ethnotheories,
processes of intergenerational cultural transmission, attachment styles,
and foundational schemas of the Aka and Ngandu, illustrating key simi-
larities and differences in the cultures of the two populations. Although
the Aka and Ngandu are neighbors in the rural southern regions of
Central African Republic, making a living from the same tropical forest,

and with "similar high fertility and mortality rates, frequent social, economic and long-term interactive relationships," they live in very different physical and social settings, with distinct modes of production, male-female relations, and patterns of infant care that affect how, what, and from whom social learning occurs.[2] In this chapter we will see how learning occurs by Aka and Ngandu children in very specific and differing ways. Embedded within the narratives of Blondine, Therese, Nali, and Konga are Aka's and Ngandu's parental ethnotheories, modes of cultural transmission, and patterns of learning.

## The Work of Childhood

Culture is learned through various avenues, parental actions and care, adapting and preparing children for adulthood. Culture is embedded in parenting practices that affect childhood development and transmission of key cultural models, foundational schema, the "ideas, knowledge and values" that provide a "foundation" for cultural models (that is, ways of thinking, explaining, anticipating others) in a variety of domains of cultural life.[3] The ethnographic background described in this chapter reflects the foundational schema of the Aka and Ngandu. Foundational schemas for the Aka include: age and gender egalitarianism, values of sharing, flexibility of social roles, respect for the autonomy of individuals, and trust of others. Foundational schema for Ngandu include: sharply delineated gender roles, age and gender hierarchy, deference and respect of older individuals (parents, older brothers and sisters), obligations to specific others (clan, lineage), material basis of social relationships, a strong belief in sorcery, and a general distrust of others.[4] The women's narratives of their early childhood memories reveal how and by whom the Aka and Ngandu children were taught these key foundational schemas.

### Ngandu Children

Ngandu children grow up in a boisterous environment, seeing an assortment of various neighbors, relatives, and playmates nearly every day. Ngandu babies are indulged (although caregivers are not particularly quick in responding to infants' bouts of fussing or crying), played with, and held by their parents and others a good portion of the day. Ngandu toddlers are taken care of by allomothers ("other mothers"), usually their older siblings, and from these "other mothers" they get high-quality, intensive care, spending the first years of their lives in a rich social environment.[5] At around the age of 18 months to 2 years, the child is weaned by the mother, who may bind her breasts or put fingernail polish or something bitter tasting on her nipples to discourage nursing.[6] The weaning infant is fed rice or manioc gruel to help supplement their diet, and spends time playing with groups of children of various ages and both genders, while their mothers are busy working in the fields or elsewhere. Young Ngandu children are spending the majority of the day with other kids and sleeping at night on a separate cot with their siblings. From this age until late childhood the time a child spends with their mother or father is limited.[7] Toddlers and 3- to 4-year-olds are taught to be obedient and respectful to adults, and girls may begin to carry small loads on their heads, or babies (sticks, bunches of leaves, or their younger siblings) on their backs, play-practicing their mother's activities. (See Figure 2.1.)

By age 4 or 5, young girls are beginning to learn household skills. Childhood ends earlier for the little girls who take care of younger

FIGURE 2.1 | *Ngandu kids and the work of childhood.*

siblings and help with the cooking and cleaning. Little boys have a more carefree time, but may help on occasion by running errands or performing other small tasks.[8]

Children at ages 6 to 8, girls in particular, are increasingly obliged to help in "woman's work"—sweeping the house, collecting water and wood, working in the fields, and caring for siblings. At this age, girls are more inclined to be around adult women in the fields and homes, while boys spend time with other males, and as both boys and girls get older they are less likely to be hanging around the younger children in the village, especially when a younger sibling takes on the care of any new infants.[9]

Young boys, as noted, have fewer responsibilities than their female peers, but may also be called upon to wash clothes, sell petrol, or engage in some other work activity to help supplement the family income, particularly as the Ngandu become more involved in the market economy, their children become a vital part of the household labor force. Older children are playing with their same-sex peers and, by early to mid-adolescence, are spending much of their time with similar age friends rather than adults, save for the girls, who are spending much of their time during the day in work activities alone, in the presence of other adults, or with their siblings.[10] But even so, it is not uncommon to see groups of children of various ages and both genders running about the neighborhood, playing games (such as soccer), or playing house. And as they grow older, they enjoy participating in dancing and singing games, when the "moon is bright and the night is clear." Childhood for many Ngandu children is a fun and busy time of exploration, friends, and social activity, in spite of the hard work and chores. They still find time, after their work of the day, to play, and this play is important. It is a way of learning social skills, a time to begin building social networks, a time to learn subsistence-related tasks.

Social learning for Ngandu children is early, and occurs relatively quickly. Many aspects of culture are transmitted though conservative transmission mechanisms (vertical and group or "conformist" effect mechanisms).[11] The social transmission of patrilineal ideology among the Ngandu seems to be an adaptive aspect of culture. Ngandu children acquire this strong patrilineal ideology not through trial and error, of course, but through mechanisms that enable the rapid acquisition of culture.[12] Children learn from other children (their older siblings, friends, and peers) and as well from their parents, grandparents, and other adults. Parents have the primary role in teaching their children important cultural values. Deference and respect for males, elders, and authority figures (key foundational schemas) are strongly enforced from early childhood onward.[13] Children are expected to obey their parents, or they can receive quick and at times painful repercussions. "If I was playing the dancing games with my friends, it was fun, but if my mother asked for help and I refused, my mother hit me" (Blondine).

It is important to have an understanding of the conservative nature of partilineal clan ideology. Ngandu children learn early that you rely upon specific people, particular members of your clan. This helps to promote social unity and conformity. The Ngandu strongly believe in conformity and have cultural sanctions to promote and maintain individual, intergenerational, and clan hierarchy and solidarity. The family, extended family, clan alliances, and ancestors are more important than the individual. By late adolescence and early adulthood, Ngandu have learned they are tied to specific others, and have invested time and energy in cultivating and maintaining social relations, learning who one is obliged to and allied with, and whom one can rely upon.[14] Ngandu children also learn early on the material basis of social relations; for example, the Ngandu males often show their love for their children and wives by giving them gifts. They are very loyal and devoted to their families and work hard to take care of them. For the Ngandu, social relations have to do with maintaining a gendered hierarchy of commitment and obligation, respect, and obedience.

As social hierarchy is highly valued, any potential display of disregard for it becomes a potential for social disruption and reorganization.[15] Male deference to, commitment to, and respect for authority figures must be maintained. Intergenerational transmission of property and social status is crucial; the interests of the family depend upon maintaining the interests of the clan. Economic activity, social continuity, delayed production, and consumption, long-term planning, and concern are bound within the partilocal lineages, social commitments, and the importance of remembering those to whom you must show deference and obedience, the group to whom you are bound and committed.[16]

## Aka Children

Aka babies are held nearly constantly, often carried on the side in a sling of cloth, snuggled skin-to-skin close to their mother or other caretaker. Therefore breastfeeding is self-directed and frequent, and the physical and emotional proximity between the infant and caretaker is enduring and intimate.[17] Aka fathers, for example, have been characterized as being the most nurturing fathers in the ethnographic record.[18] Whimpers or fussing brings a quick response from their parents or others. Aka babies are rarely let to cry for any length of time. During the night the infants sleep in the same twig or bark bed as their parents and young siblings. Throughout the day, infants are in close proximity to their mothers and fathers, as well as being held, indulged, played with, and cared for by an assortment of children, parents, grandparents, and other adults, although the mother is the primary caretaker.[19] From infancy, Aka childhood is characterized by independent exploration, experimentation with different cultural activities, play, indulgence, and social learning in a rich and intimate social environment.[20]

Aka are taught from late infancy to share, and as adults they do so frequently, nearly every day, with whomever may be in the camp that day. This way of thinking is so pervasive that often times most of the wild game they've captured or fruits and vegetables they've collected or small items they buy or are given are distributed among camp members.[21] Since it is the woman who generally distributes the most food, it is generally the mother who teaches her children to share.[22] This extensive sharing serves as a leveling mechanism, promoting egalitarianism and maintaining good social relations. From early infancy onward, Aka children also learn the sacred value of autonomy. Babies not only nurse on demand (self-directed nursing, as the mother's breast is usually bare and available), but by the third or fourth year of life, are weaned when they choose to stop breastfeeding. (Although weaning may also be directed by the pregnant mother as she prepares for the birth of the next child.)[23] Once weaned, 3- to 4-year-olds are either carried when their parents go gathering or on net-hunts, or are left in camp. If they stay behind, a grandparent, other adults, or older children and siblings will watch after the group of "left behinds." (See Figure 2.2.)

The Aka cultural value of autonomy is clear not only in self-directed breastfeeding and weaning, but as well in self-directed play and learning. "I don't like it when our children play with machetes, but if the baby decides to play, I leave it. And if the baby cuts themselves and if they see the blood, they themselves will decide not to play with the machete" (Nali). (See Figure 2.3.) In all the years of research by others

FIGURE 2.2 | *Aka "left behinds."*

and myself, no one has ever reported seeing an infant or young child hurt themselves while playing with the machetes. No doubt parents would intervene, as I have seen them do when a child crawls toward a hot fire, if the machetes were very sharp and a danger to the child. Parents rarely correct their children, and when they do, discipline generally involves chastising or teasing, and although they may ask their child to do something for them, they do not punish the child if their request is ignored. Hitting a child can be cause for divorce.[24] Even into adolescence, there are no expectations from others in terms of work or behavior save for the expectation surrounding sharing, with social sanctions for any unwillingness to share.[25] Aka parents seldom tell their children what to do or not do, nor discipline them very much, because Aka have a great and fierce respect for the autonomy of the individual, infants and children included. This is linked to a respect as well for "creative" or "innovative" freedom and autonomy, often seen in singing, drumming, dancing, and storytelling.

The autonomous young Aka children, *moanna*, play, take part in or initiate subsistence activities—for example, "cooking", digging for

FIGURE 2.3 | *Aka baby digging a hole with a machete.*

yams, playing "husband and wife, mother and father," or building little huts—and spend a lot of their time into late childhood in the company of their parents, other adults, and play groups of children of both genders and various ages.[26] Children, in part, are learning from other children through play. As Nali explains, "Children play in order to know how to live. Children play to know how their parents do things." Play, and the social learning that is a part of play, is the work of childhood.[27]

From 6 to 8 years or thereafter, boys are called *mona bokala* and girls *mona ngondo*. The child's activities and interests expand beyond the parent's hut. By this age they are able to keep up with adults and often choose to accompany them as they gather forest fruits and vegetables or when the family goes on a net-hunt.[28] Generally the male follows his father, and the female follows the mother, but although they usually learn from their same-sex parent, knowledge acquisition is generally self-directed; with autonomy paramount, the children decide which knowledgeable adult to follow and to learn from. As the adolescents told me: "My father taught me the work of women, to prepare food, and my mother taught me this too and how to hunt and kill the animal" (a young adolescent female). "Father taught me how to care for babies, to soothe and feed them" (adolescent male). These were not unusual cases. Like Nali and Konga, children at this age are taught about social relations and subsistence skills, and they learn the fluidity of Aka gender tasks and roles.

By age 10, Aka have acquired most of the knowledge and skill necessary for life in the forest: how to net-hunt, fish, gather plants, honey, prepare food, take care of babies, build huts, make baskets and medicines for illnesses.[29] But, although they may have acquired extensive knowledge, they are generally not using this information until adolescence, when they are more physically mature, have greater strength and more time to experience these different activities. They can come and go as they please, travel to other camps, work or not work, begin sexual activity, build their huts, get their teeth pointed, receive scarifications for beauty— how, where, and when they want. Childhood is an indulgent time, and this extends to the young adolescent as well. Individual autonomy, freedom of choice, and individual expression is paramount. Throughout their childhood (and beyond), Aka continue to be indulged, held, slept with, and valued, continually surrounded by others in the intimate life of the camp.

# Earliest Memories and Childhood

································································································

## NGANDU WOMEN
### Blondine

································································································

I had five brothers and three sisters. I was the first child that lived, and when I was born, it was a long time before the second child was born. My mother, Bridgette, told me this, "Two babies died before you, and the *nganga* told me after you were born to take palm leaves, build a house and live outside in that house for two months. If I had entered our own home before the two months were over, you, the new baby, would have died also." My mother said the babies' deaths were because of a type of *ekila*, [sickness, caused from] the breaking of the manioc root when it is pulled from the ground.

My first memory was when I was about 3 years old. I remember fighting a lot with my friends because my friends provoked me. You play with your friends, but when you play they always want things that you have. I hit them and kicked them because they made me so angry!

When we were not fighting, we played. We would play with sardine cans like they were something special. We went into our little house that we made and played. We pretended we were like a man and wife and this was our house, just like our parents. All my friends came when my parents were gone and we would play. The boys constructed the house. I was the wife and my friend was my husband, I gave him water to drink. I pretended I had a baby. Sometimes we played like we were having sex, just laying on top of each other, but we were little and didn't know what we were doing. One time I took a cricket and pretended it was meat, I was preparing a meal for my husband and friends. I cut it up, put it in water and boiled it. I said, "Here my husband, here is a fine meal for you." The boy threw it into the bushes! I jumped up and hit him. I was so mad! I ran home crying. But we played together again.

Sometimes we cut banana leaves, or other leaves, and put a bunch tied together on our backs and pretend it was our babies, our banana babies! My best memory was when my mother made me a banana baby, put it on my back, and then took a stick and a banana leaf and made it like an umbrella, so I was like an adult woman with a baby. My friends played house with babies like this too. They would pretend to have a home and lay their babies down to sleep and nurse them when they cried. This was when we were very young.

I was 6 years old when my mother became pregnant. I was so angry! I never saw the birth. But when she came home with the baby I thought, "This is my brother and I will care for you." I carried him and only played with my friends when my mother came back from the fields and took him. I took good care of all my brothers and sisters. I washed them and washed their clothes. I gave them water to drink when they were babies and they cried. It was serious, hard work. I thought, "These children are a lot of work, and when I grow into a woman I will only have two children!" Women here have a choice if they only want two or three children.

I remember at this age, when I was little, my mother was always telling me, "You will soon begin to do the work of a woman." One day she took my arm and took a big piece of maize and she showed me, holding my hand, how to plant the corn. My child's work was to wash clothes, get water, prepare food, sweep the house, and work in the fields. During the day when my mother left for the fields, she sometimes left food. I would eat it and share it with my siblings. I liked the work of a woman. It is the right work. But the hardest thing was to work in the fields. My mother forced me to go to the fields and to work hard all day. I came home sore and in pain. One time I was in so much pain that my mother took me to the hospital. That is my most difficult memory. But I ask the same things of my girls, to work.

It was at this time that I was going to the fields every day with my mother and she said, "This part of the field is for you." My mother suffered a lot because of me, she was very busy with me, she cared for my health, gave me food to eat and some money for clothes. She taught me to be brave in the fields and told me, "Someday you will marry and work in the fields for your husband and you must serve him well." I thought this was a very good lesson of life, because I was big and strong for the work, and this is good for a husband.

Life was not too difficult when I was a child, except when my first father died, when I was still very little, just a baby. My mother was given to the younger brother of my father, but I did not know that this man my mother married was not my real father. It was not until I was a grown woman that I knew my real father had died when I was little. The hardest part of my little life was that I was sick a lot with parasites, the pain in the side, and an illness like epilepsy.

I remember that my parents loved me and gave me lots of nice clothes, good food to eat and good care, and also my aunts and uncles on both sides. It was important that I was healthy and that I just played with my friends. Lots of my friends died when I was young, but I still have some of the same friends that were my friends then. My mother taught me many things. But the work of childhood when I was very little was to play, to amuse ourselves. When you are small you just live. The most important and good memory was the playing. I was free.

## NGANDU WOMEN
### Therese

I was born in Nambélé. My father comes from Boseke and my mother from Nambélé. My father is Mbati, my mother Ngandu. My husband Adrienne was from Boda, a long ways away. He was Bofi. I grew up here in Nambélé and I lived with my grandmother because my parents were in Congo. When I married, I lived here in the same neighborhood as my mother, father, and grandmother. I remember when I was young. Back then there were no iron pots like there are today, so our mothers would carry water in clay pots and these pots would break a lot! I played with my friends, and we would make little clay pots like our mothers'. Life is different now than long ago. Children in those times did not play too much because it was so dangerous. There were men who would come in the night and kill people. There were wars between the villages, so the children could not play in the streets or walk in the forest. Black people fought amongst themselves. They fought because of jealousy and missing of being civilized.

In the past, the Mbati fought with the Ngandu to take this village of Nambélé. In the time of President Boganda, the Mbati came here to fight the Ngandu to show who was the strongest, to know this, who was the strongest. My father told me of this. He told me that at this time there were many bad black and white men. I was with my parents and we fled into the forest because of these bad men and the fighting. The people of the past, there were no laws and they were not afraid to kill. We were afraid. Life was difficult. The French military came and took men to force them to work. So my father and mother took us children and we fled into the forest. We ate and hunted and stayed there all day. At night we would quietly come back to the village and shut our door tight and try to sleep. There was so much fear in those times! My father was taken by force by the military near the frontier to search for gold. For a long time he worked there, and my mother went and looked for him while I stayed with my grandmother. My parents were gone a long time. My grandmother, her name was Pricilla, took good care of me and taught me how to farm, to get water, to plant and harvest manioc roots.

................................................................................

## AKA WOMEN
### Nali

................................................................................

When you are very little, you do not have much memory. But I remember when my mother had milk in her breasts and when I cried, my mother gave me her breast and I would drink this milk. I nursed and nursed. But later when I had lots of teeth, I saw her stomach swell and swell. I didn't know why. I asked, "Mother, why is your stomach so swelled?" I thought she was sick, but she said to me, "No, this here in my stomach is a baby." I myself decided to stop taking her breast. "Now I am so big so I will stop taking this milk from my mother." When she was pregnant with a baby, the taste of the milk changed and I was no longer hungry for this milk.

My mother began to have the pains of birth. Suddenly she stood up, she wanted to go to give birth in the forest but she couldn't walk! I saw all the women come, and they said, "Push! Push! Push the baby and the baby will come!" I saw this birth! I asked my mother, "Why is there so much blood? What animal has hurt you?" When mother pushed out the baby, she cried and I cried with my mother and the women said to me, "No, do not cry." I didn't know why my mother had so much pain. But after my mother pushed out the baby, and I saw this baby girl for the first time, I said, "Now I have a sister." My mother gave me this baby. I was so happy to see this new sister! I was not jealous. I carried her if my mother had a little work and I gave her water if she cried.

After the baby was born, we all went to the forest to hunt. We walked and walked and walked. My father carried me and my mother carried the baby. I was so happy. When we got to the place of the hunting, the net would be spread out. My mother and I hid behind a tree and watched. My father and other men made noise to scare the animal out. I remember I took a net and captured chickens, and they cried when I caught them. I remember I had a basket and together my father and I looked for yams. I loved walking in the forest with my father.

We spent lots of time in the forest. I love life in the forest because you can find everything: meat, nuts, honey, mushrooms, natural yams, and caterpillars. There is so much to eat! It was better in the forest than the village. In the forest it was like a vacation. Sometimes in the village there was not enough to eat. When there was not enough to eat, at night I would cry and my mother would go the next day into the forest to find yams for me. If my parents went to look for yams, I would take a little basket and a machete and I would try to dig for them too. The hardest time was I had a friend who ate a yam and it was like poison. You wash it and prepare it exactly right. It is good but after you eat it you vomit and have diarrhea. My friend died of this yam. I was so sad. This was the first time I saw a person die of this poison yam.

I played so much with my friends in the camp when I was little! I played in the forest, but I stayed close to the camp. We would swing in the forest with the vines. We played in the river too, we would make drum sounds in the water. We would dance the *molembai lembai* [dancing with leaves tucked into their wraps or loincloths] and sing. I remember dancing and singing so much in the forest. I imitated the dance of my parents. Sometimes I would build a little hut close to my parents and play with my friends, and we would pretend we were married. I would take a piece of wood and pretend I was a mother, and I nursed my baby. I carried a small basket on my back. This is my best memory when I played with this baby and a little boy. I went in the hut with my little husband, I prepared food for him and nursed my baby. The play of my parents. I loved the forest, the play in the forest.

### AKA WOMEN
## Konga

I remember taking my mother's breast. My mother said to me, "You nurse too much!" So she took her breasts and bound them up. I wanted to nurse and my mother said no. I cried and cried and my mother said, "After awhile you will forget about this," but still I cried and cried. My mother gave me lots of good food to eat to help me forget. My father and mother went for honey and mixed it with water and gave it to me, and when I would cry for the breast my mother would give me *dzambo*. I had sadness for a few days, but my mother gave me so much food to compensate for this loss of milk that after awhile I forgot. I had to quit the breast because my mother was pregnant. My mother's stomach swelled and after a time, she went and gave birth in the forest. I waited in the camp and then my mother came back with a baby. I thought, "This is the baby my mother gave birth to. This is my brother." I was happy.

My best memory when I was little was playing in the forest with my friends. I had so many friends and we loved each other. I remember singing and dancing and swinging in the trees. We would build a little house and pretend we were married, finding yams and feeding our babies. Our little husbands would go hunt for rats and bring them back, and we would grill it and eat together. Our parents would call for us, but we were playing so we did not come! This was our good fun.

After I was born my mother had another child, and this child, when he was a little older, he became sick with *ekila* tortoise. He was so skinny he crawled on the ground, even when he was older. The *nganga* could not heal him. This child died. He found death and death is death. These are my sad memories and when I suffered.

When I was this young girl, my father was a great *tuma*. When he hunted he always brought back meat. He hunted the gazelle and the elephant. Before an elephant hunt, all the hunters gathered in a camp and danced all night. They take a big pot full of powerful medicine and put all their spears into this pot. Every night they dance and sing all night long. When they sleep, they sleep apart from their wives—no sex before the hunt. And if a woman sees her blood [menstruates] she cannot touch the men, the spears or prepare food. She cannot touch anything the men touch. Before the hunt the men chew on the special bark to take away the fear of the hunt. The *tuma*, only he wears a special cord around his arm, and this cord makes him invisible, so that the elephant doesn't see him.

The other hunters are behind him, and if he has a brave son or the son of his brother, learning to be a *tuma*, this boy follows behind the *tuma* and the other hunters after. Once he sees the elephant, he has his cord on and he disappears so the elephant does not know he is there, he slips underneath the elephant and spears him in the heart. Then he runs and hides behind a tree calling for his son to put in the second spear. He tells the other hunters when to put their spears in. The elephant roars and charges and crashes through the trees, the elephant would be so mean and angry! Then the elephant would turn and look for my father, to kill him. But with the second spear, the animal falls down and dies. After the elephant was dead, my father would reappear and come and call everyone to come and divide the meat and help carry the elephant back to camp. I loved elephant meat! If he killed an elephant, everyone ate so well! It could take two weeks to eat all the meat of this elephant. There are no *tumas* now, the times have changed. Before there was much meat to eat, my father was a *tuma* and killed elephants. But now it is hard to find meat, and there is so much hunger for meat. The palm oil is finished, the meat is finished. There is so much hunger.

# Lessons of Respect and Learning to Share

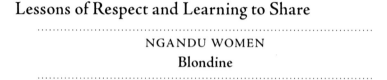

NGANDU WOMEN

## Blondine

My parents taught me many things when I was little, just 3, they taught me to be careful. My father and mother told me, "Never play in the forest because there are snakes there and they can fall from the trees." So I played with my friends in the village. They taught me when I was little how to prepare food. When my mother came back from the fields with a big pot of manioc, she would call me over, "Blondine, watch me. This is how to break the leaves of the manioc. This is how to arrange and prepare the manioc."

The lessons given by the parents, the stories at night around the fire that my parents taught me, this they said to me, "If you go to walk in the forest at night, bad people will get you and kill you, so you have to stay close to home. If a person has a bad heart, they are sorcerers and cause illness, so it is important to be a good person." My parents told me once about someone [who] died and after research they knew it was sorcery, why the person died. After that, I was very afraid of sorcery. I was afraid of the danger at night. I was afraid of the spirits that walk at night. These are the bad people that God throws out of heaven.

My father taught me to respect people. Day after day, at night listening around the fire, my parents taught us the proper things. My father, Joseph, he said to me, "If you refuse to stay and help mother, that is wrong. And you must bow your head and not look at people or speak to them until they notice you, then you can speak to them with respect and look at them." My father gave the instructions to respect my siblings, my friends, my aunts and uncles, because if you do not show respect you will not be spoken to. He taught me because he loved me. He also bought me lots of nice clothes and food because he loved me so much.

My parents also disciplined me. My father spanked me a lot because he was irritable, but my mother only spanked me a little, mostly she spoke to me about being a good person and being respectful to others. If I disobeyed, my parents told me, "You cannot go visit your friends to play. You cannot eat with your friends. You cannot go anywhere but must stay in the house." I remember another time when I was young and I went to the river to fish with my friends and we caught fish to eat. When I got back my mother said to me, "Why did you go to fish? You do not work here at the house when I need you, and go play with your friends instead, so go away and live somewhere else." So I did. I went and spent the nights with my grandmother for awhile. I spent a lot of time with my grandmother because when my mother was finished nursing me, my grandmother, my father's mother, took me away for awhile, and also because my father hit me a lot, so she took me away and I lived with her.

There is no difference in what boys and girls are taught. They are taught the same respect, but the father teaches the boys to hunt and fish, and if they want to do the work of a girl, they are hit and told they are to do the work of a man. Sometimes boys will care for babies, but only a little. Our parents taught us that the husband and wife are not the same, they are not equal, because if you see a father and mother walking together, you do not know who is the father, who is the mother, who will do the work? The mother teaches her daughters to do the work of a woman, to cook, to clean, and to care for babies. My father taught me how to wash his clothes properly, but that is all that he taught me about work when I was young.

My grandmother and grandfather taught me about medicine. They took me into the forest and showed me each plant and how to prepare it and what illness it was good for. I was maybe 10 years old when they taught me these things. They said to me, "For this illness of the stomach, *dibembe*, you can use bark or leaves, the *dibale zakoudou* leaves. You crush the leaves, mix them with water and either use the pump [for enemas] or you can drink the liquid. This is the treatment for *dibembe*." I learned many plants and bark to use for illnesses.

My grandmother was very important in my life. Sometimes she would hide away food, just for me. She said, "Now Blondine, come quietly and eat this food I have saved for you. Don't tell the others, your brothers and sisters, this food is just for you." They would see me sometimes eating the food from my grandmother and get so mad at me and we would fight. My grandmother also told this to me: "One day you will be old like I am. Old and tired. You will walk with a cane and need care and food. It is good to be old, but you will need lots of help." I said to her, "It may be good to be old, but I will never walk with a cane. I will always walk strong."

## NGANDU WOMEN
### Therese

My grandmother was the most important person in my life. At night my grandmother would give me the lessons around the fire. One time she told me this story:

> Once there was a family and the father said to one of his children, "You there! Go and fetch me water! I am thirsty!" The child went and after a long time never returned, so the father said to the second child,

"You there! Go fetch me water, I am thirsty!" This child went and like the first child never returned. The father said this to all his children, and one by one, the third, fourth, and fifth child went. None returned. So the father said to his wife, "All my children have gone and not returned. I am still thirsty, you go and fetch me water." The wife got up and left. She too never returned. The husband said, "I will look for my wife and children." He was gone a long time and like his family, he never returned.

My grandmother said to me when she finished the story, "So grandchild, the lesson is this: Take care, these are dangerous times. There is war, and people are killing people when they go for water or to work in the fields. Be very careful with your life." I remember that families would go in groups to work in the fields or to get water. Men went with machetes for protection.

I played a little but not too much because of the dangerous time. My grandfather told me, "Now play is finished, now is the time to work." My grandmother taught me lessons of being a woman, but grandfather also taught me. They taught me that you work hard and show respect to people. The most important person in the house is the man, because the man commands. The women give all the care in the house, but men command, they give money for things like soap, clothes, medicine, and other things. I was taught that women are stupid if they try to command. It is the man who commands the house. My grandmother said to me, "Give lots of attention and respect to your husband when you are married. Do not speak very much. Also give respect to your friends, your parents, and grandparents. If you see a grandmother on the road with a heavy burden, with lots of things on her head, and you see she is tired, you take the load for her. If she asks you for something, 'My daughter bring me water,' then you bring her water, you do not refuse." It is a hard work when you are a woman. That is one lesson I was taught.

## AKA WOMEN
### Nali

When you are little you don't know anything, but as you get bigger you start certain activities and you have the spirit to know. When I was a young girl, my mother made a small basket for me and we went into the forest together. In the forest my mother picked yams and she showed me the vine for the yam. My mother would say, "Come with me to the forest and we will look for yams." She would take me into the forest with my little basket, and if my mother saw a yam she would say, "Listen, one day you will be a woman and this is how you find food in the forest." She showed me the yam, "See my daughter, this is a special cord. This is the yam cord high in the tree, and if you see this there will be a yam you dig for. And when you see a mushroom, here it is, here my daughter this is a good mushroom, take this. This one is a bad one and if you eat it you will die. There is so much to learn, but after time and time you will learn." She would set out the food before me and teach me. After time I learned the difference between the good yam and the poison one. I learned the cord of the yam. I learned the medicine, the mushrooms, the plants, the *koko* leaves.

When I was bigger and brave, I began to participate in the net-hunt. My father taught me how to be brave. He taught me to hunt with dogs for the porcupine. Sometimes I left with my friends to hunt. We would trap a porcupine, bring it back to camp, and my father said, "Thank you for being brave and getting the porcupine." When we went to the place to hunt, the men put up the net, and I and my mother hid behind a tree. If an antelope came I'd be very brave and catch the antelope when it was in the net. I had to be careful because its horns are sharp. My mother or father would hit its head on a tree to kill it, and the pieces would be shared. During the net-hunt, everyone knows their own net. If an antelope goes into your net, you know if it is a gazelle or an antelope because the sounds are different. If it is in your net, everyone knows it dies in what net, and if it is yours to share, you give a little to everyone.

I learned a lot from my parents. My mother and father said to me, "You are a young girl and you need to know how to find food for yourself. If we die you need to learn to find food and learn how to prepare for yourself." My mother taught me to prepare food, she would cook a large amount and share it with everyone. My mother taught me to share. She said, "My daughter when you have food in the forest, even it if is a small amount you share it. Sharing is good." If I gave just a little and kept a lot for myself, the people would say, "Oh you are so mean and selfish. Will you do this when you are married?" Other people said, "Nali is mean and selfish and saves it all for herself." I'd be ashamed. And if my mother asked something of me and I refused, she would say, "Now it is OK to refuse, but when you are older and if we find honey or meat, we will not give it to you because you are acting like a small child."

This is one lesson I have taught my children. If my child is greedy and does not share, I say, "No, my daughter, if you find something you share this with your friends. If they ask, you share."

## AKA WOMEN
### Konga

When I became a little bigger I would watch my parents and I began to learn. My parents taught me that when you are a woman, that each day you decide what to do and together you do that with your husband. The work of males and females is not so different. If the woman is tired, the man will look for the wood and prepare the fire, get the water and cook the food. My grandmother also taught me how to get water at the river, how to look for wood, how to cut the *koko* leaves and prepare food. I stayed with my grandmother and she would prepare food, and give some to everyone, and I saw this. If you refuse to give, to share, your parents will say, "This girl here is stingy, she will not share with others. When she finds food it is only for herself." And all the others would say, "Oh she is so mean! That one does not share!"

When my mother had the baby, and she would go into the forest, she would give me the baby and show me how to wash the baby, to give it water, and after a time the baby would stop crying. I was always with my parents. When I was a bigger girl and when I was brave, I would go together with my parents on the net-hunt. I would hide behind a tree, and if I trapped an antelope or gazelle, I called to my parents to come and cut its neck, or I looked for a branch to hit it on the head. I would cut off a small morsel if my parents killed the animal, and take the head or a small piece in my little basket. In my own *huma*, I prepared this small piece and called my friends. I shared a little with everyone and we'd eat together, me and my friends. This was so good to eat this meat together!

# When the Moon is Full and the Night is Clear

......................................................................

## NGANDU WOMEN
### Blondine

......................................................................

When I was maybe 6 or 8 years old I began to work. One of my best memories was when I was nearly 10 years old. I grew peanuts and sold them with my friends and made money! I guarded my money carefully and I used it to buy clothes. When you have good clothes then the parents of a nice man will notice you and say, "Oh! Look at that beautiful young woman! She would make a good wife!" At that time in life the girls say, "No, I am too young to sleep in another house, but when I am a big girl I will marry." It depends if you want to marry or if you want to go to school. I went to school for two years but had to quit because of the work and also because the teacher hit us students too much! I think school is bad because the students get hit, but I think education is good.

My other best memory is when I was 7 or 8 and all the girls at night would get together and play, dancing and singing together in groups. The dances were *gbagba* and *amiteē*, this is a kicking and dancing game. Each night when the moon was full and the night was clear and we would finish early with our work, we would call all our friends to play. One time, when I was a little older, there was a boy I liked and he like me also. During the dance, the boy started to dance with me and I said, "Oh this boy, I am dancing with a boy!" And I knew he would say too, "Oh that girl, I am dancing with a girl that I like!" If I was playing the dancing games with my friends, it was fun, but if my mother asked for help and I refused, my mother would hit me. My mother would take me from my friends to work in the fields and tell me, "You cannot play with your friends. Now you must work." I thought to myself, "This is bad to work in the fields." But after I went I thought, "This work is not so bad because there is maize and food to eat. This work is good because I like to learn from my mother the work of women." I did not go to school for very long because of that hard work. Now it is difficult because I understand the importance of school and studies. There are other women who can speak nice French like the women on TV, and they own cars and nice clothes. I have no chance of this. But those are my memories, playing and working hard.

## NGANDU WOMEN
### Therese

I was so little when my grandmother started to teach me the work of a woman. I wanted to play, but grandmother said, "No, look at what women's work is. See how they prepare the food, and care for the family. See how hard they work in the fields. Someday you will have a husband. You need to learn that in the morning you prepare the bed, clean the bedroom from the night before. Wash his clothes and properly prepare his food. This is the preferred work of women." My grandmother taught me to farm, to take the basket and get roots, to prepare food. I cared for my siblings and when grandmother went to work in the fields, I came and took care of them. If they were hungry I fed them. Grandfather also told me when I was still very young, "Play is finished. One day you will marry and you will need to serve your husband and your friends in your home. If your husband demands something, you will need to answer him." So I began the work of women. But sometimes, when the moon lighted the night and if it was safe, we played the dancing games and *cache-cache* and I would look for fun.

### Therese's Story

I have a story my grandmother told me around the fire when I was done with my work:

There was a village once, like Nambélé, with many people, the men with their women, children, goats, sheep, pigs, all these in the village, and houses, fields, and a river. Now a man, Melee, a devil, he lived ten kilometers from the village, he was so huge! He had a form unknown, not like a human. He had a field in the back of his home, and at a certain time he had bananas, fruit, and other things in his field. Now there was a person in the village who went to see Melee's field to steal from the devil, the manioc, the bananas, all the things growing in the field. So the devil Melee, he was so mad! "Who stole from my fields? I will fly over the village and swallow all their homes, their children, the husbands and wives, pigs, sheep, all the fields and homes." As he flew closer and closer to swallow everything, he sang this song:

> Kpa, Kpa mignon nga mini bato
> Kpa, Kpa mignon nga mini mbole
> Kpa, Kpa mignon nga mini mazadji
> Kpa, Kpa mignon nga mini mai
>
> (I will swallow the people
> I will swallow the goats
> I will swallow the houses
> I will swallow the water)

As he sang he came closer and closer and he swallowed everything! All the houses, pigs, now all the people! He swallowed and swallowed and finally he ate all the village, and he arrived at the end of the village and he found a woman who was very pregnant. The devil, he tried to swallow her, first her head, but her stomach was so big it wouldn't fit in, so he tried to swallow her feet first, but he couldn't eat any more! His stomach had too much in it. He had eaten the whole village! The men, the women, children, houses, water, pigs, and trees, and now this woman when he tried to swallow, he could only get her halfway in! Her head to her chest to her belly and it was too much! So her vomited her up and said to her, "OK, now woman! You are pregnant so I cannot eat you. I will vomit a little house and a little field and a little river so you can work. I will wait until you give birth, and when your infant is born I will swallow you and your baby. But now when you are pregnant I cannot."

Now the devil, he vomited a little house, a little river and little field, and a little tree for a fire, and he vomited plates and pots to cook with, and he vomited a drum. He said to the woman, "If you give birth, you tap on the drum and I will come if I hear this drum, I will know you have given birth and I will eat you!" " Okay," said the woman. So he left to his house to wait for the woman to give birth. Now all the people, goats, and pigs still lived in his stomach. The people talked, the pigs grunted, the chickens cawed in his stomach. Soon the woman gave birth to two babies, twin boys. One was named Zanga and the other Zaou. The children were born in the morning, and in the same day, these two babies grew to the size of men. And these two children started to make knifes, spears and machetes and crossbows, and when they finished they went to their mama and said, "Tap your drum and when the devil comes, we will trap and kill this devil and save the people in his stomach." She cried and cried! "No, Mama, don't cry," said her boys, "tap the drum, and when he comes we will start a war!" So she began to tap the drum but she was so afraid! "Now Mama," said her boys again, "stay in the house and don't come out, and when he comes we will start the war and kill him!" The demon heard the drum and he came for the woman, and as he came he sang the same song, to swallow her,

> Kpa, Kpa mignon nga mini bato
> Kpa, Kpa mignon nga mini mbole
> Kpa, Kpa mignon nga mini mazadji
> Kpa, Kpa mignon nga mini mai

> (I will swallow the people
> I will swallow the goats
> I will swallow the houses
> I will swallow the water)

Now the two twins with their knives and spears heard this, and they sang,

> Komba za Komba
> Zaou na Zaou
> Zanga za nzokpe kete mingelou

> (Komba za Komba
> Man to man
> You are brave men to cut the throat of the devil)

The two twins started to throw their spears and knives, and they killed Melee, they had so many knives and spears, and he died! Their mother came out of the house and celebrated, "Thank you my sons! You are so brave! You have saved all the village! Thank you my brave sons!" She kissed her sons, she was so joyous, "You together have killed the demon!" Now the sons took the knife and cut the demon's stomach and all came out alive! The goats, the men and women and children, the houses, the trees, the rivers, the fields, and all came out into the same place. "Thank you, these two children! We thought we would live and die in his stomach! You have saved our lives!" Everyone shouted! "Now you two will be president of our country!" The people built a beautiful house and everyone helped, even the goats and pigs! Now all was finished and the people built a big fire and burned the demon into ashes! He was finished!

My grandmother told me this for a lesson: to steal is not good. The demon swallowed everyone because of one villager who stole from his fields. This is how our parents taught us important lessons. We tell our stories to teach our children and grandchildren.

..................................................................................

## AKA WOMEN
### Nali

..................................................................................

When you are a little older you can go into the forest alone and search for food, but not when you are young. There are dangers in the forest. The dangers are the serpent, and if you go far, the leopard. When I was a young girl I accompanied my father to visit the traps. As we were walking down the path, I had to go *caca*, so I said to my father, "Wait for me here I have to poop." I went off the path and there was a huge tree with a branch and the tree had fallen in the forest. I climbed up the trunk and went *caca*, and while I was up there I saw an antelope at the base of the tree. It was just lying there. I thought, "Is this antelope asleep or dead? I will go tell my father to come and get this meat." I quietly and slowly, slowly climbed down the trunk of this great tree and quietly went down the path to where my father waited, "Come quickly and get this antelope, it is either asleep or dead!"

Together we went back to the tree and he saw this antelope just lying there. My father was very wise and intelligent and he said, "Oh my daughter come quickly! This is the den of a leopard. Come quickly! She will kill you. We must get away quickly!" I was afraid, and as we were walking away we heard with our ears the leopard growl so we ran and ran. My father told me, "This is the den of a leopard, during the day she sleeps and nurses her young, and at night she hunts. That leopard has killed an antelope and took it back to its babies, and that antelope is food for her and her young. Tomorrow I will go and lay traps along the trail leading from her den, she has many trails." So the next day he returned and quietly went up the path and put traps all around the leopard's territory. "When she goes out to poop after eating all that antelope meat I will catch her in a trap." I thought, "This is dangerous work for my dad, if the leopard catches him, he will die." He returned and found the leopard on one of the paths caught in the trap. She was weak from struggling so he killed her with his machete. He heard her young calling to her but when they saw him they fled. This is my memory. My father said that leopards are dangerous but especially when they have babies.

My mother taught me how to build my own little *huma* [hut]. When my mother would start to build a hut, she would call to me and say, "Watch how I build this hut." I would watch, then my friends and I went into the forest, got the trees, cut them, and built our own huts. I built mine close to my parents and I slept there. I didn't want to sleep with my parents because they had so many children. But when it rained I would go sleep with my parents, or if it was cold or very dark or if I was afraid, I would cry out and my parents said, "What is wrong? Come and sleep with us." When I was in my parent's hut and they began to have sex, the activity of the night, I could hear them. I thought, "Oh maybe I will sleep somewhere else." They would say to me, "Go to your own hut," and so I would go to my grandmother's. The difference was that when I was little, I slept a lot with my grandmother, but as I got older I built my own hut and lived alone with my friends.

When I was little I danced. I also did a little work. I danced the *molembai lembai*. All the girls would make a bunch of leaves and dance. If a dance was in another camp, I left with my friends and we danced and danced. When the dance was finished, we returned to our own camp and danced and sang more. I loved to dance! I went for the dance with my friends, and the boys searched for girls, I said, "Now I am too young to look for men. I will wait." But the difference between the play of boys and girls, is that the boys play with a little net or a little spear and hunt for small animals. Boys hunt for rats or they throw the spear at a papaya and pretend it is an animal.

## AKA WOMEN
### Konga

Mostly I played and played and did only a little work. When I started to become a bigger girl, then my mother went to the forest to search for food and I went too. At certain times my mother would find so many yams, and we took a big basket to put the yams in. I became a yam specialist. We went with the other women, walking in the forest. They showed me how find wood and food in the forest and how to prepare it. Sometimes I would go into the forest with my friends and my parents said, "If you walk in the forest with your friends and search for food, take a little basket and a machete." And we would search for yams, wood and bring them back. We put the food in a pot, started the fire, and cooked the yams. When they were done, I would give them to my parents and to the people in camp.

At this time, I had a terrible sickness and this sickness was in my stomach and it hurt so bad! As I walked in the forest this sickness attacked me! I went to my house and after a very long time, by lots of interventions I slowly became better. But sometimes even now this sickness attacks. My mother gave me medicine and while she lived, she always tended to my health. She knew the medicine for this sickness, and I would cry in pain. But when my mother died, she took this knowledge with her. My mother died when she was young. She had a terrible sickness in her chest and treatment did not work. She died after just a few days of this illness. It was a terrible time because my father had just died also. I was so terribly sad. I had no parents. I cried and cried. I thought, "First my father then my mother. I am abandoned."

My father and mother both died, but my grandmother told me, "If you cry a lot you can become sick with an illness when you have so much pain in you heart. If you cry and have many tears, you will not see good when you are an adult. A little crying is good because you loved your parents, but too much crying is not good." I went to live with my uncle, the little brother of my father, and when he'd leave for the forest he would find mushrooms and meat, and I'd prepare it and we'd eat together. He shared with me like this until I was a grown woman.

My uncle and his wife had a little baby who died of *ekila ya kema*. It was so difficult. This baby died because my uncle had killed a monkey with a crossbow and brought it to the camp, and when he arrived at the camp, he put it on the ground, and the baby crawled to the monkey and sat close to it. Soon after he saw this monkey, the baby turned red and convulsed, and after a few days he died. The treatment is to take the skin of a monkey or the crown of the head and grill it, then make it into a powder and blow it up the nose. It enters the brain. Or you can vaccinate on the temple with the powder from the crown of the monkey's head. But babies without treatment will die. Monkeys are predators. If a pregnant mother eats monkey, she can give illness to the baby, or if a child sees someone eat a monkey, they will get this sickness. It was very hard for me. I had just lost my mother and father, and now this baby died too.

## Developmental and Cross-Cultural Perspectives

The foundational schemas reflected in the Aka and Ngandu women's narratives shape cultural models concerning parenting ethnotheories, attachment styles, learning, and teaching of cultural values and beliefs.[30] Key foundational schemas are taught early in life, are socially sanctioned and are learned and lived quickly by the child. For the Aka, sanctions include teasing or expressions of disapproval. Ngandu children face more severe repercussions such as restrictions of activity, food, playtime, and corporal punishment.[31] Cognitive anthropology suggests that cultural schemas or internal working models (IWMs) influence how people view themselves, others, and the social-natural environment. Attachment theory indicates that the IWM is a "dynamic model based upon the infant's experiences with their caregivers" whereby they develop either a secure or an insecure IWM.[32]

Internal working models as "internal representations" help individuals predict and interpret others' behavior and "plan their course of action."[33] They provide the basis for an understanding self and others. As the internal working model is based upon the infants' and children's interactions and experiences with their caregivers, by exploring these relationships within the settings, customs, and parental ethnotheories (the "developmental niche") of the Aka and Ngandu children, we can understand how the IWMs influence children's development within the larger culture, and how their culturally specific schema or cognitive models develop.[34] That is, we can understand how Aka children become Aka adults and how Ngandu infants grow into Ngandu adults, each developing culturally specific ideologies and schemas.

How does culture inform the development of the Aka or Ngandu child? The "developmental niche" emphasizes the importance of the settings in which children grow up, the cultural customs of childcare, and parental ethnotheories, how parents understand their roles as parents, what is important to them as mothers and fathers, and how these ideas and beliefs influence their child's development.[35] The developmental niche informs the internal working model of the child, which in turn determines the way the child views itself and forms attachments, relations with others and with the larger world. Culturally specific views of the environment are linked to these "customs of care, parental ideology" and ultimately the "internal working models."[36] Those parents living in, or perceiving, a secure environment where resources are seen as abundant would teach their children that the natural and social environments are generous, that other people can be relied upon and trusted. And as those around you can be trusted, and relationships are rewarding and enduring, there tends to be high-investment parenting.[37] The reverse is true for those insecurely attached, where the world is understood to be hostile and the future is seen as unpredictable, the reproductive strategy then becomes "opportunistic and facultative."[38]

The Aka generally see the forest environment as giving, sharing, and trusting, but like all relationships, at times problematic.[39] This view of the socio-natural environment has many impacts on their behavior. Aka "demand share"; they have an "immediate return system," living "in the moment": if food is gathered or game is captured, it is eaten that day.[40] Aka trust that the future will take care of itself. They have intimate and indulgent infant care patterns, because like their relationships, including with the natural environment, social relations are trusting and secure. Aka relationships and behaviors are linked to these cognitive models, contributing to and reinforcing ideologies of sharing, of having a trusting and generous view of self, others, and the natural environment. These ideologies profoundly influence the socio-emotional development of the child.[41]

The Ngandu know and spend time in the forest and view the natural (and social) environment as a source of wealth, providing them with food and a means of earning income, but they know the forest also as an unpredictable and at times frightening place. Any number of "bad" spirits, ancestral to the "more generalized spirits," can cause harm, illness, or death.[42] Sorcery is talked about nearly every day, and people are genuinely concerned about being victims of sorcery. Strong belief in sorcery alludes to a general mistrust of others and uncertainty in their particular social and natural environments, and can be seen as the "attribution of hostile intent to others," contributing to certain styles of attachment between the parent and child.[43] Ngandu practice a "delayed return system" planning for an uncertain and unpredicatable future.[44]

Men and women work hard to provide for their children and families. They plant fields and gardens, save, and invest for the future. They are generous to family and friends, respectful to each other and strangers, and take good care of their elderly kin. Ngandu devote a lot of time and energy in maintaining and building social relations and alliances, which provide security against economic and social misfortune.

The Aka and Ngandu have maintained a set of practices, parental ethnotheories, values, foundational schemas, and cultural identities that are quite distinct, and are the result of cultural models responding to the social and natural environments. There is an interaction between the environment, culture, and behavior.[45] These early influences are dynamic and strong but not forever bounded. Aka children grow into competent Aka adults, and Ngandu infants grow into competent Ngandu adults for many reasons. They learn how to be an Aka or Ngandu individual through various avenues: from their parent's behavior and care, adapting and preparing them for adulthood, from other children and adults, and from the rich social and natural setting they grow up in, a setting that is rapidly changing.

.....................................

Children everywhere must learn particular cultural values, beliefs, and practices. This is accomplished through a variety of mechanisms. We have seen in this chapter how Aka and Ngandu children learn in a multiplicity of ways and from a wide variety of people—fathers, grandmothers, siblings, and other children. Learning for these children occurs in very specific and differing ways. By studying Aka and Ngandu parental ethnotheories, modes of cultural transmission, and patterns of social learning, we can understand when, from whom, and how children learn. The women's stories in the next two chapters follow them as they grow and develop into young women. Blondine, Therese, Nali, and Konga tell us of their daily lives, loves, losses, marital relations, and sexual experiences. They share what it means to transition from childhood to womanhood, from being children to having children of their own. We also will see how the nature of their relational bonds of intimacy, love, and attachment are grounded in the knowledge of the potential impermanence of the bond. The women's narratives emphasize the nature of the diversity and similarity of lived experience as they grow up and further experience life, love, and loss.

## NOTES FROM THE FIELD
**Fall 2003**

*—Have I ever been having fun talking to the women in my research study! I have been hanging out in the "house of the three women," as I call it. It is a red-mud house on the main road, has one large room divided inside into three rooms where each of the women and their families sleep. In back is a still for brewing empacho, a clothesline and small cooking room. B. is so hilarious! She is telling me about games she used to play when she was young and demonstrates by grabbing the other women nearby, and they begin clapping, singing and dancing. She keeps feeding me koko with smoked caterpillars, which is good. L. is very sweet and quiet, she has a one-year-old baby she nurses as we talk. N. is quiet too but speaks French very well, she just looks so tired and sad, like life has been hard. T. is great! She never wants to stop talking, and her family, grandkids or daughters gather around her when we chat, to "help her remember." A. is very quiet, very pregnant and very hard to chat with. When I ask her a question she looks upwards for a long, long, long time, as though the answer will magically drop down from the sky, or suddenly appear, written on the ceiling. I can't wait to start with T., G., and the others....*

**Summer 2004**

*—The ex-mayor has bought a TV and for 100 CFAs you can watch TV, high volume from 5–10 pm. Enterprising adolescent girls have set up concession stands (think lemonade stands) and sell oranges and peanuts for the movie-goers. And as the shows get "better" (meaning violent and/or R rated) as the evening progresses, the price of admission goes up. The wonders of globalization.*

*—While I was talking with the women today, I watched this little 4?-year-old girl take a knife and cut manioc leaves for dinner, pausing on occasion to sharpen her knife and then continue chopping the bunch of leaves. When she was done with that chore, she helped to take care of her baby sister, carrying the little toddler on her back and she was just a little girl herself. I also saw a little 3-year-old girl make a pretend meal (dirt and a cricket, dead) while another little boy built a pretend house and started to make a real fire outside of his "house." Watched the older girls dance the gbagba game— about 10–12 girls form a half-circle and one by one each girl falls back into the arms of the others, who push her back upright. While they play this they sing, "I am going to be married and go far, far away and here I go!" They play this at night when the moon is bright.*

**Fall 2004**

—*I dreamt about the kids last night, that I got to visit them for awhile and told them goodbye again and they started crying "mom, mom" and I woke up and it was a goat outside my window "maaing." Funny, but hard to wake up and nope no kids, just a goat.*

—*Tried getting to Mbaiki today to call the kids, but during the night the skies cut loose, it was like a river pouring down all day. Rotten luck, I went and stood for two hours in the market to try and get a ride. But they told me, "We aren't going and even if we did, we'd be stopped at the barriers by the police and anyway the truck lost its brakes yesterday."*

—*Got to Mbaiki yesterday and talked to the kids!!!!! It was so wonderful to hear their voices!!!! They sounded great and are doing well. Whew! I am so happy to know the kids are ok!!! I ended up walking 3 hours, crossed the Lobaye in a dugout tree-canoe (that was fun), walked a few more hours, got a ride part of the way. When I finally reached a phone and called the kids, "Mom, L. is getting into my stuff and J. is bugging me and…" I loved it! Normal stuff, complaints! At $10.00/minute!! But how wonderful to hear.*

—*In this one camp there is a young girl with a terrible tropical ulcer on her foot. A Dr. visiting here from Germany (to "see pygmies") and I went to the clinic in Nambélé to find medicine ect., for her. Of course there was no medicine, no bandages, nothing, nothing. So he drives off, yelling at me in four different languages (only one I understood), screaming that I was useless. I did NOT need him to point out my uselessness. I feel useless every day when I open my door and 50 people are there to see me to "fix" their illnesses and wounds. He left most of his stuff here (which I gave away) as he literally just jumped in his truck and drove off bellowing, and that was that. But he is right about one thing—it is upsetting to feel helpless, to see so much sickness and death from diseases that in other places are treatable and preventable. He is burnt out, I think. I wonder when anger over injustice is replaced by a general anger at everything? Because then it becomes just a useless rage. My thought is if you're going to scream at the injustice in the world, scream in a way that will people listen. Scream in a way that works toward promoting change and awareness of injustice, don't just scream.*

—*On a side note, the girl healed nicely and I sent a picture of her healed ankle to the Dr.*

## QUESTIONS FOR REFLECTION

1. How do modes of production, male-female relations, and patterns of infant care affect how, what, and from whom social learning occurs for the Aka and Ngandu? How did you learn as a child? How did/does social learning occur in your life?
2. Why do you think play in childhood might be important? What do you think you may have learned through play?
3. Ngandu girls' childhood ends sooner than boys' because the females begin working sooner, having more subsistence and household duties. How might this be a reflection of systems of kinship and descent?
4. How would you characterize your culture's male-female relations, patterns of childcare, attachment styles, and foundational schema's?

## NOTES

1. B.S. Hewlett et al., 2011; Boyette, 2011; Gergely and Csibra 2006; Gergely and Kiraly. 2007; Csibra and Gergely 2006, in B.S. Hewlett et al., 2011. For research on social learning amongst the Aka and Ngandu, see B.S. Hewlett et al., 2011 and for play, see Kamei 2005.
2. B.S. Hewlett et al. 2000a, 174; Meehan 2008, 227.
3. B. L. Hewlett and B. S. Hewlett 2008, 22.
4. B. L. Hewlett and B. S. Hewlett 2008, 22; Woodburn 1982.
5. Of the high-investment care that infants receive on a daily basis, 22 percent comes from allomothers (Hewlett et al. 2000a, 174; Meehan 2008, 227). Anthropologists, such as Hrdy (2005), have predicted for some time that older siblings, cousins, and other family members play important roles as "child-minders" and caregivers (Hrdy 2005 citing Wiessner 1977; Tronick et al. 1987; Hames 1988; LeVine 1988; Konner 2005).
6. Hewlett et al. 2000, 174; Meehan 2008, 227. Weaning is both an important topic and one that has implications for psychological, evolutionary, and an-thropological theories (see Fouts et al. 2000, Fouts 2004, Fouts and Brookshire 2009a, Fouts and Lamb 2009b, Fouts et al. forthcoming; Ainsworth 1967; Draper and Harpending 1987; Hawkes et al. 1997; Trivers 1974; Akin 1985; Gray 1996; Nardi 1985).
7. B.S. Hewlett et al., 2011; Meehan 2005; Boyette, 2011.
8. B.S. Hewlett et al., 2011; Meehan 2005. See also: Boyette, 2011; B.S. Hewlett et al. 2000a; Meehan 2008; Tronick et al. 1987.
9. Boyette, 2011; B. S. Hewlett 1992; B.S. Hewlett et al. 2000; Fouts 2009a, in B.S. Hewlett et al., 2011.
10. Boyette, 2011; B.S. Hewlett et al. 2011.
11. Cultural transmission uses analogies from population genetics and epidemiology to construct mathematic models of cultural transmission (B.S. Hewlett et

al. 2011). See also: B.S.Hewlett and Cavalli-Sforza 1986a; Boyd and Richerson 1985; Cavalli-Sforza and Feldman 1981; Richerson and Boyd 2005; Freedman and Gorman 1993, in Quinlan and Quinlan 2007, 172; B. L. Hewlett and B. S. Hewlett 2008.

12. B.S. Hewlett et al. 2011.

13. B. L. Hewlett and B. S. Hewlett 2008; B.S. Hewlett et al. 2011.

14. Woodburn 1982; B.S. Hewlett et al. 2000a.

15. B. L. Hewlett and B. S. Hewlett 2008.

16. B. L. Hewlett and B. S. Hewlett 2008.

17. B. S. Hewlett et al. 1998; B.S. Hewlett et al. 2000b, 160; Fouts and Brookshire 2009a, in B.S. Hewlett et al. 2011. LeVine et al. (1977) notes that infant mortality is the prime factor that explains differences in childcare patterns between industrialized and agricultural cultures; that is, agricultural parents are being more indulgent with children because of higher mortality rates. There is no evidence that the differing forms of infant care between the Aka and Ngandu parents favor a better health outcome for the infants of one or the other people (see also B.S. Hewlett and Lamb 2000a).

18. B. S. Hewlett 1992.

19. B. S. Hewlett et al. 1998.

20. B.S. Hewlett et al., 2011; for a discussion of the potential reasons for observed differences between Aka and Ngandu patterns of childcare, see B. S. Hewlett et al. 1998.

21. Kitanishi 1998; B. S. Hewlett 1992.

22. B. S. Hewlett and Noss 2001; Kitanishi 1998.

23. B. S. Hewlett 1992; Meehan 2005, 2008; B.S.Hewlett et al. 2011; Fouts et al. forthcoming.

24. B. S. Hewlett 1992.

25. Boyette, 2011; B. S. Hewlett 1992; B.S. Hewlett et al. 2000a; Fouts and Brookshire 2009a, in B.S.Hewlett et al. 2011.

26. B. S. Hewlett 1992; B.S.Hewlett et al. 2011; Meehan 2005; Boyette, 2011.

27. Bock and Sellen 2002; Boyette, 2011. See also: B.S. Hewlett et al. 2011; Gosso et al. 2005; Konner, M. 2005; Kamei, N. 2005; Koyama 2011.

28. B. S. Hewlett 1992; B.S. Hewlett et al. 2011; Meehan 2005; Boyette, 2011.

29. B. S. Hewlett 1992.

30. B. L. Hewlett and B. S. Hewlett 2008.

31. B.S. Hewlett et al. 2011.

32. B.S. Hewlett et al. 2000a, 287.

33. Super and Harkness 1982, 373–74; B. S. Hewlett 1992; B.S. Hewlett et al. 2000a; Meehan 2008; Fouts 2009b.

34. The three components of the developmental niche model are: (1) the physical and social settings in which the child lives, (2) culturally regulated customs of childcare, and (3) the psychology of the caretakers (Super and Harkness 1992, 373–74). Super and Harkness suggest that the settings, customs, and parental ideologies mediate the child's development within the larger culture, with the

parental ethnotheories (ideologies) being the most important. The useful-
ness of the developmental niche model is that it provides the context in which
socio-emotional development takes place. Super and Harkness 1992, 373–74;
B. S. Hewlett 1992; B.S.Hewlett et al. 2000a; Meehan 2008; Fouts and Lamb
2009b.

35. Super and Harkness 1992, 373–74; B. S. Hewlett 1992; B.S. Hewlett et al.
2000a; Meehan 2008; Fouts and Lamb 2009b.
36. B. S. Hewlett 1992; B.S. Hewlett et al. 2000a; Belsky 1997, 364.
37. B. S. Hewlett 1992; B.S. Hewlett et al. 2000a; Belsky 1997, 364.
38. B. S. Hewlett 1992; B.S. Hewlett et al. 2000a; Belsky 1997, 364.
39. Ichikawa 1992 in B.S. Hewlett and Noss 2001 295.
40. B. S. Hewlett 1992; Woodburn 1982.
41. Bird-David 1990, in B..S. Hewlett et al. 2000a, 155–76; Woodburn 1982.
42. B. S. Hewlett 1992.
43. See Quinlan and Quinlan (2007) for further discussion of sorcery and parental
investment.
44. B.S. Hewlett et al. 2000a, 295; Woodburn 1982.
45. B.S. Hewlett et al. 2000a.

...................................

# CHAPTER 3

# The Components of a Good Life

I thought about the changes that took place in my body and thought, "Now this is good because I am a woman. A man will ask for marriage. I will have a house, children, and I will be very gentle to my babies. Life will be good."

—BLONDINE

Love is the work of the night; love and play are nice together if it makes a pregnancy.

—AKA WOMAN

This chapter follows the transition from Aka and Ngandu adolescence to young adulthood, as the women grow and develop, fall in love, and marry. The timing of puberty and menarche, the increasing range of adolescent exploration, socially and sexually, are taking place at a distinct period of adolescent brain development. Adolescents are able to think abstractly and innovatively, to problem-solve, invent, explore, plan, find new solutions to problems, to adapt to new and novel situations. They are developing social relationships and networks, forming long-lasting attachments and social bonds, as well as cultivating gendered roles and distinct identities, taking risks, and building reputations. Adolescents, although reproductively immature and dependent to a certain extent upon others' provisioning, are able to gain experience in social, economic, and ideological areas before experiencing the demands and responsibilities of adulthood and marriage.[1]

The women's narratives emphasize the nature of culture and social reproduction in understanding the diversity of lived experience, illustrating the interactions between biology (sexual desire, attachment, and compassion), ecology (political-economic setting), and culture (schema, ideas, cultural models about gender, sex, and love).[2] Although humans share a biological heritage with other animals, humans have characteristics that are somewhat unique (such as allomaternal care): we not only have the ability to empathize with others, to feel compassion and love, we also have the ability to rapidly acquire behaviors and knowledge, to acquire cumulative culture.[3] These characteristics make for various configurations of sexual desire, love, and attachment. As this chapter illustrates, one way to understand the social relations among men and women, and indeed many human behaviors, is by looking at the interactions between biology, culture, and ecology.

## On Becoming a Woman

Adolescence is a time of vulnerability, risk, opportunity, and anticipation, a transitional time in which a multitude of biological, behavioral, and intellectual changes are occurring. The timing of puberty and menarche, the increasing range of adolescent exploration, socially and sexually, are taking place at a distinct period of adolescent brain development, a time in which "abstract thought is possible."[4] Adolescents have the cognitive ability to learn and understand "key areas of cultural knowledge, cosmological, gender and political ideology, egalitarianism."[5] These crucial foundational schemas are, for the Aka, transmitted and framed around biological development, that is, knowledge of menstruation as *ekila*, referring to "blood, taboo, a hunter's meal, animal's power to harm and particular dangers to human reproduction, production health, and sanity."[6] Aka and Ngandu have food taboos, for instance, often associated with varying with life stages, such as menstruation or pregnancy, restricting what the individual or the entire family can eat. As a young adolescent Aka girl explained, "My parents did not teach me this when I was too little and did not have knowledge, but when I was older.... I was given knowledge of *ekila*. This knowledge comes from both your mother and father, from grandparents to grandparents. It is passed down generation after generation." An Aka adolescent female provided a lengthy list of her taboo foods, taught to her around the time of her first menses:

> I do not eat snake, turtle, or the big lizard of the forest. I will not eat the rat. This taboo is for me and for all the young girls, because if I do I will not marry. I do not eat other things because when I am pregnant

I will have a difficult time. Each family is different, and my mother and siblings have the same taboos as me. There are different taboos within each *dikàndá* [patriclan], and in the subclan there are different taboos, and within each family, each person has their own taboos. I found my taboo as the same food as my parents when they ate [the food] and their baby died.

Taboos associated with *ekila* "begin to suggest explanations for key areas of cultural practice...defin[ing] reproductive potential, productive activities...moral and personal qualities...shared so that group members experience good health, unproblematic childbirth, and child rearing and successful hunting and gathering...the basic components of a good life."[7] As adolescents and young adults learning key cultural schemas, Aka and Ngandu not only create and contest cultural beliefs and values, but also importantly conserve and carry on a "flow of tradition, bringing something of the past into the present day and perhaps help[ing to] create a sense of a more ordered, predictable, and secure world."[8]

Adolescents embody and reflect society's values and needs, promote traditions, and create a place for those cultural beliefs within the contemporary world, but this is also a time of vulnerability for Aka and Ngandu, living as they do in an environment of risk, one potentially threatening to their continued well-being. It is, however, not only their own survival that can be threatened, but the survival of those around them: parents, relatives, siblings, and friends. Anthropologists working with small-scale cultures have documented the relatively high mortality rates in these societies. Infant mortality is often 10–20 percent, and juvenile mortality 25–60 percent.[9] Researchers have also demonstrated that many children in these cultures live with stepparents in late childhood and adolescence because of the loss of one or both parents.[10] Life history theory suggests that adult and child mortality rates influence a variety of behavioral and reproductive patterns later in life. For instance, children raised in rich environments often develop a reproductive strategy where sexual relationships start late and male-female relationships last a relatively long time, whereas children raised in materially limited environments start their sexual relationships earlier and male-female relationships are relatively short-term.[11]

Life history theory is based upon the principle that "organisms encounter trade-offs in the allocation of their time and effort", and that "life history strategies are the characteristic way in which species allocate time and resources to growth, maintenance, and reproduction."[12] The life history model includes "two phases after an adolescent becomes independent of their parent, these are the pre-reproductive growth phase in which all excess energy is allocated to growth, and a reproductive phase in which all excess energy is allocated to reproduction."[13] Puberty marks the time in which reproductive life is beginning and skill acquisition learning is advancing. And as adolescents learn how to provide for themselves, they experience a change in provisioning dependence in terms of who is providing how much of their sustenance.

Adolescents, to summarize, are experiencing a shift from somatic (growth, development, maintenance) to reproductive (nepotism, mating, parenting) effort. That is, while they are learning to exploit difficult-to-acquire, high-quality resources, their energy resources are being redirected from growth to reproduction.[14] During this transitional phase, involving or characterized by "weaning of provision dependence," and changes in life history energy allocations, they are especially vulnerable. In a study on health within and between the two populations, I found this to be reflected in the low BMIs (body mass index, an indicator of the overall health of an individual) of young adolescent (10 to 15 years) children, a condition associated in the medical and nutritional literature with sickness, lowered immune functioning, and increased susceptibility to helminth (worm) infection.[15] As the weaning age of infants is a time of transition and vulnerability, so too, is this young adolescent stage.

As young adolescents shift from somatic to reproductive effort, they are learning key cultural knowledge about social relations, sexual desire, and love. Indeed, a major function of adolescence, from an evolutionary perspective, is to "attain reproductive status—to develop the physical and social competencies needed to gain access to a new and highly contested biological resource: sex and, ultimately, reproduction."[16]

## Ngandu Adolescents

Ngandu adolescents remain in the family home until the age of marriage, with both males and females spending a considerable amount of time with same-sex friends and adults. The girl will work in the field alongside her mother or take care of her siblings during the day. In the afternoon and evening when her work is done, she may walk with her friends down the street, socialize, play dancing games, and meet boys. Depending upon the strictness of her family, as she becomes an older adolescent and particularly after menarche, her movements may be more controlled. Value is placed upon the adolescent's virginity, which at least in the past was carefully guarded. If an adolescent girl becomes pregnant, the unmarried Ngandu couple may be "encouraged" to marry. If they do not marry, her brideprice decreases; brideprice is money, lifestock, and/or material items (such as pots and pans) paid to the bride's family by the groom's family, ensuring his rights to her future reproductive abilities and children and compensating the bride's family for the loss of a daughter. Likewise, a man may be required to pay a girl's family for the loss of "value," if rape has occurred. Women often marry in their middle to late teens, while men marry three to four years later. The birth of the first child occurs when the women are in their late teens or early twenties. (See Figure 3.1.)

Boys are given a freer rein and are not as controlled by the family, however at this age they not only begin to associate more with same-sex play or work groups, as they get older they also begin to associate more with older males, building social networks and alliances. As explained in Chapter One, the number and age of geographically close male kin are important. It is not unusual for older adolescent males to have several girlfriends, especially once they begin to work (and have money to

FIGURE 3.1 | *Newly married happy couple. Courtesy of Barry Hewlett.*

spend). A few marriages are polygynous, with older men having two (or several) young wives, leaving other men without spouses.[17]

By puberty, Ngandu know many subsistence activities, although knowledge and abilities are sharply divided by gender. Boys know how to sell petrol, fish, hunt, or clear fields and may also know, particularly in late adolescence, how to mine for gold or diamonds. Girls at this age know how to look after the household and infants, make meals, sell produce at the market, gather wood, and work in the fields, planting, weeding, and harvesting. Ngandu adolescents do not as a general rule tend to travel very often outside of their village, either alone or with their friends. They socialize with one another at church or walking along the road. Going out at night to socialize with the opposite sex after the work of the day is completed, is seen by many parents as not "good," for adolescent girls in particular, as "bad things" may occur.

The development of the sense of self for the Ngandu adolescent is advanced and supported within, not apart from, the larger, closely allied community of family and extended kin, a social environment providing support and resources enhancing adolescent fitness and development.

## Aka Adolescents

By the age of eleven or so, Aka boys may decide to have their teeth pointed. The girls may also decide to have their teeth pointed and may build their own hut made in exact and particular imitation of the larger parental hut. (See Figure 3.2). The huts the young adolescent females build are small and have room enough for one or at most two inhabitants. Boys entering adolescence will also build their own places to sleep and hang out in. The bachelor lean-to, built by the *bokala* (young adolescent male) is a rather precarious rectangular structure able to sleep anywhere from three to eight or more). But it is not unusual for the adolescent, particularly on cold nights, to return to the family bed of their parents or grandparents. Once a girl "sees" *ekila* (Aka females enter puberty at around 12 years of age, with menarche starting at about 15 or 16) and has built her own hut, she may begin to invite boys to visit.

Aka adolescents develop lasting friendships with one or two same-sex peers and spend most of their time with them, exploring and undertaking subsistence activities together. They do however often sleep and eat with their parents (or other adults) and stay near them during a net-hunt or when working in the fields.

FIGURE 3.2 | *Adolescent girl inside her* huma.

A favorite activity at this age is traveling to other camps to visit or dance and check out the opposite sex. A lot of energy and time goes into flirtation and looking for a prospective mate, the reason given for adolescents frequent visiting neighboring camps. Adolescent sexual activity begins early among the Aka. Several adolescents reported beginning sexual activity even before their secondary sexual characteristics developed (usually when the girls would move into their own huts). It was not clear if this was in fact sexual intercourse or simply early sexual play. However, any type of sexual play was unaccompanied by parental surveillance or disapproval. If a young couple decides to have sexual relations, the boy approaches the girl and, if she is in agreement, off they go. Yeye, a young adolescent male, said, "If a boy leaves his camp to notice a beautiful girl, he comes with his spear and puts it in the corner of her home for the sign that he has come and he needs the girl, and she comes and will meet that boy. She can have different boys on the same day and take turns. They can fall in love and get married."

As with every aspect of their lives, there is a great tolerance and respect for individual variation. Many adolescents began their sexual

*bokala—young adolescent male*

activity early, but there were those who did not. As while some preferred multiple partners, there where others, both males and females, who did not. The respect for individual autonomy and choice in sexual activity was very evident, "It is good," one older female adolescent said to me, "that Molongo is not married [and has not begun sex]. She does not want to play yet or be married." Contraceptives are not commonly used, however one young woman said that her mother gave her a hot pepper plant to eat to prevent pregnancy, as she was overwhelmed with grief from the death of her two babies and couldn't bear the thought of having more children that may die.

The visiting *bokala* regards the presence of *ngondo*'s hut as signaling her readiness for sexual relations and marriage. As adolescents, they are able to travel to other camps as they choose, enabling them to find prospective partners, establish and build social networks, and form bonds with their peers and future "helpers at the nest." Sexual freedom and exploration, as a part of social maturity and identity formation, is based upon the revered Aka value of autonomy and individual choice. This early sexual freedom allows them to practice adult roles and social-sexual relations before marriage and parenting. If the two adolescents remain interested in each other and decide to marry, they simply move in together. There is no ceremony, although the male may bring gifts to the girl's parents, such as an ax, meat, honey, or a net. The *bokala* stays in the female's natal camp while performing bride-service for a varying length of time, generally two years or until an infant is born and walking. Adolescent females are nonfertile for several years, and by age 18–20 are generally married and able to sustain a pregnancy. Aka males tend to be 19–22 or so when they first marry. Marriage is a desirable goal, and the ability to marry is seen as one of the positive aspects of being an adolescent.

## Menstruation, First Marriage, and Love

................................................................

### NGANDU WOMEN
#### Blondine

................................................................

I remember I had a friend Claudine who was older than me, and she wanted to marry when she was young because she told me that her parents were mean. When she got her first blood, she went and explained to her mother. Her mother accused her, saying, "You have slept with a man!" She took her to the doctor to have the doctor confirm whether she had slept with a man or not. The doctor told her mother, "No, your daughter has not slept with a man." Because of this, she married when she was maybe 14, and soon she had a baby. After a short time they divorced because he had lots of other women.

I learned about these things when I was young. My big friends at the market and my mother taught me:

> At a certain age you will see your blood. This is how you take care of yourself. When you have your blood you do not prepare food for men, because this is for the security of the man. If a woman prepares food for a man when she is having her blood, it can make him sick. [But mostly today women do prepare food]. If you have heavy bleeding, it is a problem with your stomach, but there is traditional medicine to take to calm the flow of blood. Use a cloth and tie it around yourself, and you wash it when it becomes soiled. This is the life of a woman. When you are at a certain age, you will have a relationship with a man and you can have a baby and this is why you have the blood. This is the consequence of being a woman.

I was about 13 when I started seeing my blood. I had pain in my stomach and back, but I took the special medicine if you have lots of pain. My mother would take the bark from a tree and boil it and give me the pump [enema]. I thought about the changes that took place in my body and thought that "Now this is good because I am a woman. A man will ask for marriage. I will have a house, children, and I will be very gentle to my babies. Life will be good."

At this age I was happy. My friends and I would talk about who we will marry and how many children we will have. We would walk down the street in nice clothes, and the boys would see us and say, "See how beautiful that girl is." When men see a woman in good clothes with nice breasts, they think, "Now you are a woman ready for marriage.

This one boy walked by the street in front of the house every day. He saw me and then came and presented himself and asked my parents for me in marriage. He came into our house and he gave money as a small gift to my parents. They said, "Now today our daughter can pass the night with you and become your wife." I understood it was time to marry. I was 15.

## NGANDU WOMEN
### Therese

When I arrived at 10 years of age, the war continued always and still my grandmother took care of me. I lived with her for years. I thought a lot about my family, but life with grandmother was good, she protected me well. My grandmother told me, "You are a girl now, but you are becoming a big woman. Then you will marry and work." Soon after this, I saw my first blood and I didn't know anything. I said, "Grandmother look at me, I have blood! Am I sick?" She said, "No, my child, you are not sick; this is the life of a woman."

Now there is a big difference. In my time if a woman was big with big breasts, this was the time to marry, when you were a woman. But now girls marry young and get pregnant and have babies. The difference exists because then we guarded our bodies. Today girls have the chance to have lots of knowledge. They want all these things and they fast want these things. They want men to get these things for them, and their mothers do not stop them. It is bad today because girls do not guard their bodies and there are many diseases.

### Therese's Marriage Story

There was once a girl who was very, very beautiful and many men asked her for marriage and she refused them all. This chimpanzee saw her and decided he wanted to marry her, so each night for many nights he put on the clothes of a man and took his guitar and sang beautiful songs outside her home. When she heard these songs and his beautiful voice, she said, "I have refused all men who have asked for me, but this one, this one who sings to me, he is the one I want to marry." She told her parents and they said, "Oh, our daughter, before you marry him, let us meet him to see what kind of man he is." She refused them, "No, I will just marry him." So the beautiful girl and the chimpanzee began to sleep in the same bed as man and wife. But the husband only came at 8 PM every night. Together they would eat in the dark and then go to bed and sleep together. Every morning he would rise out of bed and leave the house early in the morning while it was still dark. After some time had passed, her parents came and told her, "We want to meet our new son-in-law." But their daughter refused again, "He only comes at night and leaves early in the morning when it is still dark."

The parents talked together and decided on a plan. That night after dark, the father of the girl pounded boards across the door so it was shut tight and then they went home. The chimpanzee husband as usual woke up at 4 AM and went to the door to leave the house, but he couldn't open the door! He pushed and pushed, but the door would not open. So the chimpanzee husband decided to hide up in the roof of the house until he could find a way to leave. When morning came, the girl's parents came and took off the boards and called to their daughter, "Our daughter, now we are here to meet your husband. Where is he?" Their daughter said, "I do not know! He left the bed, but I have not seen him!" Now it just so happened that her younger brother was in the area hunting with a small spear for rats. He looked up and saw the toe of the chimpanzee husband between the palm branches on the roof and thought, "Oh I will shoot that rat up there!" He threw his spear and it hit the chimpanzee husband who yelled a great yell! He fell from the roof and ran off to the forest, never to be seen or heard from again! Her parents said, "Oh, our daughter! You have been deceived! You have been married to a chimpanzee!" When all the people of the village heard this they laughed and laughed, and every time the girl when for water or wood, the people would say, "There goes Madame Chimpanzee!" She was so ashamed that one day she took poison and killed herself.

The conclusion of this story is this: if you are a girl, you should know well the man you marry before the marriage.[18]

......................................................................................

## AKA WOMEN
### Nali

......................................................................................

Before my breasts began to grow, but when I was a little older, I had my teeth pointed. At the age of teeth pointing you are so afraid, it is hard because you have seen this done to others and lots of blood flies out. But it is not good if your teeth are not pointed. Pointing the teeth is for beauty. If you are a young girl, and you decide to point your teeth, the moment comes and a special person does this and takes a branch and you open your mouth then you bite down. I was so afraid when I had my teeth pointed, and the specialist told my grandfather to come and hold me down.

The person takes a knife and begins to point your teeth and you cry and spit and spit, lots of spit and blood. There was so much pain! But my mother said, "No, it is okay, after three or four days the pain is over. This is for the beauty." Then you wash your mouth out, take a leaf, the *kpangaï*, and put it on your teeth for the pain. If you do not get your teeth pointed, people will laugh at you and think you look like a chimpanzee, so you get your teeth pointed to distinguish yourself. It is good to do this. If you are a man or woman searching for a wife or husband and you see someone who does not have pointed teeth, you say, "You there, you are like a chimpanzee. You have big teeth like a chimpanzee! I do not want you."

When my breasts began to grow, I thought "Oh, now I have started to be a woman! This is good because when I have breasts and dance the boys will watch me and say, 'What a beautiful girl with beautiful breasts!'" There is a dance, special for women, the *monima*. For this dance you prepare the leaves, *molembai lembai*, and a special crème, and you put this on your face and your body. Then you take your breasts in your hands and with the bush on your bum you dance like this. The bush moves and when men see this, the men want the women! If we are not married, the men say, "Oh what a beautiful woman! With beautiful breasts and bums!" This dance is to make men notice the beauty of women. It is important to look beautiful, just for the beauty.

The young men see these young women, and when they see them dance and see their breasts and their bums, they want these girls for marriage. After the dances the boys watched me and asked me for sex but I always refused. I was so afraid of those boys! I told them, "No, when I am a very old, very big woman I will marry, but now my breasts are only little and have only begun to grow. When I am so big then I will marry and start the work of the night." I thought, "I will accept sex quickly when I am older, but now I am too young a girl."

At that time I had never seen *ekila*, but my mother said, "I am seeing *ekila* and it is difficult." She told me, "My daughter, this is *ekila* and some day you will see this blood too. The sign of the beginning is that you will have swollen breasts, and when you see this you will know that soon you will begin. This is the sign that now you are a woman." Before my blood began to soar, I had such pain in my stomach! My parents got bark and boiled it and I drank it, and a few days later the blood started. I was very angry when I began and I went to my *huma* and I stayed there for hours and did not talk to anyone! I was so angry! I was unhappy! I had no cloth and the blood was on my clothes. I was so ashamed. I did not want anyone to see me, to see the blood! I did not go out.

My mother and father called to me, and soon my mother found me. She said to me, "This is not bad, this is a sign, it means that now you need to pay attention. If you work with a man at night you will become pregnant and have a baby. When you come to be at this stage and are with boys now your blood soars. A girl with blood starts to look for men." I thought, "I have no possibility of a man so why does my blood soar? Maybe a man will come for me as a lover and fast I will become pregnant." She explained to my father that I was staying inside because I was embarrassed because of the blood on my clothes. She told me, "You hide this and be calm. You arrange your clothes and bring the cloth for washing in the river and do not speak about this." Mothers always attend well to their daughters. Everyone left the camp and I went to the forest and found a new cord and threw off the bloody clothes and took leaves, *molembai lembai*, and used that to catch my blood.

When I was little I slept with my mother and father on the same bed, but now that I saw my blood I could not sleep in the same bed as my father. If he went out net-hunting he would find no meat, and if he went out he would find no food in his traps. I sat on the ground because you cannot even sit on the bed of your father if you have your blood. But after a long time I thought, "I have become a woman." I went to dances and all the boys came to search for me but I refused. When a woman knows a man it changes them, you are changed. I refused the boys for sex because I did not want to become pregnant.

My father told me, "You are my daughter and are beginning to be a woman and one day you will marry a man. You should find a man who works well for you. He should search for food and be brave and find things for you. Because if you marry a man who does not work, you will suffer. I am your father and I married your mother. I hunted for meat. I was brave. I gave her honey. You find a man who will do the same for you or you will suffer."

At this age when the moon was clear we danced and danced. One time a *dzengi* dance was organized and so many people came, from many different camps, to see the dance. I was there, me a girl with my breasts and I had seen my first blood. I was young and beautiful. I sang and danced!

There was this boy and he said in his heart, "Who is this girl there? This is the one for me, this is the one I want to marry." He fell in love with me.

One day he gave me a small gift of fruit and he asked me for marriage. I refused the first time. I had another who wanted to marry me too! This was Kokote. He went and asked my parents, "Your daughter will not marry me, but I love her and she is the only one I want to marry." My parents said to Kokote, "You have a problem because this girl has a man who already came and asked for our daughter for marriage. But if you arrange this with our girl and she accepts then you can marry her." Now Kokote went to my camp and the other man also came and asked for marriage. Two husbands for me! But I did not accept the other man. He left saying, "The girl does not love me. I will return to my camp." Kokote came again and asked for marriage. I refused, but my parents said, "No, you are a woman and you are supposed to marry!" My parents and two grandmothers in the camp called to me, "Come and listen. In your life two men have asked for marriage and you refused! You should marry Kokote. If you marry him he will take good care of you. Kokote is brave and he will guard you well." After much *mosambo* [advice], I decided to accept him.

## AKA WOMEN
## Konga

Soon after the death of my parents, my breasts began to grow and I thought, "Oh my breasts! Now my breasts have begun to grow, and when I go to the dance, the young men will stare. When I dance they will start to dance with me. The boys will see my breasts and will ask for me to marry them." But when I went to the dances and they'd stare, I'd flee. At this time we did not have any clothes like today and I could not hide my breasts for dancing, but I was not ashamed. During this time when we heard the drums, my friends would tell me, "Come and dance! There is a dance at this camp or this camp," and we'd stay at each camp for five or six days and dance and dance. Some of my friends had lovers in those camps, and my friends went out with their boys. I would always say, "No, not me, I am too small. You go and have your fun with your boys." I refused them all. I was too small and my heart did not love any of them.

My friends had their lovers and their fun after these dances. I would dance alone without a lover, without a boy. I did not want one yet! I was too small. I have a big granddaughter who sleeps with me now and refuses to build her own *huma*, she says if she builds her own hut the boys will see, "Oh this girl is ready for marriage," and they will demand marriage. She says boys will come and enter her *huma* and she does not want this. She refuses all the boys and refuses marriage because she wants to continue her studies at school. She says if she gets married and becomes pregnant she will not be able to do this. She loves school! She tells me that if you go to school, you know how to read and write. You can sell things because you have knowledge. You learn so many good things. She tells me that when she finishes school she will fall in love with a man and marry him. We did not have this chance when I was young.

At this time I began to see my blood, I was asleep when it arrived and in the morning I saw this blood on my legs and clothes. I asked myself, "I have never known a man and why do I see this blood? Maybe I am a big woman now." After my mother's death I saw this blood, but I remember she told me when I saw her blood when I was small, "This is a sign of being a woman." I was taught that you take a cord from the forest and you cut the cord and pound it out so it is soft like cloth and you use that for your blood. When I left for a dance the boys came and searched for me, I refused when they asked for marriage. I was a woman with blood and with breasts. But at this time, I was also a girl. We were happy. All the world sang with the joy of us girls, because we'd play and sing so much in the forest.

But there was this one man, Ngouate, my first husband. He came to my camp and we were married.

## The Work and Pleasure of Sex

### NGANDU WOMEN
### Blondine

When I was young I feared marriage. But when my first husband, Issa, came, I accepted. I did not have a marriage ceremony. For the marriage ceremony the man gives money to the parents, things to drink and eat. For certain women there is a ceremony, but it depends upon the husband, if there is this possibility. The amount he gives to the parents depends on the person, and if someone offers too little, the parents say, "No, that is too little, add more to this amount." We spent the night together.

My big friends at the market explained sex to me, and I would see their husbands come and talk sweet to them. I had fear because I heard the first time to sleep with a man is hard. If a girl has never known a man, the first time is like war, because there is a lot of pain. The first time of sexual relations, I remember it hurt so badly I bit my husband's arm to stop the pain! But after a week it no longer hurt and I began to find pleasure in the work of the night. Men know the first time there is lots of pain. They try to go slow and fight it, but it is not easy for men to go slow. But after one or two weeks there is pleasure for the girl. Sex at night is for work and for pleasure, but the most important is the baby.

I was happy for the marriage. I loved him. Life was good, living together. Issa worked and bought food, drinks, and gifts for my parents. After the marriage when we lived with my parents, Issa told me, "No, we need to live in our own home." So we moved to our own home.

The qualities of being a good husband are that if he brings friends to the house, he gives lots of respect to me and he respects my parents. A good father speaks to his children. He buys shoes and clothes for them with his money. He gives money for medicine and takes them to a hospital if they are sick, it is the responsibility of the father to take the child to the hospital.

The good qualities of a wife are that she works hard. When she gets to the house she takes water and prepares a bath and food for the husband. She is the mother of the house. She has her kids and teaches them the importance of respect. She gives them food and lets the children sleep with her and her husband until they are five or six. This is a good mother. She teaches her children lessons around the fire at night or in the field when they walk with her. The work of a good woman is not an easy work. When you work in the fields, you work in the hot sun and you work so hard and with that work you get money, but it is so hard, there is pain and you are tired. You carry manioc on your head, and other things. It is heavy like a sack of cement, plus you are carrying your baby, and afterwards you can hardly move you are so tired. Both a husband and wife have important work. One is not valued above the other.

........................................................................................

## NGANDU WOMEN
### Therese
........................................................................................

My grandmother chose the man I married, and the man saw me and saw how beautiful I was and that I was a big woman. His name was

Adrienne. I did not know him until he came and asked for marriage. The man sent money for the marriage to my grandmother. When this man came to the house to ask for marriage, I refused. But my grandmother said, "No, he is good and lives good and you don't refuse him. He is nice and gives us food and you must not refuse him." The man came and we stayed in the house together during the day, but at night I would not pass the night with him in my grandmother's house. My husband would go back to his house every night. After eight months my grandmother said, "No, this is not good, you live too much at my house. You must pass the night together starting today. The first time, sleep together in my house, because the first time to sleep together is very difficult." I fled to sleep somewhere else so I would not have to sleep with my husband. The next day, grandmother said to me, "Do not fear this, this is the life of a woman. Now this day, you sleep with your husband, it is not good to refuse him. Men take a woman and the woman should give the husband food, clothes, and take care of the man with the sexual relations."

I knew my grandmother was telling me the truth; it was not a hard conversation because I was a grown woman. This first sexual relation was difficult. But after a while it was not hard to live and care for a man. This marriage was good, because my husband was a respectful man. At night in the house he was respectful to me and in the village he was respectful to everyone, and everyone in the village knew he was my husband. I have love still in my heart for my husband. Love is most important, without love there is no desire. I never looked outside of marriage for a lover. I did not desire other men after my husband died, because I wanted my husband.

## AKA WOMEN
### Nali

My mother taught me about sex, she taught me how to be with a husband. I wanted to find a man who worked hard, this is attractive. I do not know if I could love him if he didn't work hard. In marriage most often you love the man before the marriage, but not always. I did not love my husband Kokote at first. But after some time and with much consultation, I thought, "I refused this man, but my father is upset and I suffer. It is better to accept this man for marriage." Sometimes if a man loves a woman and her heart refuses him and doesn't love him, men or women can use a plant, *zambola*, that makes someone fall in love with you. If the person touches you with the plant medicine, you fall in love with them. The love plant is very strong. But Kokote did not use this plant on me.

It was difficult at first for me but after a time I became familiar with Kokote and began to love him. When Kokote entered the hut the first day, I was too shy to talk to him. We slept on the same bed, but I did not speak. It was difficult when he passed the night with me. The first time we began the work of the night, I thought, "This is my husband, we had the pleasure at night and in the morning I will prepare food for him and now everyone will know I am married to him." Kokote was my husband and for three days I was too shy to talk to him. In the mornings I would prepare *koko* and at night we slept on the same bed, but we did not speak. After three days we began to talk. Here we work hard at night searching for children. Even when your husband is tired, the men know *molomba* (a bark eaten by men that gives a "hard penis"). At first I was afraid of this work at night, my vagina was small and I was afraid to have sex too often. I am no longer afraid of this work to search for children. There is pleasure. Now when I feel desire I rub his leg. The work of the night, it is for pleasure, and for the love and sentiment of marriage.

When I married this man, I had slept here with my parents all my life. When you and your husband are married, you look for a place you want to live. But first we lived in the camp of my parents, and my husband worked for my parents. Kokote worked in the field. He found meat and brought them honey. He made snares to kill animals to bring to my mother and father. I had my first baby, Elaka, with my family. After the birth I came to live with my husband's family. I was afraid to live there, to live in the camp with Kokote's parents. This was because I did not know how they behaved, how they lived. I had seen his family before, when they would pass through, but I did not know them well. They lived far away. But when I began to know them, to understand how they lived, I was no longer afraid. His parents were very nice to me. They said, "Do not be ashamed because you are the wife of our son." I felt like a daughter to my husband's parents. After a time, I saw them as my parents. I was very sad when Kodumalou [Kokote's mother] died. She was a mother to me.

## Nali's Story

Bembé created the earth. He created women but kept only women without men. He then created men but he kept them away from the women. One day a man called Tolé took all the men in his camp and started to hunt in the forest. They had no women with them, only calabashes they put on their chests to be like a woman. They hunted animals and ate them, all the men together. The next day Tolé went alone into the forest, very early, and he listened and heard sounds he had not heard before. All the women were there. They had made a raft on the water and the women were playing on it.

Now he hid and thought to himself, these are not men, but they are like men, only they have breasts. What is wrong with their chests and they have no testicles, it is only flat. He crawled on his knees to catch one. The women were singing and playing on their raft and did not hear Tolé. He tried to trap one but they all run to their hut. So the women went to their camp, and Tolé went to his camp and told his friends, "I saw other people who have no testicles and have things pointing from their chests. Let's go and get them and find out what they are." It is because of Tolé that men know women and women know men.

### AKA WOMEN
## Konga

When Ngouate and I married, he took me to his camp and his mother and father, they loved me a lot! They said to me, "The woman of our son! Come and eat, we are your parents!" They gave me so many gifts! One time shortly after our marriage I fell sick, and the brother of my father came when he heard the news. He said, "My daughter you are sick. Come and stay with me until you are well and then you can come back." Ngouate refused to accompany us. He told me, "This marriage is over." I left with my father's brother. He cared for me and soon I was healthy. But he said to me, "Your marriage is over. Ngouate left you when you were sick and wouldn't come with us. This is a bad husband. " I said, "No, Ngouate was a good husband, but he has a bad character." I was not sad, I thought, "I will find another who will not abandon me."

There was another man that came and asked for marriage, Mopoko. Every day he would come and visit. I refused Mopoko but after a long time I was content to accept. One night I was asleep in the house. Then this man Mopoko came into my hut and slept next to me. I woke up and there he was beside me. When I saw him I did not refuse him. We spent the night together. That began our marriage together and so began the work of marriage. I prepared food and gave it to Mopoko. Each night we would have our sexual activity. I was happy now. I had another husband and all the people said, "You are married to a brave man. A man who hunts a lot and who will guard you well."

It is good to wait for the sexual activity, to keep your body and not become pregnant when you are very young. If you are not a virgin, you may become pregnant. When you are young it is not good to become pregnant because pregnancy changes your body. You will not have had time to be young and dance. If you're pregnant when you're young and you give birth, quickly you are skinny like a big woman and tired. Your body changes and this is not good. Your breasts drop like an old woman's. You can play with boys when you're young, but you do not have sex. In the forest camps little kids will imitate the sexual play of their parents. They play this sexual play and when their parents see this they say, "Why are you playing this sex play?" And the kids flee away!

My best sexual activity was with my second husband, Mopoko. I chose to marry Mopoko because he caught a lot of meat and he was very handsome and nice. Mopoko was strong and worked hard and he became good in my heart. He shared a lot of his meat with other people. I loved Mopoko a lot and wanted children with no other. I never refused Mopoko. If I had *élebé* [desire], I waited for Mopoko and then asked for the sex. We worked at night for the infants and to show I loved him. When I was young, Mopoko said I was beautiful. We were always together, walking in the forest. He never hit me. When I married Mopoko, I finished with other men. It depends on the woman. Some women search for other men after marriage and some do not.

Always I worked for Mopoko. We would go together into the forest. We lived together and worked together for many years, but he died. After the death of Mopoko I was so very, very sad. I was very unhappy. "My husband has died and I am with my children and what can I do? How can I find meat and honey for my children? I am a woman and it is the man who finds these things for his children." Mopoko died with *ekila ya ngoa*. When he was sick, with this sickness in his stomach, he had feces with blood and I didn't know what this was. I thought it was parasites and gave him medicine, but the illness rearranged his stomach and ate the stomach and his anus became huge, red, and opened like wound and he died.

There were men who came for marriage but I refused. If I married another man, he would take me to his camp and my children would stay here. If I die or my child would die, what would I do? I wanted to stay close to my children until they were grown. After Mopoko died I had no relations with other men, I lived in a little hut and suffered a lot because I loved him so much in my heart. I wanted no other man. I lived alone with my children and I was still strong. When I am alone at night I think of Mopoko and cry, even now, after so long.

But when we were together, at night, when I was in the *huma* with Mopoko on the bed, we would begin playing. Lots of caresses and tickling. After the fun, we searched for a baby. This play still continues during your marriage. Sometimes if your husband is very old, the tickling stops, but the sex continues. This is my good memory, the play of marriage in our bed.

## Sex, Love, and Attachment: The Interactive Nature of Culture, Ecology, and Biology

As adolescents shift from somatic to reproductive effort, they learn key cultural knowledge about social relations, sexual desire, and love. As noted earlier, a major function of adolescence, from an evolutionary perspective, is to develop social competencies necessary for attaining "reproductive status," access to "sex and, ultimately, reproduction."[19] But although many of our very human behaviors, such as mate attraction, sexual desire, and attachment, are influenced by interactions between our biology, ecology, and culture, few human behaviors are entirely shaped by biological or cultural factors alone.[20] Humans are not consciously influenced by, nor often think about, their evolved biology. That is, we don't look down at our newborn child and think, "What a darling bundle of genes! And every decision I make will be to ensure that my genes go on and on and are forever represented in future generations! Woo-hoo! I am a reproductive success!" We are biological beings, but we are also profoundly cultural beings.

A branch of evolutionary theory that focuses on identifying biologically based (that is, genetic) behaviors of the human mind, evolutionary psychology, generally focuses on understanding "human nature" and universals evolved during the environment(s) of evolutionary adaptation (EEA), the hunting-gathering lifestyle that characterized over 90 percent of human history.[21] The human mind is understood as having specific modules evolved to solve reoccurring problems in the EEA. These biologically based behaviors may also be part of human's phylogenetic history, as humans share a phylogenetic history with mammals and primates. This shared history contributes to biologically based propensities and an "evolved psychology."[22] Another part of understanding the evolved biological basis of human behavior is ontogenetic development. Human biology changes with age, and this changing biology influences human behavior. This chapter focuses on married couples views of sex and love; a study of children's or elderly sex and love would be very different in large part because of ontogenetic changes in biology. In short, the evolutionary psychology perspective emphasizes the importance of understanding biologically based and universal features of human behavior.[23]

On the other hand, evolutionary ecologists understand the mind as a general-purpose mechanism allowing humans to adapt to diverse natural and social environments. Behavioral diversity is emphasized over biologically based human universals.[24] Evolutionary ecology considers how organisms adapt to their environments, including their interactions with members of their own (and other species) as well as the physical environment, examining selective pressures imposed by the environment and the evolutionary response to these pressures.[25] From this perspective, humans try to optimize or maximize their reproductive fitness within particular social, demographic, or political environments. As earlier noted, a child's rearing environment, including a family's access to material and natural resources, is thought to predict when the child will start sexual activity and how long pair bonds will last.[26]

Evolutionary cultural anthropology focuses on the evolutionary nature of culture; how culture it is transmitted and acquired, how it changes, and how it affects human behavior. Culture has the characteristics required for natural selection: (1) production of variation, (2) competition and fitness effects of cultural variants, (3) inheritance (that is, transmission) of cultural variants, and (4) accumulation of cultural modifications.[27] Humans have different mechanisms to learn skills and knowledge because it would be too costly to learn everything by trial and error. Learning from parents (vertical transmission), friends (horizontal transmission), leaders (one-many transmission, indirect bias), or from all of those around you (conformist transmission) can be an efficient way to learn particular skills and knowledge.[28] Each of the transmission mechanisms has specific properties. Some mechanisms lead to the conservation of culture (vertical and conformist), whereas other mechanisms (horizontal) lead to rapid culture change. Many cultural beliefs and behaviors, especially those associated with family and kinship, are seldom linked to adaptations to the natural environment and are highly conserved by the mechanisms of cultural transmission. In short, culture matters.[29]

How does this help to explain Aka and Ngandu sex, love, and intimacy? Love and compassion are universal, but how they are experienced and expressed in intimate relationships varies dramatically. Both Aka and Ngandu identify love (*bondingo*) as an important component to marital relations. Sex is an expression of love, desire, and the longing for children.

Sexual desire *(bonguedi* among Aka, and *élebé* among Ngandu) and sexual activity is the "work of the night." Although less arduous and more pleasurable than the "work of the day," the work of night is work nonetheless; as one Aka male succinctly put it, "Bila na bonguedi [sexual desire is work]. The work of the penis is the work to find a child." Similar to the work of getting food, the work of searching for a child is not easy; "Getting food is more difficult, but both are lots of work. Sex life is not as tiring as work during day; the work at night is easier because you can make love then sleep."

The Aka were the most emphatic on these points. One young Aka male explained, "I am now doing it five times a night to search for a child; if I do not do it five times my wife will not be happy because she wants children quickly." Aka couples engage in the work of the night frequently during the week, but also frequently during the night: One 35-year-old man with two wives reported having sex three to four times a night with two days of rest in between. A 25-year-old man complained, "It is work to find children and get children to make a large camp like my father." He said he was having sex four to five times a night.

Ngandu males and females expressed the same sentiment that sex is "to search for children." However, among the Ngandu both males and females complained frequently of the tiredness that they felt in the work of the night: "Sex is a work, when I give sperm it is a work, I get tired after sex." One Ngandu male was particularly emphatic: "Having sex three times a night is to look for a child, NOT for pleasure." More females of both Aka and Ngandu explained that, although sex was work and sometimes pleasurable, the "infant is the most important."

Cultural-ecological factors are important for understanding the particularistic themes found within the women's narratives: the nature of patrilineal descent and social organization, the nature of social relations, and the political-economic setting. Both Aka and Ngandu men and women expressed love as part of their intimate relationship with their spouse, but how love was experienced and demonstrated varied substantially. The nature of culture and social reproduction is important in understanding the diversity of responses within the marital bond.

Both Aka and Ngandu mentioned having sex on a regular basis as a sign of love, but for Aka men and women, working hard and physical proximity are ways of showing love toward their spouse. Among Ngandu, women occasionally mentioned that gifts of cloth or jewelry from their husbands were signs of love. Ngandu men felt their spouses' love was demonstrated by their respect for his demands and authority within the household, and by such tasks as serving him a meal, washing his clothes, and giving him money. Material exchanges are an important part of maintaining social relations.[30] For the Ngandu, the love and commitment felt toward a loved one seemed to be tied to not only the maintenance of formal hierarchy and obligation, but also expressed through gift giving of male to female (as noted previously) as well as service of female to male.

The importance of fertility and childbearing for the Aka and the institutionalized "right" of the Ngandu males to have sexual access to their wives in order to have children by them is in part resource driven. A 58-year-old woman explained to me, "I am old and no longer have desire; when I was younger I liked it. I had sex for children and pleasure. I do not like sex now but if I refuse to sleep with him, I have to pay money to his family." However, although the desire and right to conceive are important and powerful emotions, the issues of intimacy, sexual desire, and love are complicated and are certainly a part of their marital lives that they value.

......................................

Adolescence is a time in which a multitude of biological, behavioral, and intellectual changes are occurring. The bio-cultural model helps us to understand the women's experiences of love, attachment, desire, and sex. Cultural models dramatically influence the motivation for sex and how often sexual desire is expressed in intimate relationships. Sexual drive may be controlled by our basic physiologic makeup, but the expressions of intimacy, love, attachment, sexual desire, and activity are certainly affected by our emotions and cultural models.[31] At the same time, Aka and Ngandu foundational schema regarding gender hierarchy and very different culturally constructed niches (that is, sedentary versus mobile lifestyles) contribute to the very diverse ways adolescents and young adults learn about, experience, and express love, desire, and sexuality in these two cultures.

In this chapter we have seen how adolescents develop the intellectual ability to learn and understand key cultural schemas. Their lives reflect changing biologies and social identities, a maturational process and time of intensive socio-cultural learning and physiological development. The enduring cultural features of these two populations were described in the previous chapter—the pervasive and intense value Aka place on autonomy, sharing, physical, and emotional intimacy, their trusting view of the natural and social world, and the resiliency, respectfulness, deference, and industriousness of the Ngandu—help us to understand how they develop culturally specific identities, ideologies, and schemas as the women describe their adolescence and young adulthood. In the next chapter, we will look at how their relationships of intimacy, love, and attachment are grounded in an understanding of the potential impermanence of the bond.

## NOTES FROM THE FIELD
### Fall 2004

*—T. came by and gave us a chicken, so now our dinner is tied up in the "salon" trying to escape. Poor thing. Spent the day with B. who has been talking to me about many "woman" things. She is very blunt and very curious about how things work for me—that is, sex, childbirth, menstruation etc. It was kind of embarrassing, but made me think of all the questions I ask her...I think every question you as an anthropologist are going to ask someone, you should be willing to answer yourself. Anyway, she also told me this: "If you are married, many husbands may not even know if you are seeing your blood, but they may notice your cloths hanging to dry and then they know*

*you are not pregnant. Some women hide their cloths from their husbands, and keep this time secret." Well, I did wonder.*

—*As we were in the village camp today, E. (I think she is about 10 or so?) started making dinner, cutting the leaves. M. was playing with this baby, then B. came and took the baby to cart around. Now B. is yodel-singing to the baby who apparently wants to eat, she tried to nurse the baby, even though she is so young herself and she has no breast development. Always amazes me how comfortable the kids of all ages, genders, are around babies, but especially the young adolescent girls, who love to play with them.*

—*Sick all day today, not sure with what. Everyone is sick here, even the goats are coughing and sneezing. I really miss the kids, talked to them yesterday and they are doing great!*

## QUESTIONS FOR REFLECTION

1. Adolescence and young adulthood are psychologically, physically, and socially intense times of learning, development, and exploration. Based on the women's narratives, how would you characterize Aka and Ngandu developmental environments? Are both groups able to develop secure attachments to others, have a "good self esteem," and find happiness? Why or why not?

2. Do you believe love, sex, and attachment are universal and biologically based behaviors? Or culturally and socially constructed human behaviors? Or both?

3. How would you explain Aka and Ngandu differences concerning sex, love, and attachment? How are their ideas different or similar to other cultures you are familiar with?

## NOTES

1. Bogin and Smith 1996.
2. This refers to an integrated evolutionary approach, a heuristic model used to understand the interactions among ecology, culture, and biology (B.S. Hewlett and Lamb 2002a). Excerpts from this chapter were previously published in B. L. Hewlett and B. S. Hewlett 2008.
3. B. S. Hewlett and Lamb 2002a; B. L. Hewlett and B. S. Hewlett 2008. See also: Hrdy 1999; Tomasello 1999.
4. Lewis 2008, 299.
5. Lewis 2008, 299.

6. Lewis 2008, 299.
7. Lewis 2008, 299.
8. Markstrom 2008, 357.
9. B.S. Hewlett et al. 1986b; B.S. Hewlett 1992; Hrdy 1999.
10. Chagnon 1997 B.S. Hewlett 1992.
11. Charnov 1993; Chisholm 1993, 1996; Belskey 1999; B. L. Hewlett and B. S. Hewlett 2008.
12. Trevathan et al. 1999, 139; Kaplan et al. 2000, 163; see also Charnov 1993.
13. Kaplan et al. 2000, 163–164; Charnov 1993.
14. Kaplan et al. 2000.
15. Jenike 2001, 224–225; see also Hurtado et al. 2008.
16. Charnov 1993; Ellis forthcoming. For a more detailed analysis of adolescence in cultural, developmental, and evolutionary perspectives, see B.L. Hewlett, forthcoming.
17. B. S. Hewlett 1992; Spradley and McCurdy 1975.
18. Ngandu women in particular often taught me their values and beliefs through parables. In this case, the "moral" of the story has to do with marriage, obeying parents, and not refusing men.
19. Charnov 1993; Ellis forthcoming.
20. B. L. Hewlett and B. S. Hewlett 2008.
21. B. L. Hewlett and B. S. Hewlett 2008; Bulmer 1994.
22. B. L. Hewlett and B. S. Hewlett 2008; Bulmer 1994.
23. B. L. Hewlett and B. S. Hewlett 2008; Bulmer 1994.
24. B. L. Hewlett and B. S. Hewlett 2008; Bulmer 1994.
25. Bulmer 1994; B. L. Hewlett and B. S. Hewlett 2008; Belskey 1999; Chisholm 1993.
26. B. L. Hewlett and B. S. Hewlett 2008; Belskey 1999; Chisholm 1993.
27. B. L. Hewlett and B. S. Hewlett 2008; B.S. Hewlett and Lamb 2002a.
28. B.S. Hewlett and Lamb 2002a; B. L. Hewlett and B. S. Hewlett 2008.
29. B.S. Hewlett and Lamb 2002a; B. L. Hewlett and B. S. Hewlett 2008.
30. LeVine 1977
31. And possibly influenced by particular ecological conditions, such as high child mortality rates and a diversity of infectious and parasitic diseases (B. L. Hewlett and B. S. Hewlett 2008).

# CHAPTER 4

# The Harsh and Delightful Realities of Marriage and Motherhood

With the baby I thought, "Now I am a mother of this young child. I am responsible for my husband and my baby. I am now a woman."

—THERESE

I had such fear to have more children. I gave birth and they died. There is so much pain when a child is born and then dies. There is so much pain in my heart with all this death. I think of the death of each one.

—NALI

The women's stories in the preceding chapter offer a glimpse into the rarely explored daily lives, loves, marital relations, and sexual experiences of men and women in relatively egalitarian small-scale societies. The nature of their relational bonds of intimacy, love, and attachment are grounded in the knowledge of the potential impermanence of the bond. From childhood, grief has been an inevitable and inexorable part of these women's lives. Reproductive histories were collected from both groups of women and, along with their narratives, detail the joy and grief of being a mother in this environment of risk, where 45 percent of all children die before the age of 15. By examining the context and nature of responses to loss, it is possible to identify human universals of grief and see how various demographic and cultural contexts contribute to the different ways grief is experienced. Grief, as a part of our adaptive design, is a "cry for survival," a time when corollary social networks of kin and other caregivers are established and a reorganization of attachment figures takes place.

At the core of these narratives are dominant interactions of social status, ethnicity, and gender, determining people's health status and access to health care. Each woman's story highlights her own unique experience, her sense of agency or lack thereof, her individual script embedded within social, political, and economic structures, as they learn what it means to be women, and mothers, of the Congo Basin.

## The Work of the Night

Aka and Ngandu societies place a high value on children, and although neither is a child-focused society, children are highly desired, and much time and energy are spent "looking" or "working" for them. Forty to fifty percent of the populations of Aka and Ngandu are composed of children under the age of fifteen. Children are in many ways the life of the village and camps.

Aka and Ngandu believe that frequent sex is linked to pregnancy and fetal development. The Aka emphasized the importance of male contributions to fetal development, explaining that male sperm is essential to pregnancy and fetal development. Ngandu people I spoke to indicated both men and women contributed fluid to make pregnancy and fetal growth. Among the Ngandu beliefs vary regarding the extent in which the mother is believed to contribute to the development of the fetus; some suggest that women also ejaculate "sperm" during orgasm, aiding in the physical development of the baby, and others said they did not have to climax each time during a night, as when women were excited they also contributed substance. Male sperm creates and "builds" the baby in utero, but, as noted, it is possible for the woman to contribute also. Birth defects and/or miscarriages are the result of infrequent sexual (sperm) contributions by the father.

One Ngandu male explained, "Both men and women have sperm or substances [*malima*]. That is the reason why *SIDA* (HIV/AIDS) is transmitted between a male and female, both combine to make child." However, "both men and women contribute *malima*; if one spouse is sick, a pregnancy will not happen." Among various explanations of how babies are created and "formed," the general consensus is that "women have *malima* as well as men, and it takes two sperms to create a baby.... [I] do not know how the female gives, but I think it is necessary for a woman to come [climax] sometimes, but not each time, to create a baby." The same word, *malima*, describes both male and female substances secreted during intercourse.

Aka have a similar understanding of fetal development in that it takes the "sperm" of both partners to create and "build" the new life, however more Aka seemed to feel that it was primarily the sperm of the father creating the child. An Aka couple explained, "Women do not give much to the baby; it is men, especially at first, that give good development of the baby, [so sexual activity continues] twice every night until the baby is very big [about six months]. You then have to slow to once a night." It is the cumulative "sperm" throughout the pregnancy that creates the child, not conception occurring on one night; that is, a new life is conceived and "built" over repeated encounters throughout the duration of the pregnancy.

Although sex is viewed as pleasurable, pleasure is secondary to working for or "building" a child or to demonstrate love toward a mate. Ngandu men and women were somewhat more likely than Aka to mention pleasure as an important part of sex life. Ngandu women often told me that, "Sex is pleasure, work, a sign of love, and necessary for infant growth." But there is as well a responsibility of the parents of both populations to protect the newborn child by observing the postpartum taboo, as long as one to two years following the baby's birth. This allows those babies that are born to survive, ensuring that the new infant has intensive care and investment by its parents. Postpartum restrictions and taboos also protect the health of the mother by ensuring that subsequent births are spaced farther apart.[1]

# Learning to Love and Learning to Mourn: Child Birth and Child Loss

......................................................................................

## NGANDU WOMEN
### Blondine

......................................................................................

After Issa and I lived together for a while, I knew I was pregnant because I did not see my blood and if I smelled or tasted certain foods, I vomited. One time the baby inside of me cried out for me to eat earth so every once in awhile I ate a little morsel of earth, it is what your heart desires. One day your heart desires meat and one day, *koko*, and so that is what you eat.

When I was pregnant I thought a lot about the pregnancy, *diboumou*, "What will I do? Will I die? Maybe I will have a baby born dead. What is this birth like?" I spoke to other women a lot and I asked my friend, "How does this go? Do you suffer a lot? Is it very painful?" My friend said, "Yes, there is pain, yes you suffer, you need to have a strong heart to push out this baby." And I said, "Aieee! This sounds too difficult!" I had lots of fear and I spoke of this pain of birth to my husband and I cried, and he said, "This is not good to cry while you are pregnant."

My mother taught me the ways of pregnancy and birth when I was younger, but still I was afraid. She said to me, "My daughter you will suffer a lot for a man because you will be pregnant and you will give birth to this baby." I asked her, "How is this possible?" She told me, "You wait for months and months and then when the baby is formed and ready, the baby finds the right position. When the baby is right and ready to soar, then it is like when you go to the toilet, it is the same pain. The baby soars and the *caca* also flies out." I was afraid. I had heard the cries of other women giving birth and from these cries, I knew of the pain. I had so much fear!

Once you find a baby, in the first month the baby is just blood, the second month, blood. In the third month of pregnancy, the baby becomes like a person with a head, hands, and feet. At five months the baby begins to push and turn in the belly of the woman. Some women give birth at seven months and some at ten months. Before this, the blood is red, and when the woman makes love with her husband, the sperm is released into the red blood, and the blood begins to turn color and becomes black. After the blood becomes black, the baby begins to transform into the form of a person. When you eat good food, the baby grows very good, and if you eat bad food, the baby doesn't grow. The husband needs to keep making love, to give sperm to make the baby grow because the baby will not grow if the husband does not give sperm. But then at seven months, the husband stops making love because the baby is good and formed. If the husband does not stop giving sperm at seven months, the baby will drink the sperm and die. Or the baby will drink the sperm and become very big and it will be hard to give birth.

There are certain traditions you do when you are pregnant. My mother made me a cord to put around my stomach and under my arms, this is for protection against certain illnesses. Here in my village certain men and women know when you are pregnant, and if you eat outside without a protective cord, these certain people see you, then the baby soars and leaves your body, *èkonzi* [baby is miscarried]. When this comes from your private parts, you make a traditional medicine to treat it, but if you feel the water coming, this water provokes to kill the baby and then the baby is born dead. The pygmies make a cord and so do some people in the village. It is very dangerous here in the village for pregnant women. I have seen also *gnauma-ti-ya*. I have seen this with another woman in the village. It is a small animal with many long teeth. It looks like a small mouse. This animal kills the baby inside the woman. If you take medicine it sometimes kills the animal, and the animal comes out. I was afraid when I saw it.

One day the pain began. I walked and walked. I tried to sleep but the pain was too great. I thought I had worms, so I used a pump and nothing happened, then I took medicine from bark for the worms but still the stomach and back pains continued. I never told anyone. I went to the fields but the pains continued! I walked back to my house because of the pain. I pissed myself and I thought, "Why have I done this?" I started to cry and my neighbor asked what was wrong and I told her, "Regard this, all day I have had pains from parasites in my stomach and then all this piss." But my neighbor said, "No, that is the *ppo* [birthwater] of the baby and the pains are the *zeki* [contractions], not the pains of parasites. You will soon give *dibota* [birth] to a baby." I cried and began to tremble. I could not sit and so Issa took me to the hospital. "You are in too much pain." Normally mothers are there to help and give food, bananas, and manioc, but my mother was away and came only after I had the baby.

During the birth I lay flat on a bed with my legs up and the matron told me to breathe good. I yelled and yelled! The matron told me not to yell but I yelled anyway! I thought, "This is pain! This is serious, Mama help me! This is terrible! I am suffering, this is too hard of work for a woman!" During the birth my husband was outside in a room and he heard my cries and said, "Oh my wife cries! What is happening?" Issa was afraid for me. Then the baby's head came out and I said, "No!" And then the shoulders and the rest, and I said, "Oh thank you for being born!" When the head was coming out, it was a terrible pain! But once the head was out the rest was easy! When I saw the baby for the first time I had joy. I thought, "Now I am a mother of this baby." He was named Marcel. My husband's mother gave him this name.

After the birth there was still lots of pain, lots of blood, and I took special medicine. The first time I offered my breast to my baby, I did not know how to give him my breast, and when the baby started to nurse, I pulled away because it hurt! The matron gave me alcohol to put on my nipples to wash them. I gave the first milk, *mai ma mabele ma tella*, to the baby. Certain women throw away the first milk because they think they have the sickness of the breasts. This is when the mothers are pregnant and the breasts become huge and swollen, so after birth they throw out the first milk. I took *bouï* to help with the milk, and then lots of milk came. I also took *ékama* for the pain after the birth and to help heal the breasts.

My mother and my sister came for two weeks, and my mother gave me food and wood and water, and bound my stomach and cared for me. After she left, I lay the baby in a bed until I heard the baby cry, and I would nurse, and when the baby was satisfied I would lay the baby down and commence with my work. I carried the baby in my arms until the baby had a strong head and was big enough to be carried on my back. I was happy. Now I was a mother and responsible for this baby. On the day of birth all the people said, "Now that woman there is a mother of a baby." This was my best memory. But after not too long a time, my husband abandoned the baby and me, and I was alone.

My second marriage was good for a while. The second infant was born quickly! I worked all day and walked to the fields and on the way back the pain became serious! I started trying to walk faster but because of the pain I could not. I stopped and there by the tree, my baby said, "Mama, I am coming now!" And the baby fell onto the ground. The rain came down and the baby was covered with the mud. I screamed and a neighbor came and helped cut the cord and take care of me. This second baby was a girl named Rocine. After I had this infant there were people with jealousy and they sent a poison arrow and the baby and I suffered. I went to the hospital and they gave me medicine, but there was no change, so my parents called for a pygmy. I didn't know this person but a pygmy came and told who did this to me. This pygmy was a specialist and he had a vision and looked over my body and he saw a poison dart in my stomach, *ndoki*, the bone of a gazelle. He sucked out the poison dart. Then he vaccinated my stomach and afterwards the pain and suffering left me. It was a very strong poison and I was very sick for days. Sometime after this, I went to the fields and when I returned, my new husband Levi said, "My wife, look, I have bought nice clothes for you!" I was happy.

The father's role with the birth is to buy clothes for the baby, give money for petrol to light the birth, and to carry the baby in the house to help the wife. If something happens to the wife or baby during childbirth, it is the fault of the husband because he was negligent in getting care for his wife and unborn child. It is his responsibility. Now because of state health education, the right way to give birth is at the hospital. But because it is so expensive, most women have births at home with the matron helping. A good father also knows that after your pregnancy and birth he does not pass the night with you and he respects this period [postpartum taboo]. Women should wait two years before becoming pregnant again. If the father cannot wait, then he wears a condom so the wife does not become pregnant. There was a new baby born recently in the back of the house and it does not even have clothes yet and is very small because the husband did not provide. This is shameful of the husband.

The best number of children to have is six. When you have lots of children, there is lots of help for the family. The family is wonderful, if you are sick, your children can help. But if you have too many children and you are tired, you use the pump to abort the baby, but it is very bad to do this. Or you bury the placenta upside down to prevent more babies from being born. If you have a baby with a deformity, you think this is the baby of a devil. It happens, but you say, "I will take care of you anyway." When a woman can't have a baby, you use the pump to clean yourself and take traditional medicine, because it is due to sorcery that you can't have children. Babies are named after two days, the name comes to the father's mind and he names the baby. Sometimes it is also the grandparents who name the baby if the woman is without a husband.

When your baby is two or three months old you crush corn and manioc and put this in water, like a mush, and put in a little sugar and you feed this to the baby, the *bouï de koulou*. This is because even at two or three months the breast milk is not sufficient and they cry a lot, so they are fed this and then they are happy. If a woman who has a nursing older child and is pregnant and after the birth she has a small infant, she nurses the two like twins. When the older child begins to walk you stop nursing, you put bandages on your breasts and say, "See this child? I have sores and it is time to stop!" And if the child cries you feed it a lot of food, you hold him and sing to him. He is angry but also very sad because now he can no longer have his mother's breast.

If you do not have enough milk for your baby, you go and get bark from a tree, soak it in water, and you drink. This medicine, *mogouga*, makes you produce milk for your baby. That reminds me, there was a certain woman with a little brother, and he had a wife and they had a baby and the wife died. It was because of sorcery. He never paid the bride price. It is the tradition here, but he had a hard time searching for the money. She died and she was not sick. She walked with strength. She was young and had a small baby. She walked down the road one day and she fell and cried, "Oh my heart! My heart!" and died. Her parents said, "Someone has stolen the heart of our daughter!" But her father had married another woman after the death of the girl's mother, and this second wife was a sorcerer. The second wife took care of this girl when she was young, but she took the heart of the young woman because of the money. She told the young husband, "If you marry this woman our daughter, we will get money." But the fiancé married her with debt, because he could not find the money for bride price for the family. Their baby was four months old when this young mother died.

Her younger sister sent a message from the funeral saying to send the baby, but after awhile she no longer could nurse the baby because she had her own baby. She sent the baby back to the young husband's sister to take care of. But this woman had not nursed a baby for five years and she had no milk. So she took the bark and cut it up and put it into water and when the color changed she drank this *mogouga* everyday. After two days she had milk for the baby, but only a little milk. At first it was the yellow milk. But the baby nursed and nursed and soon the white milk came. This is the proper thing to do, to take care of this baby who lost its mother. It is not hard. It is the culture here to give to this child. The father of the baby helps her with money and other things. Other women help also. If she is in the fields, her younger sister gives her breast to the baby. But if too many women give their breasts to the baby, it will become sick [allomaternal nursing].[2]

I gave birth to another baby girl, Florence, but at nine months Florence died. She died of *ekila ya kema*. When she began to crawl she got *ekila*. This makes the baby have convulsions, and the baby holds its hand tight like a monkey and the baby arches its back and there is a high fever. It attacks the baby for two days only and the baby dies so fast! For *ekila ya kema*, it is if you eat a certain monkey and the baby nurses, then it becomes sick with *ekila*. I was very sad because I loved this baby so much! I suffered when she died. I put nice clothes on Florence and I took a banana leaf and put her in the grave.

After a time I thought, I can become pregnant again. But it was three years before I was brave enough to try to have another baby. I became pregnant and during this time I had two infants that I lost when I was pregnant with them. Once because I had parasites and when parasites stir up in your stomach, you lose the infant and it takes a long time to heal. The other was because I did not wear the protective cord. No one was there to make the cord of protection and the baby died of *èkonzi*. This is when you eat outside and someone sees you eat and then you lose your baby. One baby I lost at four months in the pregnancy, and the other sometime a little after that. One was a boy and one was a girl. I had terrible pain and so much blood. I passed out on the bed. My whole bed was covered in blood and after the baby came out, I took the baby and washed it and buried it close to the house. I was very sad with all these losses. They were my babies.

··········································································································

## NGANDU WOMEN
### Therese

··········································································································

For three years I lived with my grandmother and with my husband. During this time it was very good. My husband brought us lots of meat, fish, and gifts for my grandmother so it was a good time. My husband had given the money for marriage to my grandmother and grandfather. He gave them snares, goats, and alcohol [the brideprice]. This means, "I love my wife like I love myself." This ensures that your husband loves you and it is like a reward for your parents, for losing you, their daughter.

Four months after spending the night together I became pregnant. My grandmother knew I was pregnant because I had no blood and I was tired all the time and I was sick. Sometimes I would spit a lot and vomit. I had a fever like parasites and I asked my grandmother, "What is happening?" And my grandmother said to me, "You are just pregnant, that is all."

My grandmother made three cords for protection of the pregnancy: one around my chest, one around my waist, and one around my lower leg. The cord around my chest was for *ngdouma* only, when you get big swollen breasts. The one around the stomach is to prevent the baby from soaring, *èkonzi* , and you start wearing this as soon as you know you are pregnant. There are two other medicines, one from a tree, you take the bark and boil it and then drink. Grandmother got a *nganga* to make the cords and paid money for it. You can have either a pygmy or villager make the cords.

During the pregnancy I could not eat meat without vomiting, so I ate manioc, caterpillars, and bananas. When I was very pregnant and when it would rain very hard, I smelled the smell of earth and it smelled like a good taste. I became hungry for this earth and ate the earth, but only a little. When I was pregnant I respected *ekila*. You know *ekila* when you have a baby and if you eat a certain food, it directly makes your child sick. Then you know that this food you have eaten is *ekila* for that child. I had *ekila* monkey. I had many *ekilas—ekila* fish, *ekila* rat—and when I ate fish or rat and gave birth, blood came in my nose, so I knew I had these *ekilas*. When I was young, my mother and father showed my *ekila*. I never had it until I married, got pregnant, and gave birth. I had one granddaughter, Yvonne, who had *ekila* fish too. Yvonne had a big wound in her mouth and breathed fast when she was born, and this was because of *ekila*. I treated my granddaughter with *boulou* (burnt leaf crushed into powder), but after awhile, the medicine did not work and she died. *Ekila* is difficult.

Before the birth I had a pain in my stomach and I cried, "Grandmother, what is this great pain?" My grandmother said to me, "It is okay, it is only your baby coming to be born." I walked and walked around the house and I cried as I walked. There was no hospital. I was going to have the baby in the house with my grandmother when the baby was ready. Grandmother called for a woman who knew about helping women give birth. The water of the baby, *ppo*, came and I lay down on a mat. I had lots of pain. I cried and trembled. The woman said, "Do not cry, push, push, push!" And the baby was born. A little girl baby, Ellise. After the birth, this woman put the baby on my stomach. Then I pushed out the placenta, and it was buried outside the house. The *diki za zounda* [umbilical cord] was cut with a piece of palm and tied. The first time I saw the baby I was happy and my grandmother was happy to know this baby! Grandmother took water and washed me. Ellise cried and wanted to nurse. But at that time you threw away the yellow milk into the fire or a demon could come and lick it and your baby would die. With the baby I thought, "Now I am a mother of this young child. I am responsible for my husband and my baby. I am now a woman."

I was married and had a little girl baby. I lived with my husband in our own house. I cared for my husband and my baby. This was my life at that time. There were no bandits or war. There was no longer fear in the village. I waited two years and then had a son, Basil. When I was pregnant with my son the pregnancy was no problem. But when the birth pains started, he would not come and the matron had to reach into my stomach and take him, he was such a huge baby! His head did not pass through. I pushed and pushed until I was too tired to push any more. So the matron went into my stomach and pulled him out. When Basil was born he had no spirit. He had died, so they gave air into his body and after awhile he cried! After he came out I had no sense. They made me get up and I sat there out of my senses. They gave me a bowl of manioc and my husband tried to feed this to me. I could not eat, but when my grandmother gave food to me, I ate so much! When the baby was born I had no sense, and when the baby cried, my grandmother gave her breast to this baby. I was just too tired.

I had six infants one right after another and three died. One died when she was a big woman and two were young. One was my first child that was born. The girl, Ellise, she was 15 years old when she died, her stomach swelled up, she was sick for two months and then she died. The second child, Augustine, she was a grown woman and she had many children. The third was my son Christian. He was married and he and his wife got into a fight and his wife bit him. He began to have sores all over his body and he died. When your child is an adult and they die, there is a lot of suffering because you have lived with this child together for a long while and you know him. With a baby you do not yet know him well because your life together has only just begun.

There is too much death here. Our neighbor's little sister Evette died, and our neighbor suffered because she loved that girl, she was happy with her. She died without children. Her husband had AIDS and gave it to the girl. He came and asked Evette for marriage. He presented himself as strong and healthy. He did not know he was sick. AIDS doesn't move quickly and if you do not get examined, you do not know. The husband was sick a long time. They lived together near here and he lost his health. He became very sick. So the girl's parents paid for a *nganga* [traditional healer]. The *nganga* told him, "This is not sorcery. This is AIDS." Afterwards he became skinny and he transmitted this to his Evette. She was just a young girl. The husband died before the girl. Evette knew she had AIDS. She saw her husband die of the disease. He had diarrhea and sores all over his body. My neighbor told me her little sister said to her, "I will also die like this." Six months after he died, Evette died. Many suffer from this sickness. In my time, you did not see this disease. You respected your body. But now the girls stay all night and marry quickly and sleep with many men. In my time, if the parents knew a good man, they would choose him for their daughter. He would come and they would present the daughter to him. Now many girls die here because of AIDS. In my time there was nothing like this disease.

................................................................................

## AKA WOMEN
### Nali

................................................................................

After the marriage we worked hard at night! Quickly I became pregnant. I did not see my blood and in time I began to change in my body. I thought, "With this pregnancy soon I will have a baby for Kokote." I knew this was pregnancy because when I ate food, my heart became sick. I never vomited but my heart detested certain foods like manioc. I ate a little earth, I would take a little piece from the termite mound, put it in the fire and smoke it and then eat it! When you are pregnant you eat these things! When I was pregnant and the baby hit me inside my stomach, I thought, "Oh this is the formation of my infant, he has begun to develop!" I had seen a birth before. I watched as she cried and had pain, and my mother told me, "You will have this pain. Then the water of the baby flies out and soon after the baby comes." I remembered this when I began to have pain.

When the pains started, I cried and cried for my mother! I had so much pain. This is the pain of the baby. My mother and the other women in the camp saw the water, *mai dogba*, and looked at the color and said, "Oh my child, the baby comes!" Then they took me to the edge of the camp, and told me to Push! Push! I felt the pain and the pain was so great! The head started to come and I said to Mama, "Hold me! Hold me!" And she said, "Push! Push!" I concentrated and pushed so hard and the head arrived and the baby fell to the earth. My mother cut the *tongou* [umbilical cord], washed the baby, and buried the *ekoukou* [placenta]. She wrapped the baby in a cloth and carried the baby to our house. (See Figure 4.1. ) I threw the yellow water, [*mai ya ekila*] the first water, into the fire. You spill it into the fire so the baby will not get *ekila*, then you can give your breast to the baby. The yellow water is the color of *ekila*, the color of all the animals that you eat who give you *ekila*. I spilled it out into the fire and when my baby cried, my mother gave the baby her breast. After the first day I gave the baby my good white water of the breasts.

When I saw the baby for the first time, I was so happy! This was the girl of our marriage! We love our babies. If you have a baby, you carry them all the time on the side so they can nurse. You wait for sex after the birth. You do not share a bed until the baby starts to walk for the first time, if you do, the baby will become sick with *dibongô*. If the man touches the baby after sex, the baby will have yellow diarrhea and become skinny and die. This is the responsibility of the parents.

I had many children. One child died of a certain *ekila*, *ekila ya ngoa*, when just walking because I ate pig meat. It is the meat with the sickness and after you eat this, the meat kills the child. My fourth child died of this same *ekila*. My other child had just started to crawl and he was attacked with *mabangi*, because there was an epidemic at that time. So many children died during that epidemic. After the death of

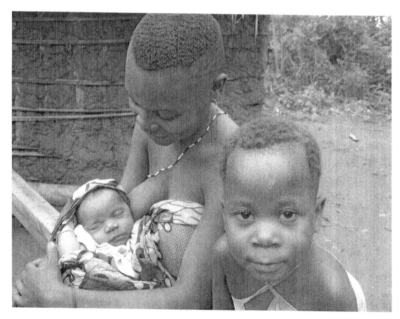

FIGURE 4.1 I *Young Aka mother and her children.*

all these children, I went and looked for a *nganga* to see why I lost my children. Was it simple sickness or sorcery? The *nganga* said, "It is a simple illness."

Each time I took leaves and put them into the grave, and laid my baby on these leaves. Some women take the dirt from the grave and mix it with water and crushed *mossassanga* leaves and spread this on their bellies so that when they sleep with their husbands they will become pregnant with the same baby. But I had such fear to have more children. I give birth and they die. I said, "No more sex with you, Kokote," because I was so afraid of the death of more children. When he asked me for sex I would say, "No. No more work at night. I will become pregnant with a child and this child will die." He said, "Please, let us continue when you find the courage. We will begin again when you find the courage." For a while we stopped our work at night. I had two children who had lived and then those children who died when they began to crawl. There is so much pain when a child is born and then dies. There is so much pain in my heart with all this death. I think of the death of each one and my heart bleeds. Kokote was mad after some time of no work at night, and there were problems in our house. We fought over this sex problem. So we began again.

Now I am pregnant, soon I will give birth, and many years will pass and I will have so many children. When I give birth, the mother of Kokote cannot help, she is too tired. [Both Nali's mother- and father-in-law died two years after this baby was born.] My oldest daughter Elaka has married, she has gone to the camp of her husband. It is Kokote who will be occupied with me, who will have to help, to give food and care for the child. There is no other person. My friends in the camp will help when the moment comes, but they are occupied with their own children. It is not good to become pregnant when you are older, or too quickly again, because you fear your birth will have lots of blood. You risk death. With the loss of blood you will be sick and die. For the infant, the little baby you already have, this baby will have a sickness and this will take the baby. You risk this baby, and also the other may die. Some women, if they are pregnant again quickly, they take a traditional medicine to abort the baby, the bark of a tree. You do this so that the baby you have may live. I will not do this, if this happens I will guard this new pregnancy and be occupied with the baby I have in my stomach. I refuse to abort any because when you do this, you kill this person in your stomach and that is bad. You give birth and it is a person and with this creation, this person, you kill this.

I will not lose this child. I did not want to become pregnant again. I am afraid this baby will die as the baby before died. After the birth I will take the baby immediately to the *nganga*. I will guard this baby day after day. When you have an infant you carry them a lot. When you go to work in the fields you take your child, always. If he cries when you leave, you take him with you. You dance with your child. You walk with your child. Always. If you go with your husband for honey, you go with your child. This is for the health of the child. After this child, I am done. I am an older woman and have enough children. We work at night, but I do not think I will become pregnant again. It is up to *Komba*.

........................................................................................................

## AKA WOMEN
# Konga

........................................................................................................

When I became pregnant, Mopoko said, "Oh, my wife, you are pregnant!" He decided to find food for me to eat. He found caterpillars, grubs, meat, and honey. I loved to eat them because I was pregnant. When I became bigger and bigger, I ate a huge amount! Mopoko was so happy I was pregnant! When the pain started I cried for my mother, but she had died. The moment of birth came and I had some pain in my stomach! Mopoko took a pot and filled it with hot water, put my feet in it and touched my stomach. That helped the pain. But this was the pain of the baby. A woman saw me, the water from the baby, and said, "Come with me for this birth." She told me to push. I pushed out the baby and when its head came, I cried. She said, "No, no, push!," and the baby fell onto the leaves.

The woman carried the baby to my home and I lay down. The baby cried and I thought, "This baby has been born and I am happy." I had this child, a boy, in my parent's camp. When the child walked, we went to live in Mopoko's parent's camp. I was afraid. If this child found death, they may accuse me, "What happened to this child, what did you do to your child?" But I took the child and my parents-in-law saw this child and they knew this child was for their son. For the women it is to carry the child and to give it her breast. The man has to work hard for the child at night, to give the pregnancy. A man has the sperm

FIGURE 4.2 | *Washing an Aka newborn in the forest.*

and the woman guards the infant in her stomach for the man who has worked hard for the child.

It is not good to have a baby and become pregnant again too quickly. If you have a baby you do not sleep in the bed with the father. When the baby walks, then you again sleep with your husband and begin sex again. After you give birth and you have pain in the body, first you find your health again before beginning sex. If you get pregnant too soon, the first baby will become sick with *dibongô*. You will cause the death of your baby. If the baby is in the bed and the father comes for sex, and the father's knees touch the baby, the baby will become sick. If the baby nurses and you have a baby in your stomach, the baby in your stomach will hit the nursing baby. He will have diarrhea, become so sick and tired and die.

I lost children before they were born, one because I ate the meat of the village men without wearing a protective cord. Once when I was pregnant, just a small pregnancy, the pregnancy fell. There was a small animal and when I felt this animal in my stomach, I took medicine and I drank it. This small animal is called *kata*. *Kata* is like a mouse. It is the size of a baby's finger but has a big mouth with many teeth and a tail. When you drink the bitter medicine, your stomach moves and this medicine kills the animal and it comes out of you. I have seen this with my eyes. It has happened to me, but when I took the medicine it did not work, because the baby was still so small it died because of the *kata*. My other children lived except one that died when he was an adult.

## The Adaptive Design of Grief

However vulnerable and helpless humans may seem at birth, as they grow, learn, explore, and develop attachments with others, they are very active agents in promoting their own continued protection and care, necessary for survival.[3] Attachment and the ability to be empathetic to the needs of others, to "read" their minds, is a part of our evolved psychology, in which we have learned to love, form attachments, express our desire, and intimate feelings for each other.[4] We also have an evolved psychology of grief, the ability to feel pain and mourn the loss of those we are attached to, our loved ones. This section expands upon Aka and Ngandu experiences with death and grief in personal and cultural contexts. During the time of my research, on loss there was one, sometimes two deaths per week. Each night in the village of Nambélé, one could hear the "grief wailing" of the bereaved accompanied by drumming, singing, and dancing, or during daylight hours, see Ngandu women walking alone down the main road, crying and loudly sobbing, "announcing" the death of a loved one. Several times I saw mothers carrying the bodies of their children followed by friends and family, a slow, sad procession walking down the main village road.

### Woodburn's Model

Woodburn has conducted one of the only studies of death in hunting and gathering societies. He suggests that, by comparison to farmers and pastoralists, foragers have relatively temporary grief; social continuity is not stressed because of their immediate return system. By comparison, he hypothesizes that farmers and pastoralists, with delayed return systems, have prolonged grief for particular kin (that is, lineage-based kin).[5] In the study I conducted with both Aka and Ngandu adolescents and young adults, I found that both populations experienced and remembered many deaths. Individual Aka adolescents, on average, could easily list eighteen deaths occurring in their lifetime, and Ngandu individuals remembered about thirty. One adolescent listed fifty-two deaths in his relatively short life.

I found general support for Woodburn's hypothesis regarding distinctions between the views of death in immediate and delayed-return cultures. Death rituals were longer among the Ngandu farmers (delayed return) than among the Aka (immediate return). Among the Aka the body is buried quickly, generally the same or next day, whereas among the Ngandu the body would be laid out for viewing for a few days, and rituals existed to remember the individual (adults only) for several years. Burial of Aka also involved less physical time and effort. Also, both male and female Ngandu remembered significantly more males, patrilateral males, in particular, than did the Aka. This is consistent with Woodburn's prediction that farmer's grief should be greater for particular individuals (that is, lineage members).[6]

Although some of the data support Woodburn's model, other data question his propositions. First, his descriptions give the impression that hunter-gatherers experience less ("temporary") grief than farmers and pastoralists. It is true that Aka buried their dead quickly and listed fewer individuals, but they remembered many dead family members, and there was no indication that their felt loss was more "temporary" than the Ngandu. Second, both Aka and Ngandu knew a cause of death for each individual. Woodburn suggests foragers are not as concerned with knowing the cause as are farmers. Aka may not act as concerned as Ngandu, in part, because so many Ngandu deaths are attributed to sorcery, and the Aka do not have as strong a belief in sorcery as do the Ngandu.

## Explaining Diversity and Unity

Some studies, such as Woodburn's, emphasize cultural diversity, but others emphasize universal patterns of grief.[7] Here I examine factors that influence diversity and uniformity in feelings of grief in the Aka and Ngandu communities. Three cultural-ecological factors are important for understanding the particularistic responses to grief: the nature of patrilineal descent and social organization, the nature of social relations, and immediate versus delayed systems of thought.

Strong patriclan social organization among the Ngandu provides a mechanism to defend and protect material (land and crops) and reproductive (spouse) resources. Consequently, the number, age, and sex of geographically close kin, especially males, is important (male-male alliances). The Ngandu accumulate goods and property (planted crops) that must be guarded from mobile Aka and other farmers. Also intra- and intergroup hostilities over women are not uncommon, which leads to conflict and violence.[8]

By comparison, Aka are mobile, and intra- and intergroup hostilities are infrequent. Consequently clan organization is weak. Patriclan organization leads to remembering a greater number of specific others.[9] In this case, Ngandu remember more individual deaths overall, in particular males, who are important for resource defense. Aka, on the other hand, remember both male and female deaths from both sides of the family, because it is important for them to be flexible in response to wild food resource availability. For the Aka, the number, age, and sex of geographically close biological kin, specifically male kin, are of less importance, as there is little need for resource defense (of accumulated goods, property holdings) and male-male alliances. The strong ideology of the Ngandu emphasizes deference and respect for elders, males, and ancestors. Ancestor spirits are shown a continued respect and deference, and they maintain an active place in the lives of the living.

For the Ngandu, social relations and the commitment of a delayed-return system extend beyond death. It is equally important that the formal obligations and commitments extended to the living are also extended to the dead. Economic activity, social continuity, delayed production and consumption, and long-term planning and concern are bound in the sense of the patrilineal lineages, social commitments, and the importance of remembering those to whom you are bound and committed, even beyond the grave.[10]

Aka have, as noted, "immediate return" values and social organization. There is a minimum of investment in accumulating, in long-term debts or obligations, or in binding commitments to specific kin or to other partners. Commitment, as Woodburn suggests, ends at the grave.[11]

Another cultural difference that exists between the two groups is the material versus emotional basis of social relations. Several have written about the material basis of social relations in Bantu-speaking Central Africans.[12] Social relations cannot continue without a material exchange. For the Ngandu, the grief felt over the loss of a loved one seemed to be tied to the grief over the loss of what that person had provided for the individual. Equally so, the diminishment of grief for bereaved Ngandu was often tied to their receiving the distributed articles of the deceased person. Consolation came with the inheritance of the material items of the deceased (clothes, money, medicine). As a 13-year-old female explained, "I was made happy again because after his death [older brother of her mother], I was given clothes and money." Another young girl whose grandmother had died "because she was just tired of life" was given a pot to cook with to earn money, which she said had helped to lessen her feelings of grief, but also changed her life, as now she had to begin working. For some, however, grief continued to be felt intensely in spite of receiving material items, as in the case of one young boy who lost both his father and mother in the same week, and at the age of 8 was sent to live with his mother's younger brother. "He is like a father, he gives me food and I live with him and we go fishing, but," he sobbed, "no one is like a mother to me, I miss my mother and still feel very sad because my mother and father are both gone."

Aka expressions of grief seemed to be bound more directly to the relationship they had with the deceased, which was not expressed as a provisioning one. What consoled them after their loss was simply being with family. Within the intimate circle of family and friends, the Aka adolescent found comfort in the face of the finality of death and the sadness of their loss. When in camp, as noted in the previous chapters, Aka are always in close physical contact, often sitting as close as space allows. This physical closeness was a source of comfort in grief also, as mothers, fathers, or other kin held the young Aka as they grieved. A young adolescent male deeply grieved over the loss of his uncle:

> I loved him a lot and he went with me into the forest to hunt and walk. When a person dies, it is finished for their life. All is finished. The spirit soars to Komba. It does not matter if it is a baby or adult who dies, I feel the same sadness and my father consoles me. The person I love a lot, I grieve for the most. When I am sad I keep crying, but the death is finished and the sadness decreases, but I still love the person.... When I played with my brothers and sisters, I felt happy again and the sadness diminished.

In contrast to the Ngandu, none of the Aka stated that their lives became harder after the death of a loved one. They did, however, list the family members in camp who consoled them, gave them food to eat, and helped them to "be happy again."

A few of the adolescents expressed fear at the thought of their own or a loved one's death, but the majority did not fear death. As one 16-year-old wryly noted, "Death is for all the world, young and old." Many expressed this same sentiment, regardless of their age. A 12-year-old related that she had no fear of death as "many people die and I see this, the body and lots of death and I know death so I do not have fear." One 15-year-old, however, disclosed that he was in fact afraid of death because "with death, it is finished and what happens to the people who die is a mystery, and for this I am afraid."

## Ngandu

For the Ngandu, there was no sense of a timely or good death (that is, only the old or "bad" should die) versus a bad death (suicide, murder). However, most expressed that they felt "saddest" when an adult dies (regardless of age) because they cannot return, whereas a child up to the age of 10 can come back. For the most part, the spirit that was good (shared with others, was "nice") "flew up to God," sometimes but not often described as "heaven," but the bad spirits (those who had been sorcerers and had eaten people) went "into the forest to cry." Heaven was described as being like a large village, exactly like the one they lived in, but without sickness, hunger, death, or sorcery. Bad spirits also included the children of sorcerers as young as 2 or 3, who are born with the "sorcerer's substance" or organ in them, and who had begun to eat people with their father (or mother) sorcerer. They were "bad children" who did not become reincarnated but rather flew up to God, who threw them back down to earth where they would "cry in the forest." No one mentioned that the bad spirits went to hell or purgatory, but rather to the forest, where they cried at night because "they felt bad about not being with family and God." Bad spirits could continue to cause problems for people, scaring them and causing sickness, especially at night when they would walk about. For the adolescents, the forest at night was a frightening place. One 13-year-old female quietly divulged, "The forest is good, but has bad spirits. I am afraid of the forest."

The influence of the church could be seen in the ceremonies surrounding death. If the family was heavily involved in their religion, then there would be no ceremonial wailing, singing, or dancing, but rather a quiet church funeral. If, however, the family was only moderately or not at all involved in the church, they would set the body on a table in the yard of the family, lay out mats for people to sit upon, and family, friends, and acquaintances would come to view the deceased and grieve. The grief wailing would often begin in early evening and continue for much of the night. The men would drum and sing, with women joining in the singing. The men would also dance but the women generally would not. This would also continue late into the night. Food would be served, or people would leave to eat and then return. Children would be present, and families would come and go throughout the evening. The greater the prominence of the deceased, the longer the grief gathering would continue, with family and friends coming from some distance to participate. Therese describes what happens "with death":

> When you lose a husband or wife, the parents of the dead person ask for meat and for coffee for the funeral, and the family of the dead person must provide this. You, the husband or wife of the dead person, must sit on the earth, and you do not change your clothes for one or two weeks. You don't wash yourself, you sleep, eat, and sit on the earth. You eat but not very much because you have no appetite. You sleep on a mat on the earth, and if it rains you sleep on the floor of the house. Then the parents of the dead person come and say, "This is enough. Wash yourself and your clothes. You have grieved enough." They give you new clothes and water and a chair to sit on. You suffer in grief. This shows your grief.

If the deceased is a child under the age of 10, the child could "return," that is, be reincarnated and born again. The child would often return to the same family, but not always. The family would recognize their "lost" one by some physical or personality trait that they had had in their previous life (a scratch or birthmark, perhaps a way of laughing). Infants (less than one year old) were immediately wrapped in palm leaves and buried next to the outer wall of the house. The mother then spread earth from the grave onto her abdomen to help ensure the child's quick return.

For older deceased children, there would be no grief gathering as with adults. Mainly immediate family and playmates or those who had helped with the care of the younger child would attend. The body, the *kwa*, would be washed by a close female relation, laid out in nice clothes, wrapped in a clean sheet, placed in a wooden casket, and interred, *loungozo*, close to the house. For those who were not strongly affiliated with a religion, there would also be a one-year ceremony, honoring the memory of the deceased, with singing, dancing, drinking, and eating. The one-year ceremony is to "see family and we dream of them. We have a ceremony to remember and dream of them again." For those belonging to the church, occasionally a quieter Catholic mass would occur, one year later, to remember.

# Aka

For those who die, the spirit "soars" to *Komba* if good, or gets thrown back to earth to cry in the forest if bad. For the Ngandu adolescents, the forest at night became a frightful place. However, for the Aka, the forest is seen at all times as "mother, father, provider, lover," in spite of the "bad" spirits who roam at night, and none of the adolescents expressed any fears regarding these spirits crying at night in the forest. When people "soar to *Komba*," the place is described as being like a camp in the forest and, as with the Ngandu, without sickness, death, or sorcery: "All the camp is there, all the family is there." There is no Aka word for heaven or paradise, but rather several of the Aka adolescents used a Sango word for heaven to describe their thoughts regarding an afterlife. Few of the adolescents interviewed seemed to have been influenced by the Christian notion of paradise, God, and people being punished for their disbelief. All seemed to believe in the reincarnation of young children. As one young male explained to me, "All the spirits are the same, the babies and the adults, but the ceremonies are for the adults because the babies return. They return to the same mother, but adults do not return."

The funeral, one young girl explained, "is to say goodbye, this is the last moment on earth. This is for the person who dies, to say goodbye, it is in their memory. The burial place is close to the house, but when we leave, the place stays in camp. We visit the place of burial to remember the person." The death of a young child or baby is often thought of as a temporary goodbye until that child returns, either to the same mother or to another women in the same camp. However, as one adolescent said, "The sadness is still the same."

As with the Ngandu, the causes of death among the Aka were broadly listed as *ekila* (of which there are many types), accidents (such as falling from trees), and sorcery.[13] After a death in camp, as I was told by a young adolescent boy,

When a person dies, the men, women, and children all cry a lot. They all stay in a group and talk about the person and then begin the funeral and dance to *djengi* (the forest spirit). The women wash the body and the men find the bark, *dikoko*, to bury the body in. The men arrange the burial place and put the body into to the ground and cover it with dirt. After the burial there is a little ceremony, they dance, they sing, they cry. This is on the same or the next day. It is short, they dance for two or three days, and then it is finished.

There was no sense of there being a "timely," "good," or "bad" death, justified by old age or accusations of murder. The one-year ceremony, the *peli*, is a "little ceremony of the time of their death and when the date arrives of their death, there is a lot of feeling, of emotion for that person. The people dance, eat, and sing together. It is for the memory of that person" (young Aka woman). It is also a time that signals the end of the grieving period for widows. At the one-year ceremony, widowed women shave their heads, wash, put on clean garments, and have a close female relative rub them with a special oil. They are then ready to marry again. During my first field study, in the rainy season, far in the forest there was a large "memorial ceremony" in which many camps gathered to sing, dance, eat and drink, and remember their lost loved ones. This apparently occurs only when someone (or several) people of prominence have died. As an elder Aka man told me, "I can live in the forest, I eat well, I have family, life is good...but then there is death and life is finished."

Diversity exists in the experiences and expressions of grief, but there are also several commonalities. Evolutionary psychologists are interested in identifying genetic or biologically based universals of the human mind that evolved during the environment of evolutionary adaptation (EEA, the long period of human hunting and gathering) in response to recurrent adaptive problems. One recurrent problem faced by humans was the regular death of individuals who had assisted them in many ways (subsistence, defense, childcare, physical and emotional health).[14] Given the adaptive problem of recurrent loss, the grief response to that loss and the cross-cultural commonalities existing between the Ngandu and Aka might suggest that humans have "grief" modules of the mind that are in part the flip side to the attachment or proximity module.[15] Infants cannot care for or protect themselves, so they seek the proximity of others by crying and reaching for these individuals.

Infants who sought proximity, in the EEA, survived.[16] In much the same way, perhaps the crying, mourning, and grief expressions following loss might represent an evolved psychology for the communication of need following the loss of an individual who enhanced survival. Like the crying and fussing of an infant, expressions of grief may be helpful in communicating the needs of one who has experienced loss.

When survival is threatened, following loss and the physiological responses to this psychological assault, grief becomes an important emotion that elicits a response from others who may benefit reproductively from the individual experiencing grief. For the grieving person, the soothing of grief, the social interaction of compassion, leads to closer bonds with both existing figures and the establishment of new corollary social networks—all of which serve to enhance the survival of the individual. Grief is a "cry for survival."

Several common patterns are found in the data from the study of Aka and Ngandu: grief is a response to loss (obviously this is seen in other cultures as well as in nonhuman primates); the expression of grief tends to illicit a response from others; those responding tend to be genetically related to the grieving adolescent; and the "soothing" of the grief expression and the practices of response in helping to diminish the grief emotion follow specific cultural patterns. An integrated biocultural approach helps us to understand the interactions between culture, ecology, and biology, and provides an opportunity to examine not only grief but also intimacy and attachment from a holistic perspective. Aka and Ngandu comparisons provide insights into how ecological, psychological, and cultural structures and relationships influence the manifestation of individual patterns of love and grief—whereby the context influences the experience and expression of grief, attachment, and love.

Mortality and grief are difficult topics to research for many reasons. Talking to people about their experience of loss is hard, but equally troubling are the reasons for the deaths. That is, many deaths are due to treatable and preventable infectious and parasitic diseases. With increasing populations, lack of consistent access to health care, depletion of the food resources of the forest from increased logging, over-exploitation by sedentarized populations, and loss of lands to conservation projects, it may well be that health risks for both the Aka and Ngandu will increase.[17] Currently, the Ngandu have limited access to primary biomedical care, with for example, rural health clinics (government sponsored) providing childhood vaccinations, maternal care, and general health services. These services are not always available or affordable for the Aka. This in itself should lower farmer child mortality rates, but concurrently Ngandu children are more likely to be anemic because of less meat in their diet, and more likely to be exposed to malaria and parasites because of a more sedentary lifestyle.[18] Ngandu have higher HIV/AIDS infection rates than foragers, which leads to greater adult mortality. Rural clinics tend to favor the Ngandu over the Aka, whereas clinics set up by missionaries and aid efforts by Cooperazione Internationale (COOPI), UNESCO, and other NGOs tend to favor the Aka over the Ngandu. For both populations, access to health care is often denied by an inability to pay for the services or medicines.

Health issues faced by both the Aka and Ngandu are determined by forces that not only "re-order cultural expressions and meanings" but also serve to make the both populations vulnerable to disease.[19] Too often organizations working to give indigenous cultures better access to the "legal, educational and social systems within the dominate culture, to give them voice and agency," as well as health care, although "driven by humanitarian aims" instead serve to undermine and devalue their very particular cultural values and belief systems.[20] Rather than trying to understand the "historic foundations and contemporary processes" of marginalization, aid organizations, development programs, and national and international policies operate as "powerful forces within a position of dominance," abetting human rights abuses.[21] To effectively combat practices of structural violence and marginalization, the battle must begin from a foundation of knowledge and respect for the values and beliefs of the Aka and Ngandu.[22] Too little time and effort is given to understanding the cultures and needs of local people.

..................................

In this chapter we have seen that the structural violence borne by the Aka and Ngandu—marginalization, disparate access to health care, education, lack of political and economic power—not only leads to many premature and avoidable deaths, but also is embedded within the social, political, and economic machinations of an increasingly globalized world. Through the narratives of the Aka and Ngandu, it is clear how foundational schema regarding gender hierarchy and different culturally constructed niches (that is, sedentary versus mobile lifestyles) contribute to the very diverse ways human emotions and behaviors are experienced and expressed in these two cultures. The next chapter examines the gendered roles of the Aka and Ngandu women, their husband-wife relations, household equity, and the valuation of women, as determined by subsistence patterns, cultural ideologies, and local economies.

................................................................................................................................................................................

## NOTES FROM THE FIELD
### Winter 2000

*—We are at a camp in the forest, camp Boningo. This morning a young mother with a two-week-old baby died. I was told the baby will be taken care of by the husband's mother, who also has a young baby, so she will be able to nurse the little baby. All day people have been gathering in this camp. The women are sitting under a tree and are sing-wailing their grief. I went earlier to take a bath with some of the Aka women, and we met this other young mother walking along, holding her baby with tears just rolling down her face, and every once in awhile she would also cry-sing her grief to her baby. After our bath we sat huddled together with the baby of the young mother. The drums have been beating all day. A group of young adolescent girls sat down together and made the leaf bushes to put on for the dance, and after they got up and together began dancing the shuffle-dance. They sang their yodeling song as they danced. Others joined in and they harmonized as they sang this grief-crying song. I don't think I have ever heard such a mournful sound. There is another young woman sitting apart from the others, just holding onto her baby so tightly. The husband of the dead woman is sitting outside their hut, next to her burial mound of red earth. This is too hard. But somehow the funeral dance ceremony seems to be as much a celebration of life as it is a ceremony to grieve the death of the young mother.*

*—Heard the grief wailing again all day today in the village. A message was relayed from house to house that a man from that quartier had died. So I heard the song of grief—there was a woman sitting on the ground yelling, crying and around her in a circle other women singing and crying. Every day we've heard this. S.'s little boy died two days ago, then his sister's little baby died the next day. Last evening I heard two kids going by crying along the road because someone they knew had died. I have sick, wounded people coming here to my house daily, wanting us to treat them. Today it was a man with a terrible burn on his leg. Have also seen a boy who got shot in the eye with an small arrow, a baby with high fever who convulsed, a young girl with a terrible burn on her head, another young girl with an open, infected,*

huge wound on her lower leg, an older lady with yellow fever? who ended up dying three days later, and on and on, so much. It's terrible and no medicine or clinic with anything to treat the people.

—Today the body of the man who died arrived. We could hear everyone wailing again when the truck came. We were at E.'s and all the little kids went running out to watch the truck go by and then came in and told us, "A dead body just went by." Later as we walked down the road, everyone all of a sudden started bellowing and came running by us, as they'd found a sorcerer out. This woman had been slowly killing her husband (sorcery). This was discovered when she was made to drink the poison oracle. So then the man's brother tried to knife her but failed, and she was taken off to prison. And M., the man who has the palm wine "bar," told us his wife gave birth to their baby, but it was born dead.

### Winter 2002
—Had to quit the death and loss study. Too hard. This little boy started crying thinking about the loss of his mom and dad, said he had no one who "was like a mother to him". I just can't do this any more.

### Fall 2007
—Today walked into village camp and M. was sitting there looking old, tired and sad. So I asked him what was wrong, and he said his wife M. had been terribly sick and he had left the forest to come and get medicine for her, but on the trail, he told me "C. the villager" stopped him and made him go back to the camp and get the koko leaves or something, not sure what as by now M. is having a hard time talking. He went back to his camp, got whatever it was for C. and then came here, and by the time he got here it was night. This morning he was going to get the medicine, but it was too late, G. came from the forest and told him M., his wife, had died during the night. And he sat there, quiet, with tears running down his face.

—Don died Monday from an embolism. I just want to go home. Three nights ago at about 8:30, E., J. and A. knocked on the door and told me there was an urgent letter/message from B. He'd emailed the Embassy and from there T. printed out the message and gave it to someone coming to Mbaiki, so a lady there has the letter. Awful, awful night. I knew it was terrible news, so thought all night of the kids. I just sat there waiting until it was morning. Was able to finally go and try calling on the phone. By some stroke of great *luck I got through and B. told me the news. I was outside when I called, everyone heard me and E. kept telling everyone not to stare at me, as I'd just heard my father died. He told me to be calm before I called my Mom and kids. Mom is doing OK, the kids are all really upset. They need me and I am here. There is nothing worth that, being away from them now. Nothing. Not being there when they need me is the worst feeling in the world. I'm leaving as soon as I can. It's so hard to think I will never see Don again. He was the only dad I ever knew and now he is gone. E. came soon as it was light and told me he was there because he knew I "was suffering." People here are so kind, so strong. They know grief.*

**Fall 2010**
*—Spent the morning talking to T. who is doing great! We sat behind her house and like before her grandchildren and daughters hover nearby and add to the conversation. L.'s baby died. Last time I was here, she was nursing her and she was a fat, healthy one-year-old. Now she is dead. L. lowered her head down and said, "That is the way of life here." I can't even imagine, it is too sad here, too often. Went to see N. today as well, in the village camp. I asked if she was not feeling well as she seemed tired/sad. She told me K.'s mother had died. She had ash on her face as she was mourning. We sat under the lean-to and talked just a little, I am so sad for her as she was so very close to her mother-in-law.*

---

## QUESTIONS FOR REFLECTION

1. As young children and adolescents, the Aka and Ngandu have experienced the multiple deaths of loved ones. Do you think this previous experience with bereavement and loss prepares the mothers to cope with the loss of their children?
2. Would it be difficult for you, in an environment in which half of all children die, to allow yourself the luxury of love, knowing, and possibly fearing, that your child may die?
3. Is a mother's or father's love a privilege or an innate emotion?[23]

---

## NOTES
1. For a more detailed review of attachment, sexual desire, and marital relations, see B. L. Hewlett and B. S. Hewlett 2008.
2. Allomaternal nursing is common cross-culturally, but it is poorly understood and few systematic studies exist. Studies that have been conducted suggest

"kinship, infant age, mother's condition and culture impact the nature and frequency of allomaternal nursing" (B. S. Hewlett and Winn, n.d.).

3. Tomasello 1999; Hrdy 1999.
4. Tomasello 1999; Konner 1983. For a more detailed examination of attachment, loss and grief see Bowlby 1999 [1969], 1973, 1980 and Ainsworth 1967.
5. Woodburn 1982. For a more detailed analysis, see B. L. Hewlett 2005.
6. Woodburn 1982.
7. Archer 2001; Babcock 1991 Bowlby 1999 [1969], 1973, 1980; Parkes 1972.
8. B.S. Hewlett 1991.
9. Woodburn 1982.
10. Woodburn 1982.
11. Woodburn 1982.
12. LeVine et al. 1996; see also Rupp 2011; Moïse 2010; Joiris 2003, 73; Bahuchet and Guillaume 1982; Takeuchi 1998.
13. For a more complete study of causes of death, see Hewlett et al. 1986b.
14. B.S. Hewlett et al. 2000a, 25.
15. Bowlby1999 [1969].
16. B.S. Hewlett et al. 2000a, 25.
17. Ohenjo et al. 2006.
18. B.S. Hewlett nd Studies comparing the health of foragers and farmers indicate that large differences thought to occur in rural forager-farmer health, mortality, and fertility do not in fact exist.
19. Kenrick 2005.
20. Kenrick 2005.
21. Farmer 2004, 8: "structural violence," a term coined by Johan Galtung, describes "a broad rubric that includes a host of offenses against human dignity: extreme and relative poverty, social inequalities ranging from racism to gender inequality, and the more spectacular forms of violence that are uncontestedly human rights abuses.... Amartya Sen has referred to such destructive forces as 'unfreedoms.'"
22. Kenrick 2005.
23. For further and insightful readings on this topic, see Hrdy 1999 and Scheper-Hughes 1989.

# CHAPTER 5

# The Consequences of Being a Woman

Men do not understand the sense of marriage. It is very dangerous to take other wives. I will leave and find another. It does not work, many wives divorce because of it. It is very mean to take another wife. Men depend upon their women for their life, for clothes, and food and to take care of their children.

—Sylvie, Ngandu woman

My first husband found another wife and I was mad and jealous and fought with him and said this is not possible, so I divorced him.

—Djaba, Aka woman

This chapter discusses domestic violence and its relationship to complex and larger issues of gender, hierarchy, agency, power, marginality, and globalization. We will explore what constraints and opportunities are afforded within the lives of the forager and farming women, and the strategies individuals employ in their diverse social worlds. Therese, Blondine, Nali, and Konga define what it means to be a woman in their relationships, homes, and communities, and explain the formation of gendered roles within families, friendships, martial relationships, and society.

## Egalitarianism, Hierarchy, and Gendered Relations

The close community of the Ngandu and Aka begins with the family, where the acquisition of cultural skills, socialization, production, and reproduction occur. Men and women participate in subsistence activities to support their households; both groups work hard for their families. Individual variation exists in the relationships between husband

and wife, and as well between the Aka and Ngandu generally. The roles of the Aka and Ngandu, their social identities, day-to-day activities, cultural beliefs, roles, and ideas about what it means to be an Aka mother and wife and what it means to be a Ngandu mother and wife are influenced by subsistence patterns, systems of descent, postmarital residence patterns, local economies, and political systems.[1]

Gender stratification and the sexual division of labor are determined in part by the type of subsistence production and by the role of social as well as biological reproduction.[2] In egalitarian societies, like the Aka, women and men are viewed as having complementary positions in relation to each other. This correspondence in gender relations is seen in the fluidity of gender roles in which both men and women are laborers and providers, sharing childcare and subsistence tasks. As mobile hunter-gatherers, there is little or no accumulation of material items, wealth, or land, therefore there is nothing to store, protect, or pass on as inheritance. Where subsistence is connected to female intensive farming, as with the Ngandu (and most horticulturalist societies), the value of a woman is found both in her ability to produce an heir, another laborer and clan member (important for male-male clan alliances), and in her ability as laborer and provider, increasing household production and economy.[3] More wives (polygyny), translates into more heirs, more laborers, more clan members, and greater household income, serving to strengthen family, clan, and community. As there is an increase in production, there often follows an increase in gendered inequalities and stratification, as well as changing social structures, kinship patterns, and the valuation of women.[4]

Ngandu women are the primary contributors of household income and of calories to the diet—food obtained from the fields they have planted, weeded, and harvested throughout the year.[5] Women spend an enormous amount of time working. (See Figure 5.1.) After a day in their fields harvesting manioc, they carry heavy baskets to the river to soak the tubers. The manioc must be then dried in the sun, pounded into flour, and finally prepared for meals.[6] Women take part in an informal market economy, selling the products of their farms, such as manioc, peanuts, corn, plantains, palm oil, and forest products, and trading them with the Aka. A few also distill and sell "moonshine" or meat their husbands brought to them, or traded for with the Aka. Men's work tends to be more seasonal, and men are also generally involved in the weeding and harvesting of any coffee crops, if the Ngandu family

FIGURE 5.1 | *Ngandu woman doing woman's work.*

has coffee fields. However, much of this "men's work" is done by the Aka.[7]

There is a marked inequality within Ngandu households. Men are served first and are served larger portions of food; women cannot touch guns or spears (or any hunting implements); women infrequently occupy political positions, such as village police. Violence against women is not uncommon.[8] Women often marry in their middle to late teens, whereas men marry three to four years later. When the marriages are polygynous, co-wives either share the same house but live with their children in separate rooms, or live in separate houses in the same compound (Figure 5.2). Extended family members build homes close to one another, often on the same property. Ngandu lead rather private lives in their homes, and family meals, household work activities, and socializing take place in the yards behind the homes.[9]

The Aka are one of the most egalitarian cultures in the ethnographic record—an egalitarian status in part related to their subsistence patterns of net-hunting and gathering, where both men and women equally contribute to the diets and work of the households.[10] Seasonal movements influence the contribution by men and women: when the Aka are

FIGURE 5.2 | *Polygynous Ngandu family. (Courtesy of Barry Hewlett.)*

working in the villager's fields and living in village camps, the women bring in more "village" food like manioc, maize, and palm oil, as food is exchanged for labor. The men's contribution increases once the couple and any children move back to their forest camp.[11] Women frequently join in the net-hunt, and it is not uncommon to see a women with a knife or spear in hand and a baby nestled in a sling at her side. In some cases Aka women go net-hunting without men, but usually the whole family participates (See figure. 5.3). Men join in the gathering of forest plants, tubers, and nuts. The women generally have control over the distribution of food sources, both meat and plant, although both men and women have equal access to available resources. Aka men provide intensive

FIGURE 5.3 | *Aka woman on a net-hunt with baby. (Courtesy of Barry Hewlett.)*

care to infants—more than fathers in any other systematically studied culture. The Aka are characterized by extensive gender role flexibility. Women and men regularly share subsistence and childcare roles.[12]

# Differing Faces of Gendered Realities, or, The Life of a Woman

### NGANDU WOMEN
### Blondine

I was married. I lived with my husband, Issa, and he gave me food to eat and nice clothes, and we lived together but only a short time. It was a good time of life. I loved my husband a lot. The relationship was like a friendship but it was much more. One day if there is a problem, we would fight at night and hit each other, but this did not happen very often. The reason for this was that Issa gave me clothes to wash and said when he returned in the evening, "Where are my clothes and why are they not washed yet?" If I was not in the house when he returned, he said, "You are out looking for another man!" But I did not look for another man, only Issa.

During this time I took care of my child and my husband. I made money, selling fish and meat, and I bought clothes for the children and things for the house. This was my best memory. When I walked down the street people would yell, "There goes little testicles!," because I made so much money and carried it in a cloth that hung down from my waist like testicles! I had my husband, my farm and this one child and we lived. This marriage did not last long. My first husband Issa was so stingy I was blocked from getting pregnant for a time.

A friend told me about when she was married for the first time, that she became pregnant and said to her husband, "I am pregnant." He told her, "No, no this is not my baby." The husband refused her and went and prepared medicine with bark, an enema that would get rid of the pregnancy. She did not know why her husband thought the baby was not his, but for two months she guarded the pregnancy and did not take the medicine. Her husband said to her, "If you do not abort the baby then I will leave." My friend told him, "Leave then, because I will have this baby." So he left. She stayed with her sister for the months of the pregnancy and gave birth to a daughter. The baby grew and grew and when she was 8 years old, the husband returned and said, "Now I will take this daughter of mine." My friend told him, "No, it is finished. Because when I was pregnant you refused my pregnancy, and now I will not let your daughter return with you." Her husband said, "I am sorry, let's reconsider this. I will give you money and then I will take the child." My friend was mad but then said she would take the money if she could see her daughter from time to time. So the father and her daughter left. She was not sad because she knew her daughter would live well and would come and see her. Now her daughter is a grown woman with a baby and comes and visits my friend. If a woman asks for divorce, the little children stay with the mother. If they are older the father pays money to the mother and they go with him. If you have older children with divorce and the husband gives you money, you cannot refuse. But if the child cries and demands, "Where is my mama?," he can visit his mother.

Another woman's husband brought home a second wife, and the second wife was very young and very beautiful, and the first wife was very old and very jealous. One day when the husband was gone, the first wife took money and sent the second wife back to her parents. The husband came home and said, "Where is my second wife?" And he went and brought her back. But sometimes the first wife would take water and dirt and put it all over the second wife's bed. They lived in a house with two rooms for bedrooms, and another day the first wife went to a *nganga* and bought medicine. She brought this medicine back and entered the room of the second wife and put the medicine on the bed. The husband came to sleep with his second wife and his penis did not work! The husband said, "Why can't I do this work? She is young and beautiful but when I go to my first wife who is old it worked. Something is wrong here!" He said to his penis, "Why are you doing this for the first wife?" After awhile the second wife's parents came and took her away and said, "This old woman, the first wife, is causing too much trouble for our daughter. This marriage is over." The husband said, "No, I will divorce my first wife, she is no good." He divorced the first wife and stayed with the second wife.

Sometimes, even if a man and wife have lived together for a long time and the woman is old and they sleep alone or on separate beds, if the woman refuses her husband for sex, the husband says, "I will go to the chief and ask for my money back [bride price]." Women have to pay if they refuse sex with their husbands. The causes of divorce are that if you have a husband and he searches for another wife; or if you, the wife, do not obey and respect your husband; or if you do not prepare food and do not give to his parents and if the couple fights a lot and if he is mad a lot or if she is, he takes her bed and throws it out on the street. The house is the man's and the woman leaves.

In general husbands are hard. If the husband doesn't have the spirit of an economist, he works and then drinks away the money. If a man has two wives, he prefers the second because he has already spent so much time with the first. But the second is new! They are given more money and gifts. The children, he loves all the children. But if he loves the second wife more, he gives her extra money in secret in the bedroom. If it is in secret it is better; if she tells the other wife there is a problem.

After marriage you work in the fields, sell things, work in the house, and have your children. The beauty of a woman is the work of the woman. This work is not easy. When you work in the fields, you work in the hot sun and with that work you get money, but it is so hard, there is pain and you are tired. You carry heavy loads on your head and you find firewood, you wash clothes, you sweep the yard. All this work is hard work and afterwards you can hardly move you are so tired.

The qualities of being a good husband are that he takes good care of the family, he gives lots of respect to me and he respects my parents. The good qualities of a wife are that she works hard and when she gets to the house, she takes water and prepares a bath and food for the husband. She is the mother of the house. A good father teaches his children. He buys shoes and clothes for them with his money. He gives money for education and takes them to a hospital if they are sick. It is the responsibility of the father to take the child to the hospital. Both a husband and wife have important work.

NGANDU WOMEN
Therese

By this age the spirit of the girl is finished in your heart and you have the spirit of a woman. I was married and I worked in the fields and came home and worked for my children. That is the life of a woman. You, yourself, without help from your parents or others, you work for yourself and family. This is the spirit of a woman.

During this first part of our marriage we did not have disputes, but after awhile we began to have disputes. The subjects were that when my grandmother walked, my husband would ask, "Why is your grandmother walking? Is she searching for another husband for you?" My grandmother told him, "No, we are not looking for another husband." I was very beautiful and many other men wanted me, but I only loved my husband. With the fighting mostly it was only my husband and me. My grandmother would say, "No it is not okay, do not fight!" But we would fight anyway and hit each other. If he hit me a lot and it hurt, I would hit him back. Another dispute was that during the night, when we passed the night together, he wanted sex and I refused. I was too tired and I told, "No, not today, I am too tired." He was angry at me so I became angry at him.

For my husband and myself, even with all these children, our relationship changed over time. When I was very young, there were no problems, but when I was between the ages of 30–35, my husband was so jealous. If I went to water he said, "No! You are looking for another!" And he would hit me! We fought a lot because of this. This change occurred because at first I was so young, but now at 30 my husband went looking for another wife. Maybe this was why, he thought that I too would look for another. My husband did not talk to me about this. I asked him and he hit me. I discovered the second wife when he left and stayed away most of the night. People would say to me, "We saw your husband with another." Slowly I knew he had another woman. After I discovered this woman, my husband said, "No, forgive me, my wife. This is not a woman for this house. Forgive me. It is finished." But I was so mad with my husband! I fought with him and he hit me. I had such anger! I grabbed his feet and lifted him up and threw him down! He jumped up and looked for the machete. I ran from the house and he went screaming through the streets looking for me, so I went to the forest to hide. I was so afraid! I just hid in the forest then slowly came back. I asked my friend if I could sleep at her house for awhile. People intervened so he wouldn't hurt me. Slowly, slowly, I came back to my house and I asked my husband if it was okay now and he said, "Yes, my wife. All is good. Come back home." My husband stayed with me alone after that.

My worst memory was this, when my husband and I had this fight. I did not work or speak to him for many days. My husband said that he thought this, "My wife there has fought with me and now she will not speak to me. Maybe this marriage is finished." He was so sad. He said to me, "Oh, my wife I am sorry. I have a gift for you." After that the dispute was finished.

When my husband would get money, he would give some little amount to me, but not very many times. When I got money, I would hide it. I was not a servant to my husband. When I married my husband, he did not like to pay for spoons, or pots and plates so I paid for all these things. My husband made more money than me but he didn't give me much money, he did what he wanted with his money. I paid for the clothes for my children, when they were sick I brought them to the hospital and I paid money for school. My husband used his money to search for another wife. I was so mad but didn't say anything. My husband did not take care of the children. That was why I had to make the effort to pay money for school, for medicine and all for my children. I stayed with him because it takes two people to make babies in life, but if one person is weak, you have to take care of the children. You have to give your hands to work.

At this time in my life, I thought, "I am a woman. I know life and this is good. I am strong." Our children grew.

## AKA WOMEN
# Nali

I was married and in the camp of Kokote with my children. Kokote liked to walk in the forest with me and I was happy. He would find meat, honey, and fruit for me and the children. I would gather yams and prepare our food and our home. These are good memories!

Life was good, I had health and I worked and Kokote worked also. I worked for Kokote, he would ask for something and I did this for him. One time I left alone to go to the forest to find food for Kokote and my children. To look for yams, the *èsuma*, this yam is preferred, it is a good quality! To find this yam, you take a big stick and put it in the earth and you dig and dig and dig. If you see this cord the yam is way deep in the earth. You take the digging stick and you dig. You poke the yam with the stick and pull it up. It is very long so you cut and cut the yam and pull it out of the earth. Then you wash it in water and take it back to camp and prepare it and give it to the family. Your husband sees this yam that you have prepared and he says, "Oh! You are a brave woman to do this for me!" And his family says, "You are a brave and excellent woman for our son!" This yam has a very good taste. I cook it with fish or meat, and when I fix this everyone says, "Oh, you are such a brave woman and this proves your love for your husband!" It is not difficult to find, it is just a lot of work!

At times I used to go to visit my family. I might stay for a week, sometimes Kokote gave his permission and sometimes I left alone. The problem was always there if I asked to visit my family and I was there for three or four days, when I returned Kokote always asked, "Did you find a lover?" Now if I don't get permission from him, I don't go. When I was young, I would go to other camps to dance with my friends. Even when I was a young wife, I would go, and even if I was married and occupied with him, I wanted to go. But he would say, "No. Stay here, do not go to the dance in another camp." Kokote said no because he thought maybe I searched for another lover. I never look for another lover. I just loved to dance. But his spirit grew jealous. He said, "No!" Sometimes he hit me, *bok bok bok*, and he said, "You have found another husband!" When I was young in the marriage, I thought, "This is a problem," because he never wanted me to dance. Now there are so many years in the marriage and as I am tired, it is not a problem. Kokote is not jealous. But sometimes, if I am at a dance, he thinks,

"Maybe a certain man will see my wife and he is searching for another wife." But after all these years in marriage I love Kokote so much.

In marriage your heart is for your parents, your children, your husband. In our marriage when Kokote was young, he would hit me a lot, but now he does not hit me, he respects me. When he has a problem and speaks a lot, I do not say anything. He talks and talks and I say nothing. If your husband is angry and talks and the woman also talks, they will start to yell and this causes problems. I am quiet until he will listen. When he becomes quiet then I speak. This is a sign of respect. Respect is a part of love. Love is the most important thing in marriage. The heart is the most important.

## AKA WOMEN
### Konga

Always I worked for Mopoko. I learned the lesson of women. We would go alone together into the forest and find things to eat. At this time I was attacked by a sickness. I had so much pain I couldn't walk. It took three months before I regained my strength. Mopoko did not know how to find the yams of the women. The family did not eat well. Others gave, but when my children searched for food, it was not sufficient, as when I, their mother, gave them food.

But after this, I was in camp sitting there like this with my friends and I started to talk about funny stories: once the spirit of one woman and her husband started to fight because the man hit the woman, and when the woman hit him, he started to cry. We imitated this and it was so funny! We laughed!

Before, marriages were good. In marriage, many women were strong. You'd walk alone with your husband in the forest. He did the same equally with his wife. Now women are not strong in the marriage. This is the education of the mother to the daughter. When some women marry, they do not work for their husbands, when they sleep, they sleep apart at night from their husbands. Before, you got married and stayed married. Now, in marriages there are many problems. Today the marriages do not endure. The girls look for many men because they love money, so marriages do not last. This is not good. Life is hard now. Certain women sleep with men from the village for money, and before they would not do this, and this may bring AIDS. Some change is bad.

Another reason for divorce is this: when you are in a family, if the mother or father have a baby and they want to take this baby and give it sorcery, to make it a sorcerer, they take this baby and suck up the sorcery organ, just a small piece, from their stomach. This is in their mouth and they kiss the baby and put it into the mouth of the baby, like this "*boo, boo, boo.*" The baby eats it and when the child is bigger, it is in the stomach of the child. The organ gets bigger and it grows with the child and he is a sorcerer. If the child does not want to be a sorcerer, or if the mother does not want her child to be a sorcerer, she finds a *nganga.* The *nganga* examines the stomach of the child for the organ, and he vaccinates the place with a razor and sucks the organ out so it comes out from the child's stomach. Then he takes the organ and cuts it, and it is finished. But if he doesn't, it stays there and the child will be a sorcerer. A mother knows the child is a sorcerer if, when you pass the night with the baby, you, the mama, are sleeping and the child wakes you up from the bed and cries and cries and wiggles a lot in bed. The baby cries so much all night, and during the day the child does not cry. So the mama takes the child to a *nganga* to be examined. The mother is so angry at the father for this, because the father is a sorcerer and has made the baby a sorcerer. So she divorces him and finds another husband.

Another reason for divorce if the husband hits the children a lot. The mother says, "Why are you hitting my children?" They fight over the children and the mother will divorce the husband.

## Voices of Pain and Passion

### NGANDU WOMEN
### Blondine

After Issa left, my second husband, Levi, saw me and wanted to marry me. He spoke so much he had no saliva in his mouth! I loved my second husband Levi. It was a good marriage, but over a long time I came to lose respect for my husband. The most important feeling in a marriage is respect. If you love your husband, you show him respect. But after some time of marriage, if he drank a lot of *embacko*, he hit me. One time my friend heard the fighting and she came and said, "Why are you hitting your wife? Stop this!" After a few years in the marriage, Levi would drink and he'd talk and talk and yell and start fights. Sometimes I'd yell back, but most times I kept quiet until he fell asleep. Levi also neglected me, but not like the first husband, Issa. Levi searched for another wife. He did not ask me. I thought, "This can't be, not yet." If he had asked me before, if he had said, "My wife, can I search for another wife?" and explained to me, I would have said yes. But he married another woman and neglected me. He did not give me money or food and spent most of his nights with his other wife. I was so mad because he did not ask. I hit him. When Levi brought in the second wife, I hit her too. One time a man will look for another wife. Maybe because the other woman is beautiful and he says to himself, "I will marry her." If he tells the first wife, "Is it okay? She can help you with your work," then sometimes it is good to have two wives. The second wife becomes like a sister and respects the first wife. If they both have a good heart, they work together in the fields and help each other with the work in the house and it is good. But if the second wife is not obedient and respectful, then there is war.

After much hitting and fighting, we tried to reconcile and for awhile we lived together, but when the second wife came, our husband said, "You two wives! Do not fight!!" When she'd come we worked together and prepared food for the family and we'd eat together. But then Levi began to neglect me. He slept too much with the second wife and bought her clothes and shoes and not me. I grabbed him by the neck and said, "My husband! Why do you not sleep with me? Tonight it is my turn!" When he came into the second wife's bedroom one night I grabbed his neck and said, "No! You sleep with me, not her!" If the husband organizes it good, it works so well! But if he does not, if he sleeps three nights with one and two nights with the other it does not work! Even so, when I heard them speak on the bed at night to each other, I listened and it made me so angry! I was jealous. I suffered and because of his neglect I divorced him.

After Levi left, life was so difficult. I was alone with two children.

## Blondine's Story

There was once a man named Bilo who married two wives. Bilo loved one wife more than the other. One day Bilo went to the forest, as he always went to the forest to get food, and he transformed himself into a pig and he killed himself. He cut his pig legs and cut his pig arms, and he made a big bed and put fire underneath the bed and he began to roast himself. Then he became a person again, but the animal stayed a pig on the roasting fire. He went home to his wives and left the pig in the forest. The next day his two wives went into the forest to find *makongo* leaves to use on their house, and they found this pig in the forest. They began to sing, "Who is this pig here?" and "Bilo, why would I eat you? Bilo, why would I eat you? I have seen your pig heart, why would I eat you?"

> Eh Mbilo na ndje kô na kele nande eh?
> Eh Mbilo na ndje kô na kele nande eh?
> Eh Mbilo na eneke dibale bodja ngoya eh?
> Eh Mbilo na ndje kô na kele nande eh?

One of the wives took the heart of the pig and ate it, and the other wife refused to eat the pig. When the one wife ate the heart, Bilo at home felt his heart begin to hurt and he was in terrible pain. "Oh my heart!" he cried. "What pain is this I feel?" When his two wives came home, he asked, "Who ate my heart in the forest?" These two wives refused to answer and said, "No! We didn't see anything in the forest, what are you saying?" But Bilo asked again, "Who ate my heart in the forest? Because my heart is in such pain!" Bilo went himself into the forest to see his pig, and when he arrived he saw the heart of the pig was gone. "Shit! One of my wives ate my heart! I am going to bring them to the judge of the water to verify who ate my heart!" Bilo ran home and got his two wives and brought them to a big river, and he says to his first wife, "You go into the river." His first wife went into the water. Bilo stood next to the river and his wife went into the water up to her knees, and she started to sing, "Bilo, Bilo, why would I eat you? When we have gone into the forest and I have seen the heart of a pig. Why would I eat you?"

The first wife sang and sang and the water stayed at her knees. Bilo ordered her to come out because he knew she was not the one who ate his heart. Bilo ordered the second wife into the water. When the second wife went into the big river, the water came up to her knees and this wife began to sing the same song, "Bilo, Bilo, why would I eat you? When we have gone into the forest and I have seen the heart of a pig. Why would I eat you?"

Bilo saw the water rise and he ordered her to keep singing, and he said, "Oh, it was you who ate my heart! My first wife walked into the river and sang and the water did not move, but when you sing the water rises! Keep singing!" The water rose higher and higher, up to her waist, and he ordered her to keep singing! The water rises up to her chest and she continues to sing. The water rises up to her chin and then up to her mouth and her nose and still she continues to sing, "Bilo, Bilo, why would I eat you? When we have gone into the forest and I have seen the heart of a pig. Why would I eat you?"

Finally the water covers her head and she disappears! Bilo takes the first wife and brings her back to the village. When Bilo arrives in the village with only the first wife, the first wife's mother and father tell him this sense, "Bilo, we have told you to take only one wife because you have one heart and one penis to love one person, but you didn't listen to us. This is why one of your wives wanted to kill you and ate your heart."

Two wives can sometimes work well together. If you have a husband and you are getting older, you may ask your husband to marry another. If there is a lot of work and a man takes two wives, one will work in the fields and one at home will prepare food and serve the husband. Sometimes if the first wife is old and tired of all the work, during the day and the work at night, she will ask the husband to find another wife. Then she will organize the work so that there are no disputes; one day the first wife will work in the fields and the other day in the house, and the two share the work of the day and the work of the night. But mostly it is hard.

## NGANDU WOMEN
### Therese

In the house it is only the man who makes decisions, and there were many things my husband hid from me. Women have less power in the house and less power to make decisions. Women cannot make decisions above the man. But women can get power when the man leaves and the women stay. But when the man comes home, she loses this power. It was not good with me. I was strong and I didn't have power when my husband was alive. But I never left him because of my children.

When he died it was a very difficult time for me. I did not marry again because after the death of my husband, I decided marriage was finished. I was alone with all my children. We worked together and just lived. I took the authority in the house. I made the decisions of all my children who lived with me, and when these children did not listen and respect my authority, I was angry with them. I became like a man. When my children did not hear, I would say to them, "Your father is dead, but now I am like your mother and your father, but you don't listen to what I have to say. You will listen to who? Who will you hear now?"

This is the way of women here, when my daughter Augustine married, she also did not have power in the house, just her husband Mormour. After her marriage, after some time, Augustine became ill and died. This was hardest because I lost my daughter and she was like a little sister to me. She was a grown woman with a baby and other children. I was very sad. I helped in the care of Augustine's children and we all lived in my house together. When my daughter died, her husband died shortly afterwards. Her children had no mother and no father and they came to live with me and I guarded them. Augustine had had all these children and I had four others so all total there were eight children living with me. It was a great responsibility. I farmed for them, and brought them manioc, bananas, corn, and many things. I sold the manioc to make money for clothes and medicine. For their health when they got sick I would take them to the clinic. I loved them very much. I sang to these children and we all danced together. I would drink a little *embacko* and for awhile feel happy, and when all these children saw me dance they laughed!

It was very hard for the children because they had lost their mother and father. If they heard of the death of a neighbor and go to their funeral, they remembered their loss, the mother and father they had lost. They would cry and I told them, "If you continue to cry then the spirit of your mother and father will come to carry you away." They were afraid of this so they stopped crying for their lost parents.

There is too much death here. This was not too long a time after I lost my grandmother. I suffered so much! I was a woman and I had my children. I worked in the fields with my husband. My grandmother had given my children so much care and now she was gone. She had watched over me when I was young. We had shared a life together. She died because she was so old. I had lost my grandmother and my daughters Ellise and Augustine. I suffered so much.

## AKA WOMEN
# Nali

In my marriage, after some time, Kokote looked for another woman for marriage. I did not know he did this, but after some time, people in camp talked to me and said, "Your husband looks to marry a wife in another camp and when you arrive there you will see. When you go to find yams and food, he plays with this other woman." When he came I asked him, "Where were you?" and he said, "I went to work." The next time I left for work and Kokote went to play with the other woman. So I followed him, behind him, slowly, slowly and he arrived at the camp of the woman. Kokote entered her home and I myself saw this! I entered her home too, this woman Saki and my husband. I took the woman and began hitting her. I destroyed her home and no one helped her, all said, "You have stolen her husband." Aieee! I was so angry! I hit her! When Kokote saw this fight he fled back to our camp. I took a branch and with all my force I hit him. After I hit him, he cried! The second marriage with the other woman was finished. Saki left her camp and I never saw her again. After a few days all was well again. Kokote knows it is not good to find another woman.

## AKA WOMEN
# Konga

A bad time in our marriage was when our daughter Semoli died. Semoli had just started to walk and she became sick in her chest. We tried traditional medicine again and again but she died. How we suffered at this death of our daughter Semoli! I had these older children but after the death of my girl, I never found another child. It was so difficult. I thought "Maybe the hunger for a child is finished with this one. Maybe now I am too old."

When I was young Mopoko loved me so much! When I prepared food I'd give him a big portion, and when he ate this he confessed his love for me. The young marriage, when we two were alone there were no problems. It was simple. When we were older, Mopoko continued to love me. He would say often to me, "Amê mo linga ofê mingui" (I love you very much). Now the love is only finished because Mopoko died. Love stays with him.

# Confronting the Challenge: Jealousy, Anger, and Divorce

The gendered roles of the Aka and Ngandu women, their activities, beliefs, behaviors, and ideas about what it means to be an Aka mother and wife and what it means to be a Ngandu mother and wife are influenced by culture:, rules of descent, postmarital residence patterns, local economies, and political systems.[13] Social organization of the Aka is based upon egalitarian relations in the marriage, family and extended family. No individual has power over another: important decisions are made largely by the group, with the opinions of all (or most) adults collectively considered. Both men and women have considerable freedom and political power. The camps of the Aka are small, egalitarian, and based upon a foraging mode of existence (albeit increasingly small-scale subsistence farming as well). The Ngandu, as sedentarized horticulturalists, have a much denser and hierarchal population, more technology, an informal economy with trade networks, land and material possessions. Political authority and power are organized in a ranked hierarchy of people. Individuals, particularly females, have less personal freedom. Women wield less power than men within political, community, and household spheres. For both populations, social and political organization informed by shared beliefs and values sanction what is proper and what is not in terms of power in political affaires, power in daily life, household equity, gender roles, and husband-wife relations.[14]

The patriarchal (patrilineal-patrilocal) system of the Ngandu leads to a general pattern of gendered stratification. Patrilineal rules of descent mean that the man, his children, his son's children, and his brother's children are members of the same descent group. This descent group generally lives in close proximity to one another, shares communally held property, and helps one another out economically. Property, political alliances, and material goods are inherited through these male lines of descent.[15] Men and women have to marry outside of the group (exogamy), the patrilineages, and any children a woman may bear belong to her husband and his lineage. Patrilocality increases male-dominated social links so that male-male alliances are more pronounced, meaning that once married, women are often more isolated than men and no longer find protection from their own supportive social (family-centered) network.[16] This increases the frequency of domestic violence against women.

There is a distinction, taught from the time they are toddlers, between women's work and men's work, between a man's role and a woman's place. Mothers teach their daughters to be resilient and strong, to be proud of and find satisfaction in woman's work for family and in hard labor in the fields. The relationship between a father and his children is characterized by discipline, formality, deference, and the authority the father wields over his family.

Although power is generally controlled, and embedded within patrilineal kinship systems, Ngandu women do have social autonomy and agency. In part this is derived from their being providers and from their increasing access to and participation in the local market economy. They make, sell, and exchange products from their fields, earning their own cash income, which they may or may not (like Therese) share with their husbands. As primary cultivators, they participate in and substantially contribute to the local economy and household income; women's work is therefore not perceived as being of a lesser value than men's work, although men's work is perceived as requiring greater strength and/or intelligence. Ngandu women find value, social identity, satisfaction, and beauty in their roles as mothers and wives: "The beauty of a woman is the work of the woman. Your beauty is how you work for your family." As Therese told me, "I am a woman. I know life and this is good. I am strong."

Aka patterns of postmarital residence (multilocality) and cognatic (bilateral) lines of descent influence the role and status of women in this foraging society.[17] Women are not isolated from their extended families, they return to live in their natal camps when they want. Males and females contribute equally to the household economy. Women's contributions are viewed as valuable as men's. Aka have fluid gender roles: both men and women hunt and gather, both mothers and fathers care for their children. Men and women have relatively equal access to resources and equal say in camp and household decision-making. Like the Ngandu women, they too find value in their roles as community members, mothers and wives: "I was a woman with a husband and baby. I was happy." These patterns of rules of descent, postmarital residence, foraging economy, and political systems relate to a cultural model of egalitarianism.

What is the nature of egalitarianism? As defined by many anthropological texts, egalitarianism has to do with equal or nearly equal access to power, prestige, and basic resources.[18] Both groups, by this classic definition, are relatively egalitarian societies. Based upon gender, age, and ephemeral characteristics, all people have access to basic resources. Although political power and authority is largely held in the hands of Ngandu men, Ngandu women can and do attempt to influence household, and community, social, economic, and political relationships. The nature of equality, arising from modes of production and foundational schema, is complex. More objective indicators of gender inequality and equality can be found in health and nutrition measurements. For example, the Aka are said to be one of the most egalitarian societies in the ethnographic record, but it is also true that Aka men have higher hemoglobin levels, and better dental health (fewer caries and fewer missing teeth). This is likely because men have a diet higher in protein, as they eat more protein on hunting trips and women have a diet higher in carbohydrates. (The prevalence of tooth decay and loss among women may be explained by the nutritional demands of breastfeeding.)[19]

To understand the nature of egalitarian gender relations, it is important to understand the nature of husband-wife relations. Aka couples are together often throughout the day, know each other exceptionally well, and cooperate in many activities on a regular basis. Ngandu couples, on the other hand, are not together much of the day, do not often participate in joint activities, and are inclined to know each other less well. Gender roles and tasks among the Aka are flexible, the capabilities of each are similar, gendered tasks are shared, gender roles are fluid. Ngandu gender roles and tasks are largely fixed, seldom shared, and tend to be largely inflexible. As this discussion continues, we will see that whereas Aka egalitarianism is pronounced, Aka and Ngandu male-female relations and gender roles have cross-cultural commonalities with each other and with other cultures as well.

In preliminary discussions with Aka and Ngandu about marital relationships, several people mentioned slapping or hitting their spouse. Although domestic aggression was uncommon among the Aka, Ngandu spousal violence appeared to be frequent. At the start of the research for this book, a group of women came and asked to talk to me. One Ngandu woman had showed up with a swollen eye and missing tooth following an argument with her husband. Three Ngandu women also came and wanted to speak of "brutal sex." However, I also saw the great love and respect Ngandu couples have for each other. Our friend, an Ngandu man of about 58, had lost his wife one month prior to our arrival in Nambélé. Every night we were all in the village together, we could hear him quietly sobbing in the next room, "I loved her so much and miss her being here with me. Life is not bearable without her."

Although Aka infrequently hit their spouses, when it does occur women were slightly more likely to initiate the hitting.[20] As one Aka woman explained, "I hit him when he forgot how many days he had been with the other wife." Two Aka men detailed their experiences with their angry wives: "My wife is very brave, she hits me, but I do not hit her. She hits me because I was walking in the forest and visiting other camps, and she thinks it is to find another woman." As the other man reported, "I hit my wife because she found another man, so she took a log and hit me back. We are divorced." The reasons Aka husbands or wives gave for hitting their spouses were similar: the husband or wife was "walking about" (tambula) too long, that is, being away too long and potentially looking for and finding another partner. A few Aka women mentioned that they hit their husbands when they simply proposed the idea of a second wife. One older Aka man summed up his experiences with spousal violence, "I hit her because I was jealous and I was afraid I would lose her love. She hit me also when I was walking too long." This idea of hitting in response to the fear of losing a mate is a common theme among the Aka. One man however, related that his first wife had just had a baby so he brought home another wife, and while wife number one was "jealous at first," the two wives worked together and "it was okay." Another woman actually suggested that her husband find another wife to help with the work. She said she was not jealous as she knew her husband would never abandon her and their baby.

Polygyny, in some marriages, seems to work well. Reactions to a husband or wife looking for another or being unfaithful varies by individual; however, most people were jealous, and quite a few were aggressively so. It remains to be seen if the current trend toward sedentarization, increased farming and entrance into the local market economy, changing patterns of subsistence, will in turn lead to changing marital relations.

In contrast, the Ngandu women were less likely to initiate violence toward their husbands out of jealousy or fear of abandonment. For some, domestic violence is regular, occurring several times a year and generally initiated by males. Seldom does a wife hit her husband if he initiates the hitting. The most common reason given by Ngandu males for hitting was that their wife did not respect or follow their requests. They did not wash his clothes or give him food when he asked. Their stated reasons for the violence had to do with their wives' lack of obedience and respect. As several men reported, "I hit only when she does not respect my requests."

Another common reason given for violence was refusal of sex. Indeed, one particular group of Ngandu women shared that they sometimes feared their husbands because of what they termed "brutal sex." One woman told me that,

> I am afraid of him when he comes home from being away. He wants sex with no touching, so I would be dry inside. I would love to be touched and then I would have desire, but if he touched me he would come too quickly. So he would just get excited, then get on me and have sex with force, brutal sex. Afterwards I would cry. I would also have sores afterwards and bleed. He would beat me if I refused sex, or if he asked for money, for clothes or cigarette or food, then he would beat me if I did not give it to him.

A young woman with a black eye told me, "He always wants sex and he forces me, it is brutal sex and afterwards I am hurt and bleeding. I cry because I hurt so badly. If I refuse he beats me. For women here life is very difficult, we work hard during the day and at night with our husbands, the sex is brutal and we cry and bleed."

A Ngandu man explained that he became angry over what he saw as negligent maternal care: "My wife went outside, left oil in pot on the fire in house, and my daughter went to the pot and burned her hands. I was angry that she neglected to watch the child better and hit her." A small number of Ngandu men revealed sometimes their wives hit them when they were giving more things to a co-wife (such as money, clothes) or if they caught them with another woman. In one case the wife stopped giving her husband food for three to four days to make sure the new relationship stopped. Ngandu females said their husbands also hit them when their husbands thought they were looking to have a sexual affair with another male or when they did not show public respect to their husband—one woman was hit when she spoke at church without his permission.

As with a few of the Aka marriages, polygyny was occasionally viewed positively by the wife. One woman spoke of how she and her husband were married 32 years when her husband brought home another wife, "It is this way here; if you are sick and you have lots of kids, the second wife will help. There is no jealousy between us two…but first my husband had to get my OK, and if I refused, he would not have done it." Another Ngandu women I spoke to also told me that, "after so many births and deaths (nine of her ten babies died) I had no desire for sex, and when he came one day with another wife, I had no jealousy, we are friends." Yet another Ngandu woman said, "We were married one year before the second wife came in. I did not have a baby right a way so he married another to give him a baby. Now he has four wives and I feel no jealousy. The other wives are friends to me, but they fight with each other. They are jealous of sharing his love and it is because they are young. I am the first wife and I have no jealousy."[21] Polygynous marriages seemed to work best if the senior wife is much older and postmenopausal; if the second or subsequent wife is from the same family; if the senior wife has no children; if the second wife is brought in during the postpartum taboo period; or if the first wife is not well. It also seemed to help if the husband asked permission of his wife.

Stories of domestic violence were not uncommon, but other women spoke to me of the love they felt for, and received from, their husbands and of the happiness they experienced in their marriage—and at times, contentment in polygynous marriages as well. Both Aka and Ngandu have relationships built upon mutual respect and love for one another. Love and compassion are universal and part of our evolved psychology, but how they are experienced in intimate relationships varies dramatically from culture to culture. Both Aka and Ngandu identify love as an important component to marital relations.

One way in which to understand Aka and Ngandu patterns of violence—as with patterns of attachment, love, and desire—is by looking at the interactions of both biology and culture. The violence among Aka and Ngandu males and females and their explanations for hitting are grounded in the evolved propensity for sexual jealousy. Jealousy is an evolutionary propensity. "Early in human history, males who did not react jealously" had mates who "walked too long," were impregnated by other males, passing on someone else's genes to future generations.[22] On the other hand, females who did not react to straying spouses were left to raise their offspring without paternal help.[23] Evolutionary psychology focuses on this diachotomy of competing and conflicting sexual strategies between men and women: men seeking to make use of an abundance of genetic seed, and women seeking men with "good genes" best able to provide "high ongoing investment".[24]

Jealousy is a response to the threat and conflict of the differing reproductive interests of males and females.[25] Violence is a response to the loss or perceived loss of a loved one and the resources they provide, a mate-retention strategy. Violence occurs because men and women felt betrayed, angry, hurt, and jealous. But equally important is the influence of culture. This is evident in Ngandu males' and females' explanations for violence: that is, from early childhood, lack of respect and disobedience shown to the male head of the household is sanctioned with severity. If Ngandu children disobey, they are likely to be hit by their parents or older siblings. The same goes for wives who disobey or do not respect their husbands. With Aka, the egalitarian nature of their culture influences the aggression of both men and women against one another, and in fact women were more likely than men to hit.

Aka and Ngandu were also asked about their marital histories, and divorce is a common feature of married life. The most common cause for divorce in both groups was that the spouse slept with someone else, or searched for or found another mate, but this was a more frequent reason among the Aka. As two Aka couples related, "I divorced my first wife because she slept with others, and it hurt my heart because I loved her so much." Another Aka woman explained, "My husband found another wife and I was mad and said it is not possible. Now we are finished and I refused him and we divorced."[26]

Ngandu men were more likely to divorce their wives because they did not respect their husbands. Ngandu women mentioned that their husbands left because they did not have any children. One Aka man said that two of his wives left him because they did not get pregnant even though they were having sex five times a night. The reasons for divorce and who initiated the divorce were quite varied.

A major difference between the two groups was which spouse left the marriage. Most Aka men said their wives left them, and Aka women agreed, saying they were the ones to leave the marriage. By contrast, more Ngandu men said they left their wives, and Ngandu women agreed with this. Again, the bio-cultural model is useful for interpreting this cross-cultural variability. The most common cause in both groups, infidelity, is consistent with an evolved psychology. Men risk losing paternity certainty (knowing for certain the children they are investing in are biologically theirs), if their wife sleeps with other men, whereas women risk losing access to resources or protection when their husband has an affair. Ngandu gender hierarchy and Aka egalitarianism also influenced patterns of divorce, as Ngandu men were likely to cite lack of respect as a cause of divorce, and generally Ngandu men left their wives. Among the Aka, the reasons for divorce were varied, and there was no bias toward men initiating the divorce. Love, attachment, and the betrayed feelings that so often accompany unfaithfulness are a part of our evolved psychology, a part of our human experience.[27]

The cultural beliefs and practices so deeply embedded within Aka and Ngandu male-female relations, gendered roles, equalities and inequalities, within local economies and political systems, thus far have endured. However, if the trend toward sedentarization and farming continues among the Aka, and if the Ngandu become more deeply anchored to the global market economy, these basic cultural patterns will be disrupted, just as the powerful forces of globalization have changed ways of life across the world.

## NOTES FROM THE FIELD
### Winter 2003

*—Pouring rain, like a river flowing from the sky, so I am sitting here writing in my house. There is a praying mantis on the chair right next to my shoulder. He is like a cat, washing his whiskers and antennae with his little bug arms and turning his head to look at me whenever I move. He is fascinating to watch. But if that bug makes one wrong move in my direction I'm going to squish him. However, as long as he behaves we can be friends. I must be lonely or bored…but how can I be lonely? I am constantly surrounded by people, constantly demanding things. And I misunderstood that. Ngandu place a lot of importance on relations maintained and reinforced through the exchange of material items. If I am to have a home here, be a part of the community, I have to give. It is more than greediness on their part and selfishness on mine. It is about building and maintaining relationships via material exchange. But even so, I find the constant demands annoying. I just want to walk out of my house without seemingly everyone asking me for something. Oh well. I officially named the praying mantis Pastis. I put a drop of real Pastis (I have a small bottle B. and I got in Bangui) near where he sits, hour after hour, and I think he's become drunk. When he does walk he kind of bobs up and down. Today he disappeared for awhile and then I*

saw him staggering down the path, for a long way, until he finally got back to his chair in the house. And when he is sitting next to me on the chair he rocks back and forth. I think I've turned a bug into an alcoholic.

—After several weeks of enjoying Pastisse as a pet, he laid eggs and split.

**Fall 2004**
—Worked in fields today with A. and B. and boy am I tired!! Spent yesterday cracking nuts. We walked forever to get to their fields. A very hot, muggy walk. On the way we washed clothes in the river and A. kept looking down at her legs as she said there were leeches in the river, so of course I kept looking down at my legs. A lot. Before we started A. prayed, then sat her baby down to play in the shade while she worked. We planted quite a lot of manioc, and A. said everything I planted was "mine" when it was ready to harvest and that that portion of her field was now mine. That was sweet of her. Also carried a (very small) tub of manic roots on my head and heard something crack in my neck, so am now tired and sore-necked. How do these women do this every day? With babies, illnesses, and demanding husbands? I was talking to E. about it, and he said, "Well, it's like this. When you people come from America and eat this food [manioc], it gives you problems with your stomach [gas] because you're not habituated to this food. It is the same with the woman's work. You're tired because you are not habituated to the work." Interesting analogy.

**Fall 2007**
—Today I paid for a chicken for dinner, and got eggs for lunch instead...close. Have been going to the coffee lady's place every morning. She serves coffee out of a huge pot boiling over a fire, and next to her is another big pot of oil, and she drops balls of dough into it to make beignets. I enjoy my cup of goat-turd coffee, so named because the coffee beans are laid out to dry on cement slabs or plastic tarps on the ground, then the goats poop on them, and dried coffee beans look like dried goat-turds, hence the name. Tastes fine though. So you can get two beignets for 50 cents, not a bad deal. You sit in her coffee shop on benches and she sits in the middle, next to a fire, talking, stirring coffee, dropping bits of dough into the pot of hot oil, and when someone new comes in for coffee, she takes a dirty cup, gives it a swish in dirty water, strains the coffee into it, adds four or five spoonfuls of sugar, and there you go, goat-turd coffee.

—Saw two strange things today. One was a snake-worm, a pretty dark green, about 12 inches long, but with a blunt head. A. said that it doesn't bite but *if you touch it, it gives you an electric shock and you become very sick, plus he said it is bad luck. Then there was the strangest thing. A slug-like clear blobby jelly thing, one body but composed of tons of worm-like appendages wiggling around, and each appendage had a black eye or dot at the end of it, and it moved as one body, but with all those wiggling parts oozing forward, very bizarre…*

—*Had a snake crawl over my BARE foot today. I was sitting there (in flip-flops) talking to J. and felt something soft as silk on my foot and instinctively kicked out and a loooooooong snake goes flying though the air. A. promptly killed the dumb thing and came running back to me and asked if I'd been bitten. "No, I don't think so," and a group of people came and checked my foot over for fang marks. "Well," he said, "that's good, because it was a very poisonous snake and if it had bitten you, you'd be dying." That terrified the monkey in me. All the ladies around me kept hugging me, holding my hands, saying, "Merci, merci, merci." Then this little boy comes over and sits next to me, keeping on the lookout for snakes, my little protector. Merci indeed.*

...............................................................................................

### QUESTIONS FOR REFLECTION

1. The idea of hitting in response to the fear of losing a mate was a common theme among Aka. In contrast, the Ngandu women were less likely to initiate violence toward their spouse out of jealousy or fear of abandonment. How do you think this may be a reflection of their particular foundational schema? How much do you think our "evolved psychologies" affect our feelings and behaviors? Is it surprising to you that violence, of any form, occurs among "egalitarian" societies?

2. Divorce is a common feature of married life for the Aka and Ngandu. How are their causes of divorce different or similar to causes of divorce in the United States, France, Great Britain, or Japan?

3. Women from both populations spoke about the difficulty of polygyny, but a few women also noted how beneficial it was for them if their husbands brought home a second wife. What do you see as some potential benefits of polygyny? Why would polygyny be good for some women and difficult for others to accept?

4. How do differing modes of subsistence influence the manifestation of egalitarianism in societies? Why do men and women experience different levels of personal and political freedom in foraging and horticulturalist societies?

## NOTES

1. Goody1976; Stone and James 2009, 314; Boserup 1970, 51; Beneria and Sen 1981; Engels 1975.
2. Beneria and Sen 1981, 290.
3. Stone and James 2009, 314; Boserup 1970, 51; Beneria and Sen 1981, 294; Engels 1975.
4. Goody1976; O'Neil 2009.
5. B. S. Hewlett 1992.
6. Meehan 2008, 214.
7. B. S. Hewlett 1992.
8. B.S. Hewlett et. al. 2000b, in Meehan 2008, 214.
9. B.S. Hewlett et. al. 2000b, in Meehan 2008, 214.
10. B. L. Hewlett and B. S. Hewlett 2008; B.S.Hewlett et al. 1998, 654.
11. B. L. Hewlett and B. S. Hewlett 2008; B.S. Hewlett et al. 1998, 167.
12. B. L. Hewlett and B. S. Hewlett 2008; B. S. Hewlett 1992, 167.
13. Goody1976; Stone and James 2009, 314; Boserup 1970, 51; Beneria and Sen 1981; Engels 1975.
14. Silberschmidt 1999,10.
15. Ember and Ember 2000.
16. Bonvillain 2007.
17. B. S. Hewlett 1992.
18. Ember and Ember 2000, 237–38.
19. Walker and Hewlett 1990.
20. Of Aka spouses hit, males were hit in 9 of 17 incidents, and females were hit in 7 of 10 incidents; B. L. Hewlett and B. S. Hewlett 2008.
21. For a more detailed analysis, see B. L. Hewlett and B. S. Hewlett 2008.
22. Donahue 1985, 132; Wright 1994.
23. Donahue 1985, 132; Wright 1994.
24. Wright 1994, 36, 69.
25. Donahue 1985, 132; Wright 1994.
26. For more in-depth analysis of the most common cause for divorce in both groups, see B. L. Hewlett and B. S. Hewlett 2008.
27. B. L. Hewlett and B. S. Hewlett 2008.

......................................

# CHAPTER 6

# Generations and Grandmothers

It is good to listen to old people because they have knowledge to teach to the young, and when the old people die, this knowledge is lost.

—THERESE

I lived young. Now I am older. I have my children and grandchildren. If I did not have children it would be so bad, because when you die without children, it is finished. When you die with children, your spirit continues on.

—BLONDINE

During the past few decades, there have been critical changes in the social, cultural, political, and economic patterns of life for Aka and Ngandu women. Blondine's, Therese's, Nali's, and Konga's experiences differ from those of their children and grandchildren. Traditional customs have been replaced by new ways of thinking, of being, of acting. This chapter explores what Aka and Ngandu women think of this world, so different from the world of their childhood, and what changes they have been witness to over time.

From their narratives we learn what it means to be a woman at the crossroads of motherhood, leaving behind the childbearing years, as the women describe their feelings regarding menopause and the value they find in their roles as older mothers and grandmothers. Blondine, Therese, Nali, and Konga speak of their relationships with their adult children and the enduring bonds between a parent and adult child. They describe how they actively teach and guide their grandchildren. In turn, their children and grandchildren describe what they learn from these women, their grandmothers. The women explain what it means to be an "old" woman, how the elderly are treated and valued by others. By comparing Aka and Ngandu women, we are given two different examples of both contemporary and historic life in Central Africa. The women's narratives focus on the impact of economic and political change, perspectives on aging, gender, and familial relationships over the course of their lifetimes.

## From Mothers to Grandmothers

In many societies around the world, the value and treatment of the elderly depends upon their contributions to the household and community, to ecological, economic, and environment factors as well as to cultural values and beliefs.[1] Being an "old" Aka or Ngandu woman is not determined by chronological age, as few women in either community know their exact age. Nor is it influenced by short life expectancies, as for both populations life expectancies, past childhood, are quite long. Nali is both a grandmother and the mother of a 3-year-old son. Her status as a grandmother does not make her "old" in the eyes of the community, offset as it is by her ability to continue to reproduce, and because she is active and strong. Therese is viewed as "old" but she is still a very lively and dynamic part of the household, going to work in the fields every day and taking care of her grandchildren. She certainly is not a frail, elderly woman; she is, in fact, in such good physical health that only three years ago she was able to carry a huge log on her head from the fields to her son's home. Blondine, a "young" grandmother, no longer interested in having children and approaching menopause, does not think of herself as "old." Konga, often given food and care by her own children, considers herself old, weak, and ill, and yet continues to help care for her grandchildren, on occasion offering her breast for the younger grandchildren to suckle.[2] They are each afforded varying degrees of status, respect, and care from their families and communities.

As the women enter middle age and beyond, their opportunities, influence, and access to political, economic, and social power change. Transitioning from mothers in the nest to helpers at the nest, Aka and Ngandu women at the biological crossroads of life, and beyond, have a general sense of well being. As elderly women, they may have a key role in religious and political domains, as "leaders of songs, games, dances, and initiation rites."[3] As providers of culture, traditional values, beliefs, and knowledge, their value and status may increase. As older women, they give advice to, and gain increasing authority over, their household

and kin.[4] As respected grandmothers, they are also caretakers, allomothers, of their grandchildren. Women in both populations who have
spent their lives working for their families increasingly become, as they
age, provided for and cared for by their children and grandchildren.
And, although both Aka and Ngandu women spoke of the need they
have for their children and grandchildren to provide care for them
as they age, for Ngandu women the need for the family care is even
greater, as we will see. Both Aka and Ngandu women are needed by and
have need of their adult children and grandchildren, each contributing
to the survival of the other.

Menopause and old age are universal stages of human life, but how
this time in life is understood and experienced is formed and shaped
by culture. Egalitarianism among the Aka exists not only between men
and women but also between the old and young. What this means is
that the aged are not shown increased respect simply for the graying
of their hair, weakening of their physical bodies, loss of reproductive
abilities, or decrease in contributions to the camp and household. If
they are shown respect by others, it is largely based upon ephemeral
characteristics, their personalities and temperaments. The lessons of
respect Ngandu women instilled in their children serve them well
as they become elderly and are treated more deferentially. And certainly for both populations—at the crossroads of life as menopausal,
or postreproductive women, respected mothers, widows, and grandmothers, increasingly dependent upon family care—these women's
lives are lived out in a dramatically changing world.

## Reflections from a Woman's Life

NGANDU WOMEN
### Blondine

Women can be strong. It depends on your competence and your heart.
Your heart directs you in many ways, in good ways and bad.

Some women will have a child and their daughter will have a child
too. (See Figure 6.1.) They will both nurse their babies and see each other
nursing. This is good. I have two grandchildren and I help in the care
of my grandchildren. When my daughter Rocine's baby was so little, I
offered my breast to the baby. I give the baby clothes and wash the baby.
I give my grandchild proper food and traditional medicine. It is good to

FIGURE 6.1 | *Generations: young Ngandu mother with her baby, and grandmother with her own baby.*

have grandchildren, but at a certain stage in life, it is not good to become pregnant. I have heard of a surgery that makes you not able to have children, but here it is not possible because the nuns do not accept it.

When your monthly blood stops at a certain age, it is good. If the blood has not stopped at 50, you can still have babies! I know a woman who had two children born when she was 50 years old! Here, it is maybe when you are 60 that your blood stops. It depends upon the woman. At this time, the blood stays in your body and you become so big and strong. The blood is blocked, and this is how you become strong. You also have hot blood, when your body is on fire and you have headaches. You know you begin this time in life because the signs are that you are very old and month after month there is no blood. When you arrive at this time, it is good because you stop having children. You do not have the monthly blood! You can have relations with your husband and no pregnancy! You are like a man.

Now I am always tired. My body has changed. My hair has grey. When you are old people respect you firstly because you are old and secondly because you respect them. People say, "Mama, you have many children," and they give you much respect. I was once young with children. I lived young. Now I am older. If I did not have children, it would be so bad because when you die without children, it is finished. When you die with children, your spirit continues on.

## Louise, Friend and (Ex)Sister-in-Law of Blondine

Blondine's behavior is like a man's. She goes into the forest and gets *koko* leaves and brings them to Bangui to sell. She has gone hunting in the forest with the Aka. She brings the meat to sell in the village. I think it is because she does not have a husband. This is why she has done the work of a man. She is a very strong woman. Many people know her because she jokes and laughs with people. I love Blondine because she is kind and laughs with everyone.

## Gaspard, 58-year-old Brother of Blondine

My sister is very nice. She doesn't want to have problems with people. But when you look for problems you can find them. She likes to drink alcohol a lot, and when she drinks everyone thinks she is funny. She works very, very hard, and she likes everyone without distinction. When she lived with her husband in the north, she didn't have any parents or family there with her, but she lived in such a way that the people respected her and she respected them. She likes to live a calm life. My best memory was one time when she was still married and her husband caught a huge amount of fish, and she brought this to my house and together with my children we ate all this fish. She has earned a lot of money and she is generous. She buys beautiful clothes and gives these to my children. It is hard that she has no husband. Her life is difficult.

### NGANDU WOMEN
### Therese

Now I am old. My health is not good. A woman's work in the village is to go to the fields. Now I cannot work as hard I used to. I stay here in the village and try to find wood and small work to do. My daughters and their husbands and children come and live with me sometimes. I love to care for these children, but I cannot give them much. I am very old and some days I am very sick. I am no longer strong enough to get food. But I live well through these children. They take care of me. They find food in the fields and cook it for me. For myself, I sweep the yard and make a fire. I get water for my grandchildren and wash them. I cook the coffee and share this. I clean the house and clean the plates. I take the basket and go into the fields and cut cassava leaves and firewood and bring it home. I cook and give this food to the family. I clean my grandchildren at night and light the lamp and bring it into the house. Then I sleep. (See Figure 6.2.)

This is the life of a woman here. I would like to say a good thing for the women in America. I would say, "Clean the house, clean the pots and plates, take good care of your children. People respect you if you have children. Think about your children and the future for your children. Greet your visitors well. Respect your husband. Respect the family of your husband." This is what I have to say to other women in the world.

When I was a young woman, I gave birth to many children. I was with my husband and we worked together with our children. Bokassa was president at this time, and he brought me and other women to Bangui to give us a medal, because we were strong women who gave birth to many

FIGURE 6.2 | *Ngandu grandmother still working hard in the field.*

children. Somewhere in the years I have lost the medal, but this was thirty years ago. Bokassa ordered the chiefs of villages, "When you see a woman who has many children, you take their name down in a book, and I will send a bus to bring them to Bangui. There I will give them a medal. It is very important to congratulate women because they gave birth to many children. Children are the pictures of tomorrow." People respected me because I got the medal. Children are necessary. Children are our tomorrows. I am old and have many children. I am like the root of life.

After my husband died, after many years, my chance at having children was finished. I became sick and arrived at the time of the monthly blood. I had lots of pain but no blood came. This was the time when you no longer see the blood and during this time you have a hot body, but the blood does not soar. You have a lot of emotion before and during this time. If a husband comes and asks for sex, you are so angry, and after the sex, you are still so angry! But it is done and finished. If the moment arrives, you are an old woman. It is good for women, because then when the day of the month comes, you do not worry! I am an old woman now. My life has changed. I have given birth to many children and now it is finished, but this is good! You continue with your life, same activities, you still sleep with your husband in bed, still give care, and continue with the work of the house.

The wisdom of a woman my age is that she is a big woman with the spirit of a long life. She gives the wisdom of what she knows, the farming, the children, the house, respect for others, how to live a good life. I am happy now with this part of life. Now that I am old, my children care for me, and when I am this old, tired woman, my children still need me. People need the old, because they have wisdom. They know the old stories and give good advice to the children. If you don't have children, no one takes care of you. For Ngandu people, when you don't have family, you die. If you have an illness when you are old, you are tired and then you die. But if you die at an old age with many children and grandchildren, it is good because people will cry at your funeral, and other people will say, "Do not cry. It is finished for her. No, do not cry, she had a good life with many children."

## Basil, 50-year-old Son of Therese

My father was Bofi, he was from Boda. My mother's father came from Mbaiki, he was Issongo [Mbati], so my mother is Mbati; her mother was from Nambélé, her mother was Ngandu. My father was Bofi, so I am Bofi. I speak my mother's language and my father's language. The Mbati came here to fight the Ngandu during the time of President Dacko, but my father could not fight against the Ngandu because he had lived here with them for a long time, so he fought with the Ngandu. My mother is a good woman. My father did not take care of us children. It was my mother who cooked food for all the children in the home, and my mother who gave to many people and took care of many others. She gave me good advice, to keep my wife very well and my children too.

The best memory I have of my mother is that when I was a child, she enrolled me in school. My mother took me to school because she liked that my life would be better. She wanted me to learn to write and speak French. She made *embacko* to sell so that she could buy me clothes and enroll me in school, but not my father. My mother has done many things, but this is the best memory. My mother loves me so much. She has taken care of all her children. Three died, but it was my mother who took care of all these children. My father did nothing. He was very mean. If I was sick, it was always my mother who found medicine for me. My father would drink and he would fight with my mother. One time he brought an ax to kill my mother. It was the problem of alcohol. He would drink and fight with my mother. I was 8 years old and my brother was 10. He wanted to kill my mother, so my brother and I took a branch and tried to protect our mother. Our father was so mad at my brother and me! We took our mother to a neighbor's house to sleep, and we asked the chief to give our father counsel. The chief gave our father advice not to fight with his wife, our mother. After this the chief took us and brought us home.

When I was growing up with my brother and sisters, I didn't know how to leave and my mother continued to care for me. When I got married I left my mother, but I continue to care for her because my mother took care of me so much when I was small. My mother brought me to school; now if I have work it is because of her. It is very necessary to reward my mother for everything she has done for me. If I abandon my mother, who will take care of her? My oldest sister Chantal lives in Bangui, and she comes here to Nambélé only for a while and then she returns to her husband. My younger sister Celeste lives mostly with my mother, but they don't have the ability to help take care of our mother. The house she lives in, I built for her. Building a house is very difficult work, but I don't like to have a big distance between me and my mother.

What I think of my mother is all the advice and stories she gave to us around the fire so that we would learn how to live well with people, to learn the manner to live with people. I loved these stories! Now my children are too small but when they are older I will tell them these stories because it is important to know how to do well, to live. My mother taught me to be a good man. Always I listen to my mother. If my mother tells me to do something, I will do it. As for me I couldn't refuse, because if I refuse, who will do this for my mother? My mother showed me all things.

## Chantal, 39-year-old Daughter of Therese

When I was born, it was my mother who took care of us. She did her best to keep us clean and fed. Our mother was very strong and brave. She worked hard like a man. She would hunt so that we would have game to eat. We went together with our mother to the field to see how to work in the fields. She worked hard so that we could go to school.

In the evening around the fire, she gave us stories. She told us,

Me, your mother, our generation was difficult because there were a lot of tribal wars between villages. People came from Mbaiki to fight against the people of Nambélé. They used knives and axes to kill people. Many fled into the forest to hide. We hid in the forest with our parents to escape the people who wanted to kill. We fled from the hand of war. The white people also came and commanded people here before independence. These white men came to Nambélé and took the daughters by force to have sex with them. We fled into the forest to escape these white people. It was very difficult for me. When I was a young woman, these white people came and they did bad things to the people. They took the people in force to carry their luggage and to travel with them to other villages. Another time the white people came and took us, and your mother and your father carried the white people's heavy luggage to a village. When we arrived at this place we left the luggage and fled into the forest. You see my difficult time.

She also said our generation was obstinate to their parents, she told us that "in our generation, we were very obedient to our parents. We did not refuse what they asked of us. When we hid in the forest with our family to escape the people who killed, we had to obey their instructions. If our parents said something to do to escape from the hands of those who killed, we had to obey."

The other advice my mother gave me was how to be a woman. When I was small she told me, "My daughter, in the morning you have to sweep the yard, make coffee, cook food for your husband and children, respect your grandmother and grandfather. Never be impolite to others. You give the blessing so that your life will be stable." She told us to respect people. She said to be kind to old men and women of the village and they will give you their secrets. She gave us these lessons to manage our lives. We have a lot of happiness in our house because our mother loves us very much. We live together well because our mother has made good choices for us. She shares with us whenever she has something. She is always close to us. I love my mother because she is kind to everyone.

## Mbengui, 20-year-old Grandson of Therese

I think that old people are like a library with knowledge for the children of today. When we are together in the caterpillar camp, after we have eaten the caterpillars, my grandmother tells us the old stories of the past, in the time of tribal wars and forced labor, and how she hid in the forest to escape. She taught us the dancing of the daughters of the time she was a young girl, and she told us how she was a good dancer, one of the best among her friends! She gives us good stories and songs. Thanks to my grandmother that I know these histories and stories of life. Finally, I love my grandmother, but I also dislike her a little because when she drinks alcohol she becomes dangerous and makes problems. But we respect her and love her because she is our grandmother.

## Vanessa, 24-year-old Granddaughter of Therese

My grandmother Therese, she teaches us stories of the past. She tells us,

> Our life was not your life like today. During our time, we were respectful of our parents and our life was quite different. There are many changes, like AIDS that is killing people. Me, your grandmother, we did not know AIDS when I was young. In our time, marriage was different. When a man wanted to marry, he came to ask his girlfriend's parents and they

would say yes and he would get his wife. But this man had to work hard for his family-in-law to marry this woman. When a man came to marry me, your grandmother, I fled and hid so I would not see this man. I did not have contact with him for a long time. But today if a man comes to you, on the same day you have contact with him. This is not good. When you live without control, you catch AIDS. When your life is not lived right, you will die young. Your life is different than mine.

This is what our grandmother said to me: to not go after men, to guard my life, to protect my body, to respect and listen to my parents. I have learned from my grandmother to pay attention to life.

........................................................................................

## AKA WOMEN
### Nali

........................................................................................

In the morning I go to the river, I bring water to the camp. Then I go into the forest or the field to find food. I carry my baby when I go looking for food. To be an Aka woman you have to know how to make a *yukwa* [basket]. You use this basket to go to the forest to find meat, *koko* leaves, and yams. You cut firewood, and bring it back to the camp. Afterwards you take this basket full of food, get water, cook the food, and share it with all your children, your neighbors, all the people in the camp.

After we eat, I wash my baby and clean the plates. I talk to my friends. At night I bring fire into the house and I arrange the bed and sleep. When we feel not busy or tired at night, we dance and sing. Sometimes I tell stories at night to the children. Some days I go to the field, some days to the forest, and some days I go fishing. I no longer net-hunt, it has been a long time, because Kokote bought a gun and he hunts. No one is this camp net-hunts any longer; the people who live in Boganda net-hunt, but on this trail we no longer do. Kokote and the other men trap with snares and use his gun. The women stay in the camp. Men like to live in the forest better than the village. They leave the women in camp to find meat and food to bring to their wives. Women prefer life in the village. Yes, this is a big change. I am happy with this change, life is better, my children are healthier.

The future, who knows? What a concept is the future? I want to keep farming; if I do this work, I will feed my children with what I produce with Kokote and family. Now I have this farm in the forest, and the work for the women of the village has finished. Village life is better than forest life. I go to the forest to search for food. Now it is hard to find food. Now I like life in the village because I can send my children to school and they are healthier. School for children is good. If they go to school they can find education to understand things. They can become a teacher and teach other children. They can work at this and get money, a salary. But we must be careful. When we spend too much time in one place, the people are sick a lot.

Before, we used to use traditional medicine when people were sick. You had mean people who lived close who infected you with *ndoki* and you would suffer from this *ndoki*, but if you couldn't find a *nganga* you would die of a simple illness. Now if you call the *nganga*, when he arrives he reveals the *ndoki* and removes the dart from your heart. In the morning you take a plate and give it to each in the camp. They give their saliva and the *nganga* takes the traditional medicine and mixes it with the saliva of everyone in camp. He puts this on the body of the sick person. This sickness I have seen. In the village we work a lot and we are sick with pain, the pain of work. In the forest we have many ulcers and simple illnesses. But always, I keep my children as the highest. I keep them very well with everything. I don't like anything disturbing my children. My children are like my eyes. They are necessary for life.

When I am very, very old my children will take care of me. I will stay only in the camp. I will take care of the babies when my daughters or sons go into the forest. An old person, a man or woman who works well, this person is given respect. He has lived a long life and is now tired. All the women in the camp prepare and give them food. We give old people respect because they know many things. Over time the grandparents have given us certain knowledge for our lives. Now, the young of today do not know the things of people before. The great *tumas* before they die, they give their knowledge to their sons and he would take his place at death, but now it is bad because the young do not know of these things from before.

## Elaka, Daughter of Nali

My mother said to me,

> My girl, me your mother, when I was young, I lived in camp with my parents and I was very brave and very beautiful. The men were fighting between themselves because of me. I was young and all the people wanted to see me because I was a good dancer. Men wanted to marry me

but I refused until your father Kokote came to ask me if I would be his wife, because your father admired my courage. But I refused many days. In all this Kokote did his best to marry me. Kokote brought my parents game and honey and he worked hard; his family and my parents advised me not to refuse your father but to accept to marry him.

When I was small my mother told me that she was brave and that she went into the forest to net-hunt with her parents. I saw the game that my parents killed. When my father would kill an animal, it was my mother who cooked the meat and shared it with the other people in the camp. I saw that when one of us was sick, even in the night, she found medicine for us. My mother told me that a difficult time in her life was when my father killed an animal in his trap, a big animal, and brought it to camp. My mother cooked it and shared it with all the people. But there was a sorcerer in camp who was jealous of this animal that my father had killed. After everyone ate the animal and everybody slept, this sorcerer came and ate the heart of her little sister and she died. This was a difficult moment for my mother.

A lesson that my mother told me was that, "when you will be a big girl, it is good to share things with people because people kill over food." She told me to work hard to find food for your husband and children. I love my mother because we do many things together. We go into the forest and when she finds food, she shares with me. When I find food, I share with her. She is always close to me and she gives me good advice for my life.

## Kokote, Husband of Nali

This woman was very much in love with me. When another man before me wanted to marry her, she refused that man. When I presented to her parents, they asked me to bring things for Nali. I brought all these things they asked to me, so my wife could come to my camp. When she arrived in my family's camp, she was very, very nice and kind. When I found meat, honey and she shared this with my parents. My parents were happy with her. She worked hard with my mother and with the others in camp. She is kind, but she didn't like to see me with another wife. If she finds me with another wife, quickly she will be angry and speak a lot at home.

Nali told me, "Kokote, my husband, after these years we have lost our parents, but today we have to work hard to care for our children. It is difficult now to eat, life is difficult, but we have fields to work in now to help care for our children." She said to me, "I have seen your courage. We walk in the forest together and I am happy." My wife Nali, she loves me very much, where I go she is always close to me. In our life we live very well with our children, and for me, I love her very much.

## AKA WOMEN
### Konga

I have finished the work of sex. I do not look for another lover. It is finished. I do not see *ekila* [menstrual blood]. Ndjombi, my last child, after his birth, he nursed until he was an older child and I never saw another blood. After this I had a hot body, "*doo dooo dooo doo*," and I would sweat so much, "*sa sa sa sa*." I sweated and sweated. One time I would be hot and one time I would sweat. I thought I must be sick. I did not know what this was. My mother spoke of this, when *ekila* stops, but she never told me the exact signs. "One time when you are old your blood will stop," this was all she told me. She never told me of the hot body and the sweats at night. For me, when I have the hot body and sweats, I began to know because in my stomach my blood had stopped. When you have had your children, your blood does not come out any more. It is because after all these children, your eggs are finished. All the babies in your stomach are finished so your blood stops. Mmph! This blood is done! I have had my children. I am without pregnancy, without new children. I am happy to not see the blood. I no longer think, "Oh, maybe my clothes are dirty with blood." I do not have to think this. It is finished. I am like a man.

It is good to be a grandmother now. I have a grandson and granddaughter and people say, "Oh, she is a grandmother." It is better to be a grandmother because now I watch over my grandchildren. And we all walk together. When the parents go into the forest I watch the children. I feed them well and give them care. The children we love so much. These children also look for food and give it to me. This is my age. This is what living is about. I am happy with this life. (See Figure 6.3.)

I am old. I think, now I am getting older and one day I may walk with a cane. I think old age is that you have worked a lot and now you stop. Your children may work for you and they are occupied with you, they give you food and what you need. Old age is good but when you are old, you are tired. Then there will be one day when you die. This illness I have now has filled me up quickly. Now it is very difficult. I hardly work like before, I stay in camp. I don't work like before, I am too tired. I do not have the strength to work.

FIGURE 6.3 | *Elderly Aka grandmother nursing her granddaughter.*

It is good to be in this life. It is good to be old. When you are old you walk with the little children. All the people come and respect you. If they find food they share it with you. I rest now because I am old with white hair. It is the heart that always gives to the family. To be a grandmother is good, it is the end of your life. You are young and then you are old, others are busy with you and you wait for death.

I don't fear death. Death is another chance to sleep, calmly without suffering, without work. Now there can be problems and troubles, but with death you are free of these and you rest. I think death...when you have had children and they live, you think, "I have had these children and now they will take my place." Death is this, all people die. They live and they die. But with children, they take your place after you die. I never fear death. When death comes I will attend. There is no choice.

## Mokandja, Son of Konga

My mother told me that when she was young, she was very beautiful, and that men fought because of her. Some days, she said to me, that when there was a dance she and her friends would walk in a group and dance together to show their beauty. Many men asked her to marry, and she saw many men enter into her home, but she fled from these men until my father came and married my mother. My mother told me stories of women and men who were sorcerers and who killed people because of meat and honey. She told me, "When you are big, you will kill game meat and you share this with all the people in the camp."

My best memory is when I was with my mother and father. We went to the forest and my father found honey and killed an animal. We ate well with this honey and meat together. The most difficult time is when I lost my father and I was sad. My mother was very sad. She sat alone and walked alone in the forest with only us.

I love my mother because she works a lot to give us food after our father died. She is always close to us. When we travel or work, she enjoys looking after our children. We are happy together because she takes care of us and our children.

## Moboubou, Daughter of Konga

My mother told me that when she was a young girl, she went often into the forest to find the *payo* nut. She went to the net-hunt in the forest and she caught game meat and brought it back to camp. Her mother and father ate well together. She told me that she liked to sing. She told me stories of when my father went to a camp to find another wife, that she went in the dark and fought with him and with this other woman, and took my father home and that she was jealous.

I love my mother a lot because she is always close to us. She respects us and took good care of us after our father died. As night begins, and we are close to the fire, she tells us funny stories. We love our mother a lot because she has taken the place as a father and mother.

# Lessons from the Grandmothers

## NGANDU WOMEN
## Blondine

I am now at this age when my children have children. I am a grandmother and thanks be to God. But it is hard also. I work a lot and I am so tired. I have pain in my body because of all the work. Before I worked with my husband Levi, but now I am alone and I work alone. I suffer for this.

Many children are important. It is necessary because if you have lots of children they will help you. They will build you a home and buy you gifts, when you are older. If you have many children life is good. I am a grandmother. My children have children. They are the next generation. I give them lessons. I say, "You give respect to other people. If you see an old person you give to them, you help them. You never refuse to help a person with grey in their hair." I explain the stories of my parents to my grandchildren. I tell them to guard their bodies for a long time, and when they marry to give respect to your husband. I tell them it is not good to marry for a short time and divorce. I teach them about the taboos.

Taboos come from grandparents to grandparents to grandparents. When my mother married my father, they had their *ekila* and they respected it. My mother and father taught me this taboo, "If you eat this, you will be sick." This is the manner of people learning about *ekila*. When I was an adolescent my mother and father taught this to me. Now I teach my children and grandchildren this. My parents, when I was little, cooked good food for me that was not *ekila* and they gave it to me. My parents did not teach me this when I was too little and did not have knowledge, but when I was older. *Ekila* is passed down generation after generation. When I was grown and became pregnant, I respected this *ekila*. That is a way to protect your children. When your baby is born and grows and grows and becomes an adult and begins to have children, they must respect this *ekila*. This is what I have taught my children.

The most important thing in my life is the work. I go to the fields, get manioc, make *embacko*, and I have money. These activities are important. The most important people in my life are my grandchildren. I work for them. Yes, I am happy. I don't depend on anyone. I work. I have my children and grandchildren. If a man comes, there would be disputes and problems. I am free.

................................................................

### NGANDU WOMEN
### Therese

................................................................

I was beautiful once, but now I am old and beauty has left me. After the death of my husband, I worked in the fields so that all my children could live. I thought so much of them! But this was my time of suffering, my husband's death and to care for all those children! But now my children and grandchildren are all in good health. We all sing and dance and laugh with joy.

## Therese's Story

There was once a man who married a young woman, and they lived together in the house of her parents. The man went into the house with the woman and the woman became pregnant. The parents said to the man, "Our daughter does not work in the house because she is pregnant." The wife demanded that the husband go into the forest to find meat for her to eat. So he went into the forest, found meat and brought it back to his wife. He says to her, "Listen my wife, I have found meat, prepare this and we will eat." When the wife heard this, she says, "No! I do not work!" The husband says, "My wife at least give me water to drink." And she says, "No! I do not work!" Then this husband calls for her parents and says, "Please intervene! My wife will not prepare food or bring me water to drink after I have hunted for her. She will not give me food to eat or water to drink! This is a problem!" Her parents hear this and they say to him, "But she is pregnant! She cannot do any work. You must do all the work! You prepare the food. You get yourself water to drink."

The man thinks, "This really is a big problem! Her parents tell me to do all the work! What kind of marriage is this! Why must I do the work of a woman? My wife should wash my clothes, get me water, and prepare my food." He becomes very mad. He has to do the work of a woman, and he is so angry. "My wife does not work! Her parents came and told me to work! For the daughter, they tell me to prepare food and she eats! Oh, how I suffer! I am so tired!" So the man decided to leave the house and leave the woman for a long journey. But on the way he had a thought. While his wife slept at the house with her pregnancy, he went down the road to the parent's house. He took wood and cut it into sharp points and put it on the path and covered it well, so it looked like nothing, just like a nice path. He returned to his house and said, "Now, my wife, give me water to drink." The wife sang a song, the call of the girl for her parents to come,

> **Tooeeee to tooeee mbilo e too**
> **To mbila send. Ba ba bou**
> **Ma mele-lema. Ma mele-leki**
> **Baabaa, baabaa, baba leki!**

(Hello Father
My husband does not want to help
I am so tired I have been working so hard
Hurry, hurry, I need your help!)

They began to walk and they fell into the trap! The points pierced their bodies and they died. The girl continued to sing, calling for her parents and they did not come! So the husband dissected the bodies of the parents into little morsels and started to cook the girl's parents like meat while she continued to sing. He said, "Wife! Make me some food to eat!" And she continued to sing, calling for her parents. He ordered her again, and she continued to sing. So he took the pieces of his in-laws, the heads, arms, legs, and brought them into the house. His wife said, "I want to eat a big piece!" And the husband said, "Yes let's eat!" Together they ate the parents. The wife said, "Oh this meat is so good!" And he told her, "You are eating the meat of your parents, your mother and your father. Because you did not work for me! And here you ate them morsel by morsel!" His wife began to cry, "Now I have no parents!" He replied, "Now you will work for me when I ask!"

The lesson is for the woman: if a woman is married, she is in the house to work for the man and you must do all for the husband. When you have a husband, you prepare his food, and when his clothes are dirty you wash them. When he goes out and returns, when you see him coming, you take a chair and give it to him to sit on, a special place for him to sit. This is a lesson I taught my children and grand-children.

I remember one time I drank a little *embacko* and I put a cloth on my behind. I danced and danced, just like a young woman. All my children and grandchildren laughed and laughed! I have lived for many years and arrived at this age. Now I am with all these days with my children and grandchildren, it is so good now. The hardest time is when I think of the deaths of my parents, my grandmother, my son and daughters, and my husband. I remember them all and I suffer.

I have all these grandchildren and they sleep with me in my home. I love my girls' husbands, they give me gifts and are nice. I give them all lessons! "Daughters!" I say to them, "You have a husband. You have to respect your husband. Every morning you have to leave early to farm, take care of your family, take care of your children. Children are the most important. They are life. You are to have only one husband because now there is the sickness of HIV." This I said to my daughters. To my son, I said, "Son, if you earn money, you have to take care of your wife and children. If you earn money, you need to build a house. Don't fight with your neighbors. Don't fight with your wife. When you fight you create disorder. You have to keep peace and quiet in your family."

I have so much to teach! I give many stories with songs to my grandchildren to give them a good example of a life lesson. The children don't always understand the lessons of life, so again and again I give the lesson until they all understand. I play with my grandchildren. Sometimes they leave for play when I give them lessons! So I say, "No, I have prepared food for you and also I have a good lesson!" But they still run off and I am too tired to chase after them. This is a good time.

......................................................................................

### AKA WOMEN
## Nali

......................................................................................

I am a grown woman with children. I am a brave woman. I taught my children so they would know many things, so they would know traditional medicine, but this is only a little that they know, they do not know all. I went with my children into the forest to find yams, and when I went with them, I began to dig, dig, dig for yams with a *mopana* [digging stick]. My children saw this and I said, "This is a good yam." When we would find a bad one, I taught them, "This is a bad one." I also taught my girls, "You build the men a home like mine and take the bamboo and make it just so, and if you find a man you still remember me, your mother, when you go in to the forest and find food with your friends, and when you make things and find meat and honey, you still remember me your mother. You can sell meat and find yams and bring them back and share this. You guard your life well." The boys, I told them to learn to hunt and to look for palm oil and to fish and trap and, "When your mother speaks, you listen." The father speaks a lot to the boys and tells them, "If you work for a villager, work bravely." This is what you teach your children and grandchildren.

## AKA WOMEN
# Konga

I have taught my children that dancing is important to show the joy of the heart. We dance for amusement with the drum when we have joy, and we dance for ceremonies when someone has died. So you have simple dances and dances for ceremonies. The little brother of my daughter's husband died. He died during the season of the caterpillars. He had climbed a tree to get the caterpillars and the cord broke and he fell to the earth and died. We are waiting for the moon to climb so the *njamba* will organize a dance for him. The *njamba* is a woman specialist, a dancer. She is a great dancer, a grand *njamba*, and she has the knowledge of traditional medicine. If you want to be a great dancer, you go see her and give her a pot, machete, or some payment, and if you pay her, she will vaccinate you with the medicine to possess the dance. You become a great dancer and you dance without becoming tired. When you dance, the people see you and say, "That woman there is so supple and such a great dancer!"

People also invite the *njamba* to organize a dance, she knows the special dances. She takes the bark used for the vaccination, and everyone gives her things for this vaccination and dance. The *njamba* organizes a dance when the moon climbs, the people wait for the moon because it is good to dance in the moonlight. She organizes dances for *djengi*, a dance for the men. Before the dance they attach the *molimbai* across their chest and waist to the earth, and when *djengi* dances, he moves weaving and turning and the people yell when he comes near. There is also a spirit that kills dangerous animals like the elephants, and you dance in memory of the spirit of the hunt. If there was a *tuma*, he dances with the others in the camp to find an elephant. They used to find elephants to hunt, and the *tuma* takes a spear and kills the elephant and the elephant dies. The *tuma* calls to the women to come and carry meat to camp. Then the people would celebrate with a dance, to show their joy that they have this meat. Everyone would dance for the festival, for *djengi*, to celebrate the death of the elephant. We danced to celebrate because the people were content and happy.

Old people pass this knowledge to their sons and daughters. If someone was a hunter, when he is old and no longer hunts, he passes this knowledge to his son. He says, "My son, listen to me your father. I know well how to hunt. Take this cord, prepare it and when you go far from the camp to hunt, this cord will call the animals to you." If they kill with a bow, they give the vaccination of the hunt, *ndombi*. If you point with your arm with this vaccination, you will hit the animal and the arm will kill the animal. Also with the gun and the vaccination on the hand, *ndombi*, the animal will die.

Some women can take *mbondo*, if a person is accused of being a sorcerer, and they say, "No, I am not a sorcerer and I will demonstrate to others that no I am not a sorcerer. Give me the *mbondo* and I will show I am not. If you accuse me of sorcery and I take the *mbondo*, I will die. I will be ashamed to take the *mbondo*." *Mbondo* is not just for sorcery. If you are in the hunting camps and all the people go for a net-hunt and start hunting and you kill lots of animals and then this stops, it is because there is a person there who is a sorcerer. You can't get any animals, so everyone says, "Before we killed so many animals! Now when we hunt, nothing!" The old wise person takes the *mbondo*, prepares it and drinks it next to the camp to find the source of the problem. "Before when we hunted there were so many animals. Now nothing. Is it sorcery?" He searches person by person. If it is a person he knows, he will find this and identify the sorcerer. He tells the sorcerer, "Open the hunt or you take this *mbondo*." The sorcerer has fear so he opens the hunt. Or the bad hunting may be that a woman has hunted meat when she sees *ekila*. So there is a tree in the forest, *ékama*, and you peel the bark and make it into powder. Then you go into camp and take the red tree bark and grate it and mix it with the powder of *ékama*. You ask of all the women in camp to come and give blood. The women cut their stomachs with a razor and give blood from their stomach. You take all this blood from each woman. Then you take the powders and mix all this together with the blood of all the women in camp. You put this on the nets, all the nets in camp, and the *ekila* is finished and the hunt will continue. This is the knowledge the old give to the young. (See Figure 6.4.)

For the women, an old woman passes the knowledge of how to trap fish. People do not trap this way, but I teach them. There is also a leaf the old use for fishing. If you are trapping the fish, you take this leaf and squash it in your hands and put it all over your hands, and then when you fish, the fish will come quickly to the trap. It draws the fish, this medicine that is on your hands and arms. Quickly, quickly the fish come and you take the fish and soon your basket is full.

The old woman also gives the *zambola*, the medicine to quickly find a husband. If there is a man you love, you take this medicine and

FIGURE 6.4 | *Aka woman demonstrating how to make "the clothes we used to wear."*

he will come to you quickly. *Zambola* is tree leaf and you grind it into powder and you put this into water. You wash yourself at the river with this, all over your body, then rinse. You take a little more and put it into a cream and put this all over your body very well. You stay in your home, and if the man goes for a walk and he sees you, he will say, "This is my woman. I will have her be my wife." Quickly he is your husband. The old are wise and teach the knowledge from the past to the young.

## Social Continuity and Change: An Intergenerational View

### NGANDU WOMEN
### Blondine

Thanks be to God. I am thankful because I have arrived at this age, because so many women die. I have children, I have life. Many women die because they search for men and they find AIDS and die. There is a lot of death in the village because here there are diamond men, many men who come to search for diamonds. They come and give money to the young girls and they also give AIDS. Before we did not know HIV, but after some time we received the information, now we know. If people are skinny and have diarrhea, we know it is HIV. When a man has access he will use a condom but if not he does not...Even older women will have lovers and they can contaminate the whole family. Women have lovers because if you're a woman and you are married, there are other men who want you. If you have the heart you will refuse, but if you have no heart you do not refuse. But if a woman refuses a lover, he can send her *ndoki*, women have fear of this. I have seen this happen to my friends and neighbors. When a husband is away on a trip, another man comes and has relations with his wife and without a strong heart the woman accepts. If the husband finds out he says, "Shit! What have you done my wife?" If he is a man, he hits her and throws her out of the house and then he kills her lover.

## NGANDU WOMEN
### Therese

In the past people had power. They knew how to use sorcery to transform themselves. When they went into the forest to hunt, they could use a snake. They could send a snake to kill the monkey. They knew how to transform themselves into animals, panthers, elephants, monkeys, antelope, and they could hunt. They learned how to do this. Villagers in the past used sorcery. It was dangerous to live in the past. Now it has changed, this knowledge has left.

My mother and father gave birth to me and when I grew, life did not change. But now I see many new changes; schools, learning languages like French, television, and motorcycles. In schools with education, you know what you will do. But if you are not educated, what will you do? Education in the past was beside the fire. This is not so important now. Now it is important to write, to speak many languages. My father and mother taught me beside the fire. They told me life is difficult. From the past there were many wars and conflicts against people, and they said to me, "Do not go anywhere." I had to stay with the family and at night they said, "You stay here with us because it is dangerous." It is different now.

When I was young, there were no hospitals and it was very difficult to treat people. Now it is necessary to have hospitals because if you are sick, you may have to go for treatment. When you're sick now, people bring you to see the doctor, and they can even operate on you! I had an operation and I would have died if I had not had this. They can give you life! The first thing is life and health. If you have health you have everything, but if you're sick, nothing! In my time, there were deaths, men died and women and children, but not like today. Now people die almost every day! Before there was no HIV/AIDS. Now there is lots of sickness.

Now there is the television, the movies. I saw TV in Bangui when I visited Chantal, and the priests showed us TV. This is good but there are bad things on TV also. Many people get education from TV, if you let your children see good TV, you discover many things, the good thing I saw is about Jesus. This was very nice. When the priests told me about Jesus, I did not accept it, but then when the priests showed us Jesus on TV, I believed. The bad things that I saw on TV was war, people died by killing, by fighting, their homes were burned. I don't like the children to see this fighting or killing. One day I saw a neighbor child go to the TV, they saw a bad TV. Then they came and they began to fight like they saw on TV. This is bad.

I am also thinking about a bad thing, a bad change, and that is the gun. The white people brought the gun, and some people use the gun to kill other people. My son was injured by a gun. Basil had a goat, and the mayor's wife wanted to buy the goat but she thought the price was too expensive. She told her husband she wanted the goat and didn't want to pay the price, and the mayor became angry and ordered the policeman to shoot my son.

In the past, keeping children was easy. Now it is difficult because it is so expensive. Now when you have many children and they are sick, they can go to the hospital, but if you don't have money, they die. In the past we used traditional medicine and it worked well, but sometimes it did not. Now children go to school and it is necessary, but it is expensive. When I was a child, we bartered. I would have a machete and if you had something I needed, a snare, we would exchange the machete for the snare, or for meat. This barter is a system of exchange here in Africa. We had barter because then there were no white people.

In the past there weren't clothes like today. People used bark or leaves. They walked with nothing on their breasts or they would wear skins for clothes. When I was a child, I wore a *kangbo* made from animal skin. When the white people came, they brought clothes and made us work hard and gave us small money and made us buy clothes with this small money. White people began to show black people to buy things and to abandon our bartering system. That is why today we buy with money. In the past, we bartered for food and the things we needed, but now it is money. Money is God.

There have been many other changes from the past. There was no salt, no peppers, no oil, no *cube magique*. We cooked without these things. We took *peya* and cooked with that. We used salt, *moukwa*, from the palm leaf, and we would burn it and then use the burnt ash as salt to cook, the *ingo ti basenzi*. It was not good. But now we have *cube magique*, salt, and fire. From the long past, the way past, there was no fire even! We made pots of clay, *tawa ti basenzi*; in the past we used the earth to make pots for water and cooking. There were no good houses. People lived under big trees in small houses built with the bark of trees called *bombo*. The roofs were covered with leaves and branches. They did not have good beds. The people of the past slept on a bed built with tree branches and palm leaves called a *kerekpa*, the bed of old people. At night there was no lanterns of petrol so they used *packa*, the sap of big trees.

In the past our system of education was practiced around the fire. Men and women educated their children through storeies. In the past, people communicated with the tom-tom. They did not believe in only one god but in many gods. They did have cassava, but the people also ate the wild yams,. These were not planted, they just grew everywhere in the forest, and it was the Aka who showed the people these yams. In the past I went on a net-hunt with my mother and father. They told me to hide near a big tree. I liked to net-hunt because this gave me food, but I abandoned the net-hunt when I had children. The first net-hunt was practiced by the Aka, and after this the Ngandu began to net-hunt. Then after the white people came with the gun, we no longer net-hunted.

Relationships between men and women have changed also. In the past the relationships were not so good sometimes, because many men would fight with their women. They saw women as weak and gave them much work. Now it is better, the relationships between men and women, because women are people. Women are free. In the past men didn't wash their babies or cook. That was for women to do, but now I have seen men wash their baby and cook. This is a good relationship. Today, polygyny is a bad thing. But in the past, it was good. If one man could marry three women, they would all share the work for this man, to cook, to clean, to work. Now men see women as oppressive. One wife is good, two wives are bad. Men know that if they have more than one wife, that they will have problems. They will have to give much money and they will have many children who will need many things.

The old people like me know many things about being an Ngandu woman of the past. The new young women do not have this knowledge. This is bad because they believe they can learn all they need from school. I know one young Ngandu girl who went to Bangui to go to school, and when she returned here, her parents gave her food to eat and she refused. When her parents told her to go wash the manioc roots in water, she refused. She felt the new knowledge of school was more important. It is good to listen to old people because they have knowledge to teach to the young. When the old people die, this knowledge is lost.

## AKA WOMEN
### Nali

When I was little, the Aka were in the forest. Now I see a change because many Aka come to the village and they get clothes, they eat food with salt and oil. It is not bad because they change. When I was little, the people used animal skins or leaves, and when we walked it swayed back and forth. Now we have beautiful clothes and shoes. Now we are not the same as the Aka in the past. In the past the villagers gave us hard work and we lived under the law of the villagers. We liked to live in the forest. We did not like to come to the village because the villagers hated us. In the forest it was also easier to find food. When I was young, the relationship was not good between the villager and the Aka, but now it is better. The villagers do not take our things in force. This change is because of the priests who said it is not good to fight with the Aka.

There is an older woman, Djongi, who is brave and she is like the chief of women. She calls all the women together, "Come, come and listen." So all the women come from different camps. All the women from the trail voted for her to be this woman. Father Jacque told her to be this. She calls her friends and they come and speak together, "My mothers, and sisters, I have called you together. We work so hard for the village women and they give us so little, we have fear of famine, because they give us so little. So after today, you women, you each do the work in your own fields to eat, to find food for your children to eat." This is what the Mama says to all the women.

When I was *ngondo* [adolescent], I saw *djengi* like a god, a God of the forest who provided for us. I danced for *djengi*. Now I see him as a devil because now I believe in the Holy God. The priests said that *djengi* is not a god. I have left *djengi*. I believe in only God. When I go to the forest I find meat, fish, *koko* leaves. When I believed in *djengi* I did not get more food than now. *Djengi* is not the best knowledge for my children. If I believe in the *djengi*, then my children will believe in him. But if I believe in the Holy God, then my children will believe the same. Now I do not believe so my children do not believe in *djengi*. They will lose this knowledge.

We need to lose this knowledge of *djengi* because the only God is a good man. When I die I will go to God, not *djengi*. It was the people of God, the priests who told me that *djengi* is a bad thing, a mystery, or sorcery, a traditional thing. It is good to believe in God, he is invisible but he keeps us alive. Father Jacque said that only God keeps people. In the past we thought *djengi* keeps people, but we changed because God is bigger than *djengi*. God has more power to take care of people. *Djengi* is dead to us. We only believe in God now because God is holy and there is only one God but there are many *djengis*. I like *djengi* for dancing only, for the pleasure of dancing only. But God is first. God gives strength and life and after I am dead, I will go back to God. *Djengi* doesn't give me anything, only to dance. The meat, honey, yams from the forest, all come from God. The priest told us that *djengi* is evil and will kill us by burning us if we believe in him.

It was not hard for me to change this belief because the Father said to me, "You have been created by God. When you believe in God, you will see God, but if you don't believe in God, *djengi* will burn you. He demands your blood." Many people leave *djengi* because of this, because after they dance for *djengi*, he will take them and burn and eat them. The priests told us this. The priests are white, how did they know this? But we have known that *djengi* is powerful. He is of the forest, and he had given us many things but after he asks for blood.

We lose some of our ways and we keep some. We keep closeness and love between us. We share between us, because one day I may not have something and my neighbor will give it to me and someday I will give to her. It is not only food to share, but many things. The care of our children is still the same. Our children are very important. We go everywhere with our children.

## Konga

The difference between now and before is that before we ate so well. Now, we fix food with *cube magique*, there is palm oil but the meat is less. Before, we ate and prepared food with salt made naturally. Now, when we work, the people of the village, the men and women give us money. Before, there was no commerce of *koko*, and now we have commerce. We can buy clothes and shoes. In our house we have many objects from this commerce. We have pots and pans, clothes, and a machete. Before we did not have good clothes, we wore the leaves of the forest, *ntoulu*. We carried our babies with *kangbo* [baby sling made of animal skin]. Now we carry our infants with cloth. The missionaries came to give people knowledge and clothes. But now we receive clothes through our commerce. The relationship with the Ngandu women is good now. Before we did not farm, but if there was a woman from the village, we would go together to the farm and she would take me to go work in her field. When I was finished, she would give me manioc, yams, and manioc leaves. I would take this back to my camp and prepare this food. Now it is still a cooperation of work.

When I was young there was a good dance, *molembai*. I danced and danced. I loved to dance good for *djengi*! All the people danced a lot for *djengi* because *djengi* danced very well for the Aka. There are different forms of *djengi*. There is the simple one and he dances on the earth. There is the one who dances in the air. He is a spirit. We danced to evoke him to know a father or mother who takes the spirit, the demon spirit. If I kill my mother or father to take their spirit, I will dance in the air with *djengi*, the demon spirit. When I was young I saw this complicated *djengi*, and I fled because he charged at people and they cried. Before when we danced for this *djengi*, the dance was very complicated. Now the grandparents who had the power with *djengi* have died. The children today know only the simple *djengi*. The knowledge I know about the past is that when this *djengi* danced, all the people were at a distance. This *djengi* was very dangerous. But now I see people dance and they touch *djengi*. The old *djengi* danced to have the blood of the people. He killed people to have their blood to make his power better. This *djengi* took people and disappeared with them into the forest to kill them. When the people saw one of their people disappear in camp, we remembered this *djengi* took this person. He is a forest spirit.

The simple *djengi* lives beside the forest village. He has power but his power is not to kill people. I don't know his power because women don't approach *djengi*. But men know his power. This *djengi* is not bad for women, women are not afraid of the good one. Women want only to dance with this *djengi*. Only men know when he will come. Women do have some knowledge of *djengi*, but we do not share this with our men. We know when the *djengi* is ready to come. *Djengi* makes a trail, and we take flowers to him and prepare to dance. If we don't greet him, he is angry and leaves.

I taught my children, I said to them, "When you see *djengi* dancing, you don't approach this *djengi* because when this *djengi* pushes you, you will die. But the good *djengi* when he pushes you, you will not die, but you will feel a pain like a fever." This is not bad because he wants to show you that when he is dancing, you do not approach him. I received this knowledge from my parents and grandparents. They taught me this manner of living. I got this knowledge, but the people of today do not like living beside their parents. They move anywhere. Then when their parents are dead, they will not know this knowledge of their parents.

The men love the forest better than women because of the hunting. Women like the village better. When men are hunting in the forest, they come back to the village, they take a rest and sell their animal. When I was younger, a little child, I didn't know this change, but now I see. When I was little, I liked to live in the forest better. Not just myself, but many Aka men and women. We needed to live in the forest.

Now we like to live in the village because we work to have health and we help the villagers. In the time of Boganda we began to see this change. Boganda brought the white people to Central Africa. When the white people came to Nambélé and saw many Aka living in the forest, they didn't like that. They thought the Aka were the same as the

Ngandu. The Ngandu said we were like animals. We lived in the forest in small houses, we were bare-chested. We had bare feet. We, the Aka, used the net-hunt, first to kill animals to bring to the villagers, and then after the villagers saw that many Aka net-hunt, the white people came. They brought a plant and began to shower the forest with this plant; they brought salt, and money, bon-bons, and necklaces. They did not give us hard work. But they took our blood. They tested to find sickness in our blood. If they found sickness, they gave us medicine. Some of the blood they put in their bags. I don't know what they did with this.

They wanted us to live together with the Ngandu and have a good relationship with them. The first white person was an American missionary called Barbara Wood, who wanted Aka to live next to the Ngandu in the village. The second were the Catholic missionaries who told us not to live far in the forest. The missionaries told us that if we moved next to the village, they would build us a school, hospital, and a church. The missionaries did not say to us that our way of life in the forest was bad, but that it is better to live next to the village and just go to the forest like a holiday.

People from here net-hunted for a long time, but now we don't net-hunt, maybe on the Bassako trail they do. We left the net-hunt because making the net was very hard. The young children have lost this knowledge of how to make the net. They want to use the gun. It is faster to find food. It is not bad to lose this knowledge of the net-hunt because if you lose the net-hunt, you yourself think, "How am I going to live in my life?" But people learn new knowledge. It is good to find new knowledge. Then you eat and sleep well.

Today when you say, "Find palm oil," children refuse! Before the children never refused! Before the Aka worked for the villagers, but the work was not paid well because there was no revolution. We worked so hard and got a small amount of salt; now when we work, we demand for money in the hand. If the work is good, you win food to eat. If you do not work, you have no food; if you are tired and stay in camp, there is no food without work.

Our life has changed. We lived a lot in the forest. We fled from the sun. We only came into the villages for a month. With the teaching of the missionaries today, people have started to farm. Aka people do not buy land. The land is theirs, not the villager's land. I farm a little. I cut the trees and burn them. I plant the area with tubers of manioc, taro, and maize. My children help me.

Now we wear clothes and have radios. Certain Aka carry them-selves like villagers. Women wear jewelry, bracelets on their arms; before there were no such things. The village women work so much! They work on their farms, prepare food, and care for their children. The village men, women, and children all wear clothes, and their clothes are clean. They walk with shoes on their feet, and we walk without shoes. They respect and love their children, and their children love and respect them. Their children go to school. Now we are changing. We are teaching our children respect and they are going to school. We both love our children the same. Some change is good.

Many things have changed, but not the way the fathers take care of their babies. They care for their babies like the Aka fathers of the past. The people of the past, the father held the baby and the wife would hold the other child and they would walk together. They still do this.

## Lives at the Intersection of the Global and Local Worlds

Older women's lives are narrations of changing biologies and social identities, a shifting of power, identity, prestige, authority, and privilege against dramatic historical, social, political, and economic transforma-tions. Marriages are not arranged; women's children and grandchil-dren marry whom they want. Ngandu brideprice is paid in gifts of animals, material items, and money. As the market economy becomes more pervasive, emphasis on cash crops and wage labor increase, the nature of work and daily lives of both young and old Ngandu and Aka women continue to change profoundly. Fewer Ngandu men are able to afford more than one wife and have smaller families because of rising school fees, medical costs, clothing, and food. The public knowledge and personal experience of the HIV/AIDS epidemic is increasing. Only a handful of older Ngandu women I know in Nambélé have gone to school, and fewer still speak French. Now, however, many of the chil-dren and grandchildren of both groups are able to go to school. For the first time in recent history, Aka are being taught Sango (the national language) and French. Children have the opportunity, albeit limited, to go beyond primary schooling. Indeed, two Aka boys from the Nam-bélé area are currently enrolled in their second year of high school. A few Ngandu students are able to attend the University of Bangui. Some change, as Nali says, can be good.

Fewer Aka are staying for long periods of time in forest camps. Several Aka families have small farms close to the village. Women spend more time harvesting their food from these fields rather than gathering from the forest. Family net-hunting, particularly on the trail where this research was conducted, has decreased. Aka men prefer the use of guns they have borrowed from the Ngandu. Aka husbands and wives therefore are spending less time together than in past. As the Aka labor in their own fields and hunt with guns, rather than net-hunt, the social networks, sharing obligations, and bonds, vital for creating and maintaining a tightly integrated egalitarian society, are changing. It is too early yet to see how the increasing material inequality, farming, lack of dependence upon the Ngandu, new religious beliefs, and education are changing Aka culture and life. But it is clear that the changes in sedentarization, farming practices, proximity to schools, and health care is viewed positively by many of the women.

Political, economic, and cultural networks existing between the Aka and Ngandu, the ties binding the communities together, are slowly changing as the Aka increasingly refuse to provide cheap labor for the Ngandu and work instead for themselves.[5] Additionally, European missionaries in the area have built a modern medical center catering to the needs of the Aka. One Ngandu woman explained matter-of-factly, "Now it is we who wait in long lines to be treated and are often turned away. They [the missionaries] favor the pygmies and we go sick. They do not have to pay very much and we wait behind them and are made to pay a lot." One is left wondering how the structured hierarchical relationship between Aka and Ngandu women will transform. It remains to be seen if the incorporation of religion, education, health-care, self-reliance, increasing opportunities, and shifts in "traditional" hierarchies will bring a new order of life for both groups of women.

Anthropological studies in small-scale societies that focus on the subjective experiences of middle-aged and elderly women with adult children and grandchildren are often overlooked.[6] Or if not over-looked, homogenized in several ways, by the portrayal of their lives as the deprived and powerless victims of international, national, local, and household levelling processes; or as women represented as singularly biological beings, shifting from breastfeeding mothers to provisioning postmenopausal grandmothers. Although Aka and Ngandu women provide childcare and contend with political, economic, historic, and social forces, their narratives illustrate that as middle-aged and elderly individuals, life encompasses many biological, social, cultural and historical dimensions.

In the following section we will take a look at this universal stage of a woman's life, which has stimulated research among anthropologists, biologists, and reproductive physiologists concerning explanations for the evolution of menopause and women's long postreproductive lifespan. Does their role in provisioning increase the survivability of their grandchildren, particularly around the time of weaning? Grandmothers feed, wash, babysit, even offer their breasts to their grandchildren. But so do many others: fathers, aunts, uncles, siblings, cousins, and nonrelated children and adults. Is menopause an adaptation permitting grandmothers to invest in grand-offspring, thereby increasing their own inclusive fitness? Or is it simply a by-product of a long lifespan?

## Grandmothers, Kinship, and Health

Studies of provisioning, menopause, and the evolution of long postmenopausal life spans have been researched by a number of scholars from various fields, with research evaluating hormonal levels, reproductive ability, time allocation, and provisioning.[7] Most studies evaluate evidence for one of two key hypothesis: the "grandmother hypothesis" posits menopause as an adaptation that permits nonreproductive women to invest in grand-offspring, thereby increasing their inclusive fitness; and the "embodied capital hypothesis" which focuses on the reproductive senescence of human, favoring a long postreproductive lifespan with menopause as a "byproduct."[8]

The grandmother hypothesis assumes that an older woman's long postfertile life serves to enhance daughter's fertility and grand-off-springs' chances of survival by the extra provisioning and care provided by postmenopausal women.[9] Additionally, the grandmother hypothesis suggests that menopause is a byproduct and grandmothering an adaptation facilitating increased longevity.[10] The "embodied capital hypothesis" proposes that shifting productivity from younger to older individuals selected for increased investments in longevity and survival.[11] Hamilton's kin selection/inclusive fitness theory predicts that help and provisioning will be "favored when the fitness benefit to the receiver divided by the cost to the giver is greater than the reciprocal of their genetic relatedness (B/C > 1/r)."[12] And indeed, many studies suggest that it is closely related kin who provision children, and this in turn, has a direct effect on their survivability.[13]

Among the Efe foragers of the Ituri forest of the northeastern Democratic Republic of the Congo, extensive and intensive alloparenting occurs, such that the "number of allocaregivers at one year of age has been positively associated with survivorship to three years of age."[14] For the Hadza foragers of East Africa, older matrilineal kin (both grandmothers and great-aunts) are important providers and caregivers, provisioning their daughter's weaned offspring and enhancing the child's survivorability.[15] East and Central African hunter-gatherers and West African horticulturalists in Gambia all exhibit the same pattern: having a "rich complement of relatives," a maternal grandmother especially, increases survivability.[16] It was also found in Gambia that the survival advantage to having a maternal grandmother nearby emerged around the age of weaning—a "very vulnerable phase attended by emotional stress and the introduction of new foods."[17] However, in their study of the relationship between kin and health, Draper and Howell reasoned that having older living relatives enhances the nutritional status, health, and survivability of the children of the Dobe !Kung, but they found, as I did in a similar study with Aka and Ngandu, that health and survival were not influenced by the availability of numbers of older lineal kin or specific lineal kin (such as maternal grandmothers).[18]

Beyond babysitters and provisioning grandmothers, perhaps one of the "most important function(s)" of the elderly is as Mbengui, Therese's 20-year-old grandson, said, "I think that old people are like a library with knowledge for the children of today."[19] As grandmothers, Nali, Konga, Blondine, and Therese have long experience, and as cultural "teachers," they impart this knowledge to their children and grandchildren. Grandparents are likely to have "accumulated resources, status, knowledge, and skills that their kids haven't yet accumulated."[20] They know "who is related to whom…the names and habits and uses of hundreds of species of local plants and animals, and where to go to find food when conditions are poor."[21] Old people pass on cultural knowledge, culturally provisioning their offspring and grand-offspring, and for some societies, this may be "a matter of life or death."[22]

The important influence on cultural conservation and economic development at the household and community level of these women is overlooked, as increasing interventions by missionaries, local and international NGOs, and the national government into these areas target specific categories of people, often focusing on children and women of childbearing ages, bypassing the middle-aged and elderly—primarily because policy makers do not consider the activities and contributions of the elderly.[23] Unfortunately so, for older women can make significant contributions, reinforcing cultural beliefs and practices helpful in meeting the increasing challenges of living in a dramatically changing world.

The last decades of have brought tremendous transformations for many populations of the peoples of Central Africa. These cultures have endured and adapted to many forces: the steady penentration of the globalizing world; the increased reliance upon the market economy; the increased importance of money; cash cropping and trade; the rise of education and literacy; the displacement of traditional beliefs and practices by Christianity; population growth; resettlement; deforestation; and changes in hierarchal structures of gender and ethnicity.[24] The autonomy of the Aka and dynamic resiliency of Ngandu women has allowed them both to adapt to their changing worlds.

........................................................................................................................................

## NOTES FROM THE FIELD
## Fall 2002

*—Today I think I visited the equivalent of an old folks' home. It seems in most compounds there is one older woman or man, but here, there were two smaller and one larger home and three old people. An old man sat at the far end of the long house (made of the red-mud with a thatched roof, inside the floor is the same red-dirt, but swept clean, with two rooms divided by a mat-wall). So the old man was at one end sitting there with a cane, and at the other end of the home was an old woman squatting by a bowl of the leafy green food (looks like spinach but tastes good) and when she looks up and smiled, the three or four remaining teeth are green, her whole face is wrinkled and worn but her eyes were so kind and warm. The other old lady had no teeth and really had to work her mouth around to get the words out. Both old ladies backs were straight as a rod, the one toothless lady was bent over at the waist, perfectly horizontal to the ground. What a lifetime of work and carry heavy loads on your head with a ramrod straight posture does.*

*—Last evening the termites lost their wings and burrowed into the ground, so this morning there were termite wings all over the street. The kids in the village stuck the unlucky termites onto twigs, roasted and ate them. B., N. and several other Aka came and visited today. I can't believe how many vil-*

*lage camps there are now. They are so close in and are very big (lots of people in them). They tell me it's because the Congolese are threatening them in the forest (logging, hunting), extending the border of the frontier, moving it closer into CAR (how does a country's border move?), and also the Catholic sisters and an Italian priest have told them to move closer in to Nambélé as they want to put a road in somewhere for the Aka to settle next to, not sure what that's all about, will have to check into this more.*

**Fall 2010**

*—S. had a baby!!! I wouldn't have believed it possible! I thought she was too old and sick. But there I was holding the proof, a darling little, healthy baby and S. is so happy and proud! The baby is about 3 months old. Saw L. also on the way back home, she asked us to dinner. And! She told me that the manioc I planted last time I was here was doing well and that section of field still belongs to me. We get up early everyday (thanks to the roosters), have goat-turd coffee and start the work. T. is so sweet, she keeps telling me how important it is to talk to old people like her. She is so strong and feisty. Then I get to go and visit N. and she is such an interesting person, she has such a gentle smile and chuckles so often over the questions she is asked (or dumb things I do). She had her baby, two days after I left (she and I had waited so anxiously for the baby's birth!). He is darling. K. just got into camp today and has already built herself a home, she is as old and feisty as T. She is also healthy and doing well and still always has her grandkids sitting on her lap.*

*—Holding S.'s baby, sitting in forest camp in a hut with the rain pouring down, but we are dry inside!!!!! Well sort of, the little baby wiggles around, yawned a sweet little baby yawn and then peed all over me. So very happy to be back! Saw mostly everyone and for the most part many people I know are still alive and doing well. So many changes but at least everyone is ok.*

........................................................................

### QUESTIONS FOR REFLECTION

1. How do people in other cultures treat their elderly? How do you feel toward those who are "old"? At what age do you think people are old? Is old age determined by chronological age or physical frailty or mental decline?

2. What do the women mean when they state that with menopause they are "like a man"? Is menopause viewed differently in other cultures, such as in Great Britain, Japan, Europe, or the United States? Why or why not?

3. How might the advantages of age and seniority be useful in upholding and reinforcing social practices that are beneficial in meeting the increasing demands and challenges of living in a dramatically changing world?

...................................................................................................................................

## NOTES

1. Diamond, forthcoming.
2. Interestingly, as the Aka and Ngandu grandmothers narratives suggested, "some postmenopausal grandmothers can produce milk or fluid when they nurse their grandchildren. They are not just pacifiers. Benefits for the child are clear (survival) but allomaternal nursing may also benefit the grandmother. The immunological hypothesis implies that grandmothers living in environments with high pathogen loads might want to nurse other women's infants in order to enhance their own prolactin production and immunocompetence" (Hewlett and Winn, n.d.).
3. Diamond, forthcoming.
4. Keith 1980; Brown 1992 in Kerns and Brown 1992, 18–27.
5. Moïse 2010.
6. For exceptions on studies of middle-aged and older women see, Kerns and Brown 1992, Dickerson-Putnam and Brown 1998, Brown in Stromquist 1998; Beyene 1986; Kaufert and Lock 1992; Lock et al. 1988.
7. Ellison 2001a, 2001b; Jasienska and Ellison 2004; Gosden 1985; Hawkes et al. 1997; Hawkes et al. 1989, Hawkes et al. 1998; Hawkes et al. 2003; Gurven and Kim 1997; Hamilton 1966 Hill and Hurtado 1991, 1996, 1999; Kaplan 1997, Kaplan et al. 2000, Kaplan et al. 2002; Lancaster and King 1985; Marlowe 2000; Peccei 2001a, 2001b.
8. Lancaster and King 1985, in Kerns and Brown 1992, 7–15.
9. Hawkes et al. 1997; Hawkes et al. 1989, Hawkes et al. 1998; Hawkes et al. 2003
10. Peccei 2001a, 2001b.
11. Kaplan et al. 2000.
12. Kaplan and Hill 1985, 224; Hamilton 1964.
13. See for example, Meehan 2008.
14. Ivey 2000, 856.
15. Hawkes et al. 1989.
16. Hawkes et al. 2003; Ivey 2000; Sear and McGregor 2003
17. Sear and McGregor 2003, cited in Hrdy 2004, 18.
18. Hewlett and Winn, n.d.; Draper and Howell 2005.
19. Diamond, forthcoming.
20. Diamond, forthcoming.
21. Diamond, forthcoming.
22. Diamond, forthcoming.
23. Commission for Social Development 2001.
24. Bahuchet and Guillaume 1982; Moïse 2010; Kisliuk 1991; Bailey et al. 1992

CHAPTER 7

................................

# Conclusion: Globalization and Forces of Change

The future, who knows? What a concept is the future?

—NALI

Over the past century Aka and Ngandu societies have witnessed a cascade of dramatic changes, perhaps more than in any period of their histories. Therese's, Blondine's, Konga's, and Nali's narratives introduce the characteristics of those changes as they respond to one another, rapidly changing ecologies, socio-cultural conditions, the incursion of NGOs, missionaries, local and national forces, and globalization. Their stories eminate from very diverse sets of cultural beliefs and values, life experiences, and histories, as multifaceted and enduring as the women themselves.

Writing in the 1980s, Bahuchet and Guillaume noted the decrease in the Aka's traditional forest-based mobile lifestyle, and an increasing tendency to forage and hunt from village camps.[1] As we saw in Chapter One, with an escalation in Ngandu involvement in commercial coffee production, and diamond and gold mining, Aka were relied upon as a low-cost labor force, working in the villagers' fields, to the detriment of their traditional lifestyle and knowledge.[2] Since that time, life in and around Nambélé continues to undergo considerable transformation. Settlement sizes have increased, particularly in the number of Aka village camps, camps close to roads, and missions. Fields of manioc, coffee, and other cash crops have expanded. Hardwood extraction of valuable forest trees and mining continue, often to the detriment of the rain forest.[3] To counteract multinational impacts on the forests, large areas have been set aside as conservation parks and reserves. These protected areas severely restrict " 'local peoples' access to land and resources and position them in the crossfire between forest exploitation on the one hand, and attempts to protect the natural environment on the other."[4] Over-hunting in the most frequented, nonprotected areas reduces hunting efficiency. Other harvestable natural resources of the forest are diminishing, as well. With dwindling harvestable forest products, and the depletion of forest game, coupled with an increased amount of land set aside for conservation, both populations are facing economic, social, and environmental challenges. It is more and more difficult for the Ngandu to continue to exist as subsistence farmers; they are increasingly turning to more intensive agricultural production, an economy subject to fluctuating world markets.[5]

Incorporation of the Aka into the villager's economy has implications for both Aka and Ngandu societies. Their lives are "organized around coffee, and logging economic cycles, and harvest seasons" for their own or Ngandu fields, and "less and less by a nomadic forest-based" life.[6] Some Aka families are now settling for several months at a time in village camps, only returning to the forest for brief "visits" to hunt (often with guns, not nets) and to collect honey, caterpillars, *koko*, and other forest products.[7] However intensively they enter into a cash economy, either by laboring for wages or selling forest products for money, many Aka are still unable to engage "fully and autonomously within the market economy" of Nambélé, as much of their income often ends up in the "pockets" of the Ngandu.[8] And, as "new needs are born of new values, there is a desire of both the Aka and Ngandu to meaningfully act within an increasingly changing world of which they are inherently and inextricably bound, and as for much of history, continues to be marginal to them."[9] The Aka and Ngandu continue to be profoundly affected, in many ways, by the reach of the global economy.

For the Ngandu, increases in farm sizes for cash crops leads to growing environmental problems, over-cultivation of land, "declining soil fertility" and changes in traditional forager-farmer relations. Ecological pressures and economic hardship play a crucial role in cultural change for the Ngandu, who are more "economically and commercially minded."[10] Seeking employment opportunity, men (and unmarried women) are increasingly migrating for long periods of time to the capital city, Bangui and other urban areas. Separation from their families increases the chances of transmission of HIV and other sexually transmitted diseases and oftentimes exacerbates incidences of domestic violence when the men return home for brief visits.[11]

Particular values of both populations are being supplanted by the changing values of the youth. Formal schooling and the opportunities it provides for children are replacing lessons and education by parents and grandparents "around the fire." Immunization programs reaching both Aka and Ngandu (although there are still greater numbers of Aka children who are not immunized) and water wells dug in the village and close to Aka village camps have improved the health of both populations. Life for some is now a little easier, a little healthier.

Catholic missions are continuing the "humanitarian ideals" of the former colonial powers, who sought to initiate an "acculturation process," characterized by the presence of village-style mud huts along the roads and a few on the forest trails.[12] Meant in part to free the Aka from the oppression of the Ngandu, "villigization" has led to missionaries' discouraging Aka beliefs and values.[13] Overall disapproval and opposition to dances and beliefs has been an important factor in their decrease. *Djengi*, the spirit of the forest, to whom the Aka once danced and sang "for joy," good hunting, and to maintain harmonious relations with the forest, is now said by many Christanized Aka to be a "devil." Indigenous dress (or lack thereof), the bare-chestedness of the Aka women, enabling their babies to breastfeed and comfort themselves at will, is disappearing, being replaced by T-shirts and cloth skirts donated by various NGOs or sold by the missionaries. Western-style clothing is increasingly common among the Aka men.

In exchange for salvation, "freedom from Ngandu oppression," and "encouraged" settlement, the Aka can enjoy the benefits of education and entrance into the market economy, with the opportunity to buy clothes, pots and pans, maize and manioc, to farm and harvest from their own fields, and to have access to a mission health clinic. This, along with an understanding encouraged by the missionaries that Aka are "people too" and deserving of respect, and an increase in education opportunities (generally provided by the missions) for girls and boys, are viewed positively by Aka and Ngandu women. The growth of Christianity and education are influential features of social change for the two populations, exacerbating significant divisions between believers and nonbelievers, literate and nonliterate. To that end, both Aka and Ngandu women make choices based upon costs and benefits. Whether "forcefully encouraged" to sedentarize or choosing to move closer to missionary schools and health clinics, Aka parents hope that their children will be healthier, "educated," and better prepared for life in an increasingly complex world, even though it comes at the cost of particular beliefs and practices. Globalization is creating opportunities and change in life-ways, as well as disparities in wealth, prospects, health, education, and human rights between and within these two populations.

More broadly for Congo Basin populations, socio-political, economic, ecological, and cultural changes that have and are continuing to occur in Central Africa raise a multitude of concerns, questions, and considerations. New attention has been focused on the rights of the "indigenous" populations, giving rise to the importance of prehistory and genetics to address what has become a "central and very politically loaded question": Are "pygmies" autochthones, descendents of the first inhabitants of the region of the Congo Basin rainforest?[14] Phylogenetic studies indicate that "pygmy" populations diverged approximately 70,000 years ago, "from an ancestral lineage of modern Non-Pygmy populations," possibly as a result of dramatic variability in African climates.[15] As rainfall declined by as much as 50 percent during the Last Glacial maximum, a "massive retreat of the Congo Basin forests" occurred, and hypothetically, groups of Non-Pygmy and Pygmy populations diverged at the same time.[16] Western pygmy groups (such as the Aka and Baka) diverged about 2,800 years ago as the expansion of Bantu speaking farmers settled into the region, "aggravating resource pressures, decreasing the mobility of hunting-gatherers, and increasing the relative isolation of forager groups".[17]

The genetic data indicating that Western "pygmy" populations diverged from an ancestral population fairly recently, as noted, suggests a "recent isolation and heterogeneous admixture".[18] In the contemporary context it will be important to determine what populations have a "basis for claiming customary rights" to the forests as "autochthones" of the Congo Basin.[19] Can "pygmies" be recognized as the first "true inhabitants [of the] rainforest"?[20] What of other Non-"Pygmy" groups? The Bangando of southeastern Cameroun, for example, have had a "deep historical presence in the equatorial rainforest," a fact overlooked in policy documents, where they are positioned "categorically against their Baka 'pygmy' neighbors."[21] How long does a population have to be "in the neighborhood" to be recognized as deserving of "rights," advocacy, protection, and compensation? 10,000 years? 2,000 years? 500 years?

Central to this debate of "pygmies" being the "true and first inhabitants" of the rainforest and as such, able to claim customary rights, is a related question: Were the ancestral populations of "pygmies" even able to survive in the rainforest prior to the arrival of agriculturalists? This is the "Wild Yam question." The tropical forest is often assumed to be a "green desert" unable to support populations surviving upon wild food resources alone.[22] The existence of pre-agricultural populations in the central African forests is supported by increasing archaeological evidence; a study with contemporary Bofi foragers in Central Africa and with Baka hunter-gatherers in southern Cameroun suggests that these foragers can live "independently of agriculture without difficulty" and "adapt themselves quite well" to the tropical rainforest environment by exploiting wild yam sources.[23] Forest life without "agriculturalist dependency" is seemingly possible using wild yams as a "key food accounting for 60 percent of energetic intake."[24] Distributions of other "human influenced food species" found in secondary forests attests to the "historic interaction between humans and forest ecologies."[25] Does this historical interaction of humans and "human-induced vegetations" in the equatorial forests of Africa provide the foragers, as the "first inhabitants," a "foundation of legitimacy" for claiming rights to these tropical rainforests?[26]

The socio-interethnic relationships of these two groups of the Central African rainforest involve "relations of association since antiquity."[27] Research suggests that "mutually dependent relationships between foraging and farming populations were established during the Bantu expansion 2,000 years ago."[28] Ethnoarchaeological data from Central Africa was used to examine the "potential role that environmental factors (e.g., the hyperarid phase of the Mid-Holocene period when resources declined due to contraction of habitats) may have had in the establishment of interdependent and reciprocal relationships between foraging and farming populations."[29] Archaeological evidence of metallurgical activity from the same region of Central Africa has implications for suggesting that long-term, mutually dependent relations existed between the two populations. Iron objects produced in metal workshops along the Oubangui and Lobaye Rivers may have been "highly valued products of exchange" in the forest environment.[30] Were their initial relationships economically based and driven, dependent upon resource exchange? Can they be classified today in a similar manner?

And what of their connections in the contemporary world? In southern Gabon associations between the Babango "pygmies" and Massango "farmers" illustrate a more "equal" relationship.[31] There are frequent intermarriages, they both share significant roles in "ritual activities and norms," and they "mutually visit" each another.[32] The social relationships between Aka foragers and Congo Basin farmers in the northeastern Republic of Congo are said to be formed by the influence of the "outside world."[33] Following sedentarization, and resulting from increased concentration of camps along the roadside, "infiltration of a logging company, extension of semi-permanent cocao plantations, conservation efforts and incursion of the global market economy, social conflicts have increased, transforming their social relations over time into a culturally antagonistic but economically interdependent relations."[34]

The relationship between "foragers" and "farmers" has been characterized as being one of "solidarity, cooperation and friendship" or "political-economic domination." Their relations have also been variously described as "opposing and discriminatory," "parent-child like," a "pseudo-kinship."[35] The long-term dynamics of these relationships, how and why they have changed, and regional variations serve to illustrate the mistake of categorizing their realities in stereotyped, singular ways.[36] There are many versions and variously experienced associations. No single characterization can capture the relationships between "pygmies" and their neighboring "farmers." Has the portrayal of "pygmy-farmer" relations been characterized in the same way for so long that it has become the version that is accepted as definitive, as the reality of present-day relations and identities?[37]

Anthropologists studying these populations fail to agree on these points, and fail to agree on how to refer to the inhabitants of the Congo Basin. The term "pygmies" used in local settings is derogatory. Bantu farmers refer to the foragers as "pygmies"—that is, "less culturally evolved peoples of the forest."[38] This characterization of foragers comparatively "places them in opposition" to their farming and sedentarized neighbors.[39] Does a "pure" foraging lifestyle even exist? Many hunter-gatherers, as we have seen with Nali and her family, have adopted at least part-time farming and are becoming increasingly sedentary.[40] Additionally, categorizing forest communities based upon "contrasting subsistence strategies and polar relations of power" into "hunter-gatherers–farmers," "pygmy-villagers," or "forager-farmers" negates the fluidity of their social, ecological, and political relations, and in doing so, their dignity and agency.[41] "Ecologically reductive" characterizations become the singular representation for all foragers and farmers, despite the "great diversity, complexity and changing registers" of their relations.[42]

At national and international levels, "pygmies" as "first inhabitants" of the rain forest are afforded rights under the Declaration of Indigenous

Peoples, and those rights are fiercely debated by various local, national, and international institutions, NGOs, and other advocacy groups. "Pygmy" thus becomes a powerful designation, a useful tool within a loaded political, socio-economic context. This becomes problematic for several reasons. Extensive diversity exists among groups of "pygmies": not all hunter-gatherers in this region continue this lifestyle, some live near or in cities, practice subsistence farming, and/or cash cropping.[43] The Bakoya "pygmies" of Gabon, originally seminomadic, became sedentary a relatively long time ago and now live with non-pygmy groups practicing agriculture in villages along the roads.[44] Agriculture for the Bakoya has become an important source of income and "redefines the relationship with the non-pygmy villagers."[45] In Gabon, international development, NGOs, the national government, and conservation agencies all view the Babongo forager populations (and as well the Bantu peoples) as having been in a certain region for a long duration.[46] However, field work recently carried out along the Ikoy River calls that assumption into question, showing both populations to be fairly recent arrivals, having initially emigrated from the area in the late 1800s and returning in the 1960s following the start of logging operations in the area.[47]

These findings illustrate the problematic implications for international agencies that confine themselves to one reality, one version of what it means to be "indigenous" and one version of "farmer" and "forager," in the face of manifold social, political, and economic relations. But the question still remains, how to characterize the people and describe their "social landscapes": Are they semi-nomadic forest foragers, when many are in fact quite sedentary? As "farmers" who also happen to hunt and gather from the forest? "Patron-client," "parent-child," "forager-farmer," or "pygmy-villager"?[48] Are the terms "farmer," "villager," "Pygmy," or "pygmy" acceptable in international forums, but not at the local community level? Is construction of identities, "positioning of peoples categorically against one another," useful?[49]

As "pygmies" and "farmers" within "polar relations of power," the "pygmies" are often positioned as victims.[50] And as first comers to the equatorial forests, they are thus seen as more deserving of advocacy and development efforts by outside organizations. This is not to suggest that the Aka do not experience marginalization. But by failing to acknowledge the perceptions of "pygmies" and "farmers" by national and international NGOs, the government, missionaries, and others, including social scientists, as well as the autonomy and efforts of both groups, the "success of the interventions" generated will be limited.[51] "Alternative models of forest identity are needed to acknowledge the historic, and continued, agency and engagement of foragers in local, national, and international processes."[52] Additionally, there may be other factors, as in the case of the Baka in southeastern Cameroun where, after "five years of logging companies engaging in forest recertification processes and the ongoing sustainable forest management and certification programs, there should have had notable positive impacts. The reality is these actions were short term and limited, a failing attributed to the many constraints linked to political, social, economic and institutional contexts."[53] Questions that must be addressed include: Who are these organizations? What are their objectives? How do they work? Are local people involved in any meaningful ways? Are their voices heard and emphasized?[54] National and international intervention and development programs are often mismanaged and disconnected from the people who need aid, thereby becoming forms of structural violence, contributing to the destruction of indigenous societies, amplifying inequalities, and changing traditional subsistence, social, and cultural patterns.

Coups, failed coups and mutinies, riots, unrest, corruption, mismanagement, and human rights abuses have plagued the history of the impoverished country of Central African Republic and continue to do so. Advocacy efforts by local and international NGOs, missionaries, and other organizations must be informed and guided by contextualized research and sound analysis that takes into full account the agency of both foragers and farmers.[55] International and national laws are written to uphold and protect the rights of women, children, and indigenous peoples, vulnerable victims to structural and actual violence and abuse. Numbers of people, many of them children from diverse communities like Nambélé, continue to die each year from diseases that are preventable and treatable. Both populations, "foragers" and "farmers" alike, are affected. This is not to suggest that foragers are not more or less vulnerable than their farming neighbors, but simply that both populations may suffer impoverishment, disease, and lack of access to healthcare, education, and resources. The existing realities of ethnicities, social relations, "land use, peoples access, ownership, and use of forest resources" need to be researched systematically by "international and regional organizations advocating for the legal recognition" and respect for all local peoples' need to access the resources of healthcare, education, and subsistence.[56]

In the first chapters of the book, we are introduced to the Aka and Ngandu women of the Congo River Basin. The pervasive and intense value of autonomy and sharing, their trusting view of the natural and social worlds, are enduring and essential cultural features of the Aka, enabling these women to continue to express values of their distinct culture. Within the social structure of the Ngandu, significant values of respect, reciprocity, solidarity, resiliency, and strong clan alliances have allowed them to transcend the hardships of their daily lives and effectively find their way within a challenging and changing social and ecological world. The remarkable lives of these Aka and Ngandu women—from childhood to womanhood, from earliest memories to middle and old age—describe cultures that may be lost forever or may just as likely endure. The distinct individualities of Blondine, Therese, Nali, and Konga, as expressed through their childhood and adolescent experiences, marriages, parenting ideologies, changing biologies, and present lives, bear witness to contemporary forces and adaptations, as well as to enduring traditional beliefs and values.

Social structure, development, economic activity, and rapid political and culture change reflect the degree to which the Aka and Ngandu societies have been affected by global, national, and local processes. Structuring their own adaptations to the harsh and delightful realities of their lives, these women increasingly participate in a broader social, economic, and political world. But in many studies on the effects of globalization on small-scale societies, women's experiences are homogenized in several ways: by being characterized as women of small-scale societies in sub-Saharan Africa unable to act meaningfully within cultural, social, political, and economic realms; by singular representations incorrectly defining their lives. Too often the emphasis centers on the negative experiences of sub-Saharan African women, living in what others view as deprivation, poor health, powerlessness, and poverty, at the expense of their positive perceptions and lived experiences. In assessing the life of women, a narrow range of factors are considered: biological stages (birth and weaning, menopause, provisioning during postmenopausal life), gendered roles, and household contribution. What is more, because most of these studies are driven by homogenizing approaches, these assessments are taken as inevitable for all women living in small-scale societies, ignoring women's courage, strength, resilience, and individual experience.[57] Within their gendered social categories and diverse cultures,

Blondine, Therese, Nali, and Konga have varying degrees of power, agency, and choice.

The narratives of these individual women, although serving to posit their lives within a wider social, cultural, and temporal context, suggest that they do not see themselves as marginalized, powerless victims—neither of their changing biological state, nor of a globalized and challenging world. These perspectives can be key to the development of far-reaching and contextualized policy intervention and strategies by government, missionaries, and local and international NGOs for several reasons: The focus on women's perspectives and experiences has the capacity to provide culturally sensitive and context-appropriate understandings of the impacts of marginalization, globalization, and culture change. The focus on their voices has the potential to increase awareness of and respect for their individual, although culturally influenced, life adaptations in face of adversity. Attention to their agency as women upholding and reinforcing cultural practices beneficial to themselves, their families, and the larger society, unveils their coping strategies that help to buffer the negative impacts of living in a changing and challenging environment.[58]

We have been, throughout much of history, witnesses to suffering, hope, and connection "to some other peoples...."[59] With that connection comes responsibility. Conventional "consumer values and First World living standards" dramatically, and in various ways, economically, politically, and environmentally impact the health, human rights, and cultures of populations throughout the world.[60] It is important to question and understand what our impact and role as individuals are toward those with whom we share this world. We also have an opportunity in our interconnected world to learn and find courage from people like these resilient women of the Congo Basin. What does it "mean to be a woman?" This is an unanswerable question. But Blondine, Therese, Nali, and Konga have taught us that as women they can embody and reflect society's values and needs, and maintain traditions of culture, while creating a place for those values and beliefs within a contemporary, challenging world.[61] Their stories now, more than ever, matter.

> Listen, here is a story that I want to tell. This is the life of me, a woman who lives here in Nambélé. This is the life of women and how the life for women here has been going for many, many years.
>
> —BLONDINE

## NOTES FROM THE FIELD
**Fall 2007**

*—Got scolded out today by L. of the house of three women. She said to me, "You work with us in the fields, you work with us in our homes, talk with us about our lives, eat with us, but sometimes when you walk down the street, you just say hello. You don't stop, you should come inside and talk awhile." I felt terrible. I was thinking I have only a week or so left and so much to do yet. But she is right. She is teaching me the responsibilities of friendship. The obligations of friendship are about investment of time and emotion. Good lesson for me to learn.*

**Fall 2010**

*—We are in Nambélé now, so wonderful to be back!! We are talking to two Aka boys who went to school at Mballa and now speak French and even a little English. They will work as research assistances for B. Amazing. We've seen lots of people, lots of our friends, and so many of our friends are alive and doing well. It is always a worry when we go away and then come back, to see how many of our friends and acquaintances have died.*

**Winter 2012**

*It is the season of the "Mango rains"—We are back again for a short time. Everyone is doing well, E. now has twins! What a change in Nambélé in one year. There are so many people here from all over, other villages, Cameroun, etc. because of gold and diamond mining. With the global increase in the value of gold, people here are making money, so the village population is expanding, trees are being cut down to build more homes, prices in the village market are going up, there are motorcycle taxis driving up and down the trails, there are new little bars/eating places, the medical clinic said the prevalence of HIV is now 20% here, there are hardly any goats as the miners as A. says have eaten them all, there are only a few chickens, and I haven't heard the roosters crowing in the morning as a epidemic of bird flu? wiped most of them out last year, and lots of Aka families are now living in the village camps. Oh and I met an old, blind Aka man who'd recently went on the pilgrimage to Mecca. Amazing.*

## QUESTIONS FOR REFLECTION

1. Does the historical interaction of humans and "human-induced vegetations" in the equatorial forests of Africa provide the foragers, as the "first inhabitants," a foundation of legitimacy for claiming rights to these tropical rainforests?

2. How long do you think a population have to be "in the neighborhood" to be recognized as the "first inhabitants" deserving of "rights," advocacy, protection, and compensation? 10,000 years? 2,000 years? 500 years? What about other long-term (say, 2,000-year) inhabitants? Is one group more "deserving" than the other, based upon this assessment?

3. Why have the relationships between the foragers and their neighbors endured over time? How have they changed?

4. Why do you think the terms "farmer," "villager," "Pygmy," or "pygy" are acceptable in international forums, but not at local community levels? Is construction of identities, positioning of peoples categorically against one another useful?

5. Do you feel a responsibility toward others with whom we share the planet? Why or why not?

6. What life lessons might you have learned from Nali, Konga, Therese, and Blondine?

....................................................................................................................................................

## NOTES

1. Bahuchet and Guillaume 1982, 208, 209.
2. Bahuchet and Guillaume 1982, 200; B. S. Hewlett and Fancher 2011; Moïse 2010.
3. Bailey et al. 1992, 263; Bahuchet and Guillaume 1982, 198.
4. Ichikawa 2004, 114, in B. S. Hewlett and Fancher 2011, 12.
5. Moïse 2010; Bailey et al. 1992.
6. Bahuchet and Guillaume 1982, 196–98.
7. Bahuchet and Guillaume 1982, 196–98.
8. Bailey et al. 1992.
9. Bahuchet and Guillaume 1982, 208; Moïse 2010; B.S. Hewlett nd
10. Bahuchet and Guillaume 1982, 208; Moïse 2010.
11. Van Donk 2006.
12. Bahuchet and Guillaume 1982.
13. Bahuchet and Guillaume 1982; Bailey et al. 1992; Moïse 2010.
14. Taylor 2010; Verdu 2010.
15. Verdu 2010; Patin et al. 2009; Batini et al. 2007; Quintana-Murci et al. 2008, in B. S. Hewlett and Fancher 2011.
16. Verdu 2010; Verdu et al. 2009, in B. S. Hewlett and Fancher 2011, 3.
17. Verdu 2010; Verdu et al. 2009, in B. S. Hewlett and Fancher 2011, 3.
18. Verdu 2010; Verdu et al. 2009, in B. S. Hewlett and Fancher 2011, 3.
19. Verdu 2010.
20. Hardin et al. 2010.
21. Rupp 2011.

22. Ichikawa 2010; Headland 1987, Headland and Bailey 1991; Bailey et al. 1989.
23. Mercader 2002, 2003, in Ichikawa 2010; Caudill 2010; Sato et al. 2010.
24. Caudill 2010; Sato et al. 2010.
25. Yasuoka 2006; Ichikawa 2010; Sato et al. 2010.
26. Sato et al. 2010.
27. Bahuchet and Guillaume 1982; Cavalli-Sforza 1986; Moïse 2010.
28. Lupo 2010.
29. Lupo 2010.
30. Ndanga 2010.
31. Matsuura 2010.
32. Matsuura 2010.
33. Takeuchi 2010.
34. Takeuchi 2010; Oishi 2010.
35. Takeuchi 2001; Joiris 2003, in Ichikawa 2003, 4; Rupp 2011
36. Rupp 2011
37. Rupp 2011
38. Bahuchet and Guillaume 1982.
39. Rupp 2011
40. Rupp 2011
41. Rupp 2011
42. Rupp 2011
43. Soengas 2010. For example, the Baka of Cameroun (Hayashi et al. 2010; Leclerc 2010; Tegomo 2010); the Bakoya and Baka in Gabon (Soengas 2010); the Boffi of Central Africa (Fargeot and Roulet 2010).
44. Among the Bakoya's nonpygmy neighbors are the Mwesa, Mahongwe, Kota, Kwele, and Bongom (Soengas 2010).
45. Soengas 2010.
46. Hymas 2010.
47. Hymas 2010.
48. Takeuchi 2010; Rupp 2011.
49. Rupp 2011
50. Bailey et al. 1992; Moïse 2010.
51. Bailey et al. 1992; Moïse 2010.
52. Moïse 2010.
53. Defo 2010.
54. Simiti 2010; Robillard 2010.
55. Moïse 2010.
56. Moïse 2010; B. S. Hewlett and Winn, n.d.
57. Gebru 2009; Gutmann 1992.
58. Gebru 2009.
59. Diamond 2005.
60. Diamond 2005.
61. Markstrom 2008.

# GLOSSARY

## Anthropological Terms

**allomother.** Literally, "other mother."

**allomaternal nursing.** Other "mothers" or women who nurse another women's infant.

**anthropometric data.** Human body measurements.

**autochthones.** Descendents of the first inhabitants of the region.

**body mass index.** Measure of weight controlled for height, calculated as weight (in kgs) divided by height (in cms) squared; is an indicator of the overall health status of an individual and provides an index commonly seen in the range of 12–30.

**cognatic lines of descent.** Bilateral lines of descent, meaning that female descent lines are recognized as well as male descent lines. Compare with **matrilineal** and **patrilineal rules of descent**.

**communalism.** Places a high value on meeting the needs of the family, including clan members of extended family, over the needs of the individual.

**developmental niche.** A model of child development emphasizing the importance of parental ethnotheories, the physical and social setting, and culturally regulated customs of childcare.

**delayed return system.** System in which wealth, land, material items, and food are collected (delayed production and consumption) and as long-term planning for an uncertain future. Compare with **immediate return system**.

**emic.** Insider's view or interpretation.

**ethnomedicine.** Cultural medical systems.

**ethnotheory (parental).** How parents understand their roles as parents, what is important to them as mothers and fathers, and how these ideas and beliefs influence their child's development.

**etic. Outsider's view or interpretation.**

**foundational schema.** The ideas, knowledge, and values providing a foundation for cultural models, that is, ways of thinking, explaining, and/or anticipating others in a variety of domains of cultural life.

**Hawaiian kinship system.** Uses a single term for all relatives of the same sex and generation. Compare with **Iroquois kinship system**.

**immediate return system.** System in which wealth, food and material items are not collected, or stored, reflecting a trust in the future. Compare with **delayed return system**.

**informal interviewing.** Discussion and questions as you participate and observe in the daily life of the community.

**internal working model (IWM).** Cultural schema influencing how people view themselves, others, and the social-natural environment. The IWM is a "dynamic model based upon the infant's experiences with their caregivers" whereby they develop either secure or insecure IWM (B.S. Hewlett 1992).

**Iroquois kinship system.** A child's father and father's brother are called by the same term, the mother's brother is called by a different term; the mother and mother's sister are called by one term, the father's sister is called by a different term. All siblings are given the same term as parallel cousins. Compare with **Hawaiian kinship system.**

**life history narrative.** The life story of an individual.

**key informant.** Someone who may be recognized by others as an "expert" in the research topic being studied, and/or someone the anthropologist relies upon and from whom he or she learns the culture.

**matrilineal rule of descent.** Descent traced through female line. Compare with **cognatic lines of descent** and **patrilineal rules of descent**.

**matrilocal.** When a married couple lives in the wife's mother's or wife's family's place of residence.

**multilocal residence.** When a married couple lives for a time in either the husband's father's or wife's family's place of residency.

**patriarchal.** Cultural system in which men have greater authority and decision-making power than women.

**patriclan.** Clan membership through male line.

**patrilineal rule of descent.** Descent traced through the male line so that the man, his children, his son's children, and his brother's children are members of the same descent group. Compare with **cognatic lines of descent** and **matrilineal rules of descent**.

**patrilocal.** When a married couple live in husband's father's area of residency.

**participant observation.** Key anthropological method of living with, observing, and participating in the lives of people being studied to better understand their culture.

**polyvocality.** Multiple or many voices (such as the Aka singing style).

**postpartum taboo.** Prohibition against having sexual intercourse for a some time following the birth of a child.

**rapport.** Bond shared between people based upon a mutual foundation of trust and understanding.

**semi-structured interview.** Easy flowing interviews with specific topics, partially coded questions, plan and direction.

**structured formal interview.** Specific questions asked in the same sequence; a directed and controlled form of interviewing.

## Aka and Ngandu Terms

**amiteē.** Kicking and dancing game.

**beya.** Type of sickness in an infant.

**bokola.** Young adolescent male.

**bombo.** Bark of trees used in old times to build houses.

**bongide.** Sexual desire (Aka; **elebe** among Ngandu).

**bondingo.** Love.

**bouï** *or* **bouï de koulou.** Mixture of water and rice or manioc, gruel.

**boulou.** Type of traditional medicine in which a burnt leaf is crushed into powder and put into nose, eyes, mouth.

**cache-cache.** A hide and seek game.

**dibale zakoudou.** Leaves used to treat worms.

**dibembe.** Stomach illness; infection with worms.

**dibota.** Birth (**moï** in DiAka).

**dibongô.** Sickness infants get if parents don't observe the postpartum sex taboo.

**dikanda.** Patriclan.

**diki za zounda.** Umbilical cord.

**dikoko.** Bark.

**Djengi.** Forest spirit.

**djombo.** Plant used to stop heavy flow of blood after birth.

**ékama.** Tree bark used for pain relief.

**ékonzi.** Illness that causes miscarriage.

**ekoukou.** Placenta.

**edio.** Either ancestors of certain families, or nameless generalized spirits.

**élebé.** Sexual desire (Ngandu; **bonguedi** among Aka).

**ekila ya ngouya** *or* **ekila ya ngoa.** Sickness after eating pig meat.

**ekila ya kema.** Sickness of the monkey.

**ekila ngombe.** When an infant dies of sunken fontanels and convulsions.

**èkonzi.** Illness that causes miscarriage (diouke).

**embacko.** Moonshine (homemade whiskey) made from manioc or corn.

**èsuma.** Yam that is preferred for its good quality.

**etounga.** Basket (Ngandu).

**gbagba.** A dancing game in which girls form a semi-circle, clap and sing, and one by one each girl throws herself into the arms of the girls in the circle, and the girls throw her back up to a standing position.

**gnama-ti-ya.** Name of illness caused by "small animal with teeth" (same as **kata** in DiAka), which strikes only women and causes them to miscarry.

**huma.** House or hut.

**ingo ti basenzi.** Traditional salt made from burnt ash of the palm leaf.

**kadi.** Brothers and sisters; siblings of either gender.

**kangbo.** Loin cloth made from animal skins or leaves.

**kata.** Small animal with a "big mouth and many teeth like a mouse" that causes miscarriages.

**kerekpa.** Bed for old people, made of branches and palm leaves.

**kôkô.** Term applied to all grandparents; also an edible plant from forest.

**Komba** *or* **Bembe.** The creator of all living things who retired after creating the world and its people.

**kombeti.** Term applied to the elder male of the Aka camp, who has somewhat more influence in that he is the one looked to for advice.

**konza.** Village "patron" or boss.

**kpangaï.** Leaves used to help with [tooth] pain.

**kpodo.** Illness; perhaps elephantitus.

**kwa.** Dead body.

**lango.** Aka camp.

**lou ngo zo.** Interred, buried.

**mabongo.** "Knees" sickness; occurs if mother or father have sex before postpartum taboo period is over.

**mai dogba.** Birthwater.

**mai ya ekila.** Colostrum.

**mai ma mabele ma tella.** Colostrum, literally, "water of my breasts is yellow".

**makoka.** Leaves on which Aka baby is placed just after birth.

**makongo.** Leaves covering old traditional houses.

**malima.** Sperm or substance (Ngandu).

**malonga ma ngai ma tegna.** Literally, "blood of I is over" and **ekila yamou ya mo sia,** in DiAka (i.e., menopause).

**mamboli.** Sperm (Aka).

**masombo.** Consultation, advice.

**mssassanga.** Leaves that are crushed and mixed with water and dirt from a baby's grave, then spread on the mother's belly so she may become pregnant again with the same baby.

**matanga.** Grief gathering or funeral.

**mbondo** *or* **mbengue.** Poison oracle used to verify or search for the truth, usually to identify the sorcerer who caused illness. Strychnine is made from the root of a tree by grating the bark and soaking it in water, which is drunk by a traditional healer or elder.

**mobila.** Matrilineal line.

**mogouga.** Traditional medicine that helps women produce breast milk.

**molembo.** Name of Aka dance.

**molimbai.** Palm fronds or other bushes tied around waist or chest and used in dances.

**molembai lembai.** Name of Aka dance.

**molomba.** Bark eaten by men that produces a "hard penis".

**mona** *or* **moanna.** Aka offspring, children.

**mopana.** Digging stick.

**moukwa.** Salt.

**ndala.** All grandchildren.

**ndima.** Forest.

**ndoki.** Poison (dart).

**ndombi.** Vaccination of protection.

**nganga.** Traditional Aka healer.

**ngondo.** Adolescent female.

**ngouma.** Breast infection.

**ngue.** Term used for mother; refers to both mother and mother's sister.

**njamba.** Dance or song specialist.

**ntoulu.** Clothes made from leaves or plants, worn in the past.

**ouka.** Meaning "out" as in miscarriage: **moana amou ouka,** literally, "my baby is going out."

**packa.** The sap of big trees, which hardens and burns when lit.

**peli.** One-year ceremony to honor and remember the dead.

**ppo.** Birthwater.

**tambula.** To walk.

**tao.** Term applied to father's older brother and husband of mother's sister.

**tawa ti basenzi.** Traditional clay pot.

**tongou.** Umbilical cord.

**tuma.** Great hunter of the past (generally elephant).

**yukwa.** Basket.

**zambo** *or* **nzambo.** Water mixed with honey, sometimes given to nursing child to help in the weaning process.

**zambola.** Plant that makes someone fall in love with you.

**zeki.** Contractions of birth.

# BIBLIOGRAPHY

Adichie, Chimamanda. 2010. "The danger of a single story." Video on TED.com. http://www.ted.com/talks/chimamanda_adichie_the_danger_of_a_single_story.html (accessed December 17, 2010).

Ainsworth, Mary, D. 1967. *Infancy in Uganda: infant care and the growth of love.* Baltimore: Johns Hopkins Press.

Akin, K. Gillogly. 1985. "Women's Work and Infant Feedings: Traditional and Transitional Practices on Malaita, Solomon Islands," in *Infant Care and Feeding in the South Pacific*, ed. Lauren Marshall, 207–234. New York: Gordon and Breach.

Appiah, K. Anthony, and Lewis Henry Gates Jr. 1999. *Africana.* New York: Perseus Books.

Archer, John. 2001. "Grief from an Evolutionary Perspective," in *Handbook of Bereavement Research*, eds; Margaret S. Stroebe, Robert O. Hansson, Wolfgang Stroebe, and Henk Schut, 263–283. Washington, D.C.: American Psychological Association.

Arom, Simha, and Jacqueline M. C. Thomas. 1974. *Les Mimbo: Génies du piégage et le monde surnaturel des Nbgaka-Ma'bo (République Centralafricaine).* Paris: CNRS.

Arom Simha, Natalie Fernando, Suzanne Fürniss, Sylvie le Bomin, Fabrice Marandola, and Jean Molino. 2008. "La categorization des patrimoines musicaux de tradition orale," in *Categories and categorization. Une perspective interdisciplinaire*, ed. F. Alvarez-Pereyre, 273–313 Paris: Peeters-Selaf.

Babcock, Pat. 1991. Death Education Changes Coping to Confidence, in *Loss, Grief and Care,* vol. 4, (1–2): 35–44

Bahuchet, Serge. 1979. "Pygmées de Centrafrique: Études Ethnologiques, Historiques et Linguistiques sur les Pygmées "Ba. Mbenga" (Aka/Baka) du Nord-Ouest du Bassin Congolais," in *Études Pygmées*, ed. Serge Bahuchet, 13–31. Paris: Selaf.

———. 1985. *Les Pygmées Aka et la Forêt Centrafricaine.* Paris: Selaf.

———. 1990. The Akwa pygmies: Hunting and Gathering in the Lobaye Forest, *in Food and Nutrition in the African Rain Forest.* Food Anthropology Unit 263, UNESCO.

———. 1993. "History of the inhabitants of the central African rain forest: perspectives from comparative linguistics," in *Tropical forests, people and food. Biocultural interactions and applications to development*, eds. C.M. Hladik, O.F. Linares, H.Pagezy, A.Semple, and M. Hadley, 37–54. "Man and Biosphere series vol. 13." Paris/Lancs: Unesco/Parthenon.

———. 2010. Overview of Ethnic Diversity Among African Forest Hunter-Gatherers. Paper Presented at Recent Research Among Congo Basin Hunter-Gatherers and Farmers, University of New Mexico, Albuquerque NM, Febuary 17.

Bahuchet, Serge, and Henri Guillaume. 1982. "Aka-Farmer Relations in the Northwest Congo Basin," in *Politics and History in Band Societies*, eds. Elenore Leacock and Robert B. Lee, 189–211. Cambridge: Cambridge University Press.

Bailey, Robert C., G. Head, M. Jenike, B. Owen, R. Rechtman, and E. Zechenter. 1989. Hunting and Gathering in Tropical Rain Forest: Is It Possible? *American Anthropologist* 91: 59–82.

Bailey, Robert C., Serge Bahuchet, and Barry S. Hewlett. 1992. "Development in the Central African Rainforest: Concern for Forest Peoples," in *Conservation of West and Central African Rainforests*, eds. Kevin M. Cleaver, Mohan Munasinghe, Mary Dyson, Nicolas Egli, Axel Peuker, Francois Wencelius, 202–11. Washington DC: The World Bank.

Batini, C., V. Coia, C. Battaggia, J. Rocha, M. M. Pilkington, G. Spedini, D. Comas, G. Destro-Bisol, and F. Calafell. 2007. Phylogeography of the Human Mitochondrial L1c Haplogroup: Genetic Signatures of the Prehistory of Central Africa. *Molecular Phylogenetics and Evolution* 43: 635–44.

BBC Monitoring. 2011. Central African Republic Profile. http://news.bbc.co.uk/go/pr/fr/-/2/hi/africa/country_profiles/1067518.stm (accessed December 2011).

Becker, Noemie, Paul Verdu, Alain Forment, Priscille Touraille, Yves Le Bouc, and Evelyne Heyer. 2010. The Riddle of Pygmy Stature: An Interdisciplinary Issue. Paper given at the International Conference on Congo Basin Hunter-Gatherers, Montpellier, France, September 22–24.

Belsky, Jay. 1997. Attachment, Mating, and Parenting: An Evolutionary Interpretation. *Human Nature* 8(4): 361–81.

———. 1999. "Infant-Parent Attachment," in *Child Psychology: A Handbook of Contemporary Issues*, eds. Lawrence Balter, Catherine Susan Tamis-LeMonda, 45–63. Philadelphia: Psychology Press/Taylor and Francis.

Beneria, Lourdes, and Gita Sen. 1981. Accumulation, Reproduction, and Women's Role in Economic Development: Boserup Revisited. Development and the Sexual Division of Labor. *Journal of Women in Culture and Society* 7(2): 279–298.

Bernard, Russel H. 1994. *Research Methods in Anthropology*. Sage Publications: London.

Berry, John.W. and Jan M.H. van de Koppel. 1986. *On the Edge of the Forest*. Berwyn PA: Swets North America Inc.

Beyene, Yewoubdar. 1986. Cultural Significance and Physiological Manifestations of Menopause: A Biocultural Analysis. *Culture, Medicine, and Psychiatry* 10: 47–71.

Bird-David, Nurit. 1990. The Giving Environment: Another Perspective on the Economic System of Gatherer-Hunters. *Current Anthropology* 31: 189–96.

Bock, John, and D. W. Sellen. 2002. Childhood and the Evolution of the Human Life Course: An Introduction. *Human Nature* 13: 153–60.

Bogin, Barry and Holly Smith. 1996. Evolution of the human life cycle. American Journal of Human Biology 8: 703–716.

Bonvillain, Nancy. 2007. *Women and Men, Cultural Constructs of Gender*, 4th ed. London: Pearson Prentice Hall.

Boserup, Ester. 1970. *Women's Role in Economic Development*. London: George Allen & Unwin, Ltd.

Bowlby, John. 1999 [1969]. *Attachment: Attachment and Loss* (vol. 1) (2nd ed.). New York: Basic Books.

———.1973. *Separation: Anxiety & Anger*. Attachment and Loss (vol. 2). London: Hogarth Press.

———.1980. *Loss: Sadness & Depression*. Attachment and Loss (vol. 3). London: Hogarth Press.

Boyd, Robert and Richerson, Peter, J. 1985. *Culture and the evolutionary process*. Chicago, Illinois: University of Chicago Press.

Boyette, Adam. 2011. "Middle Childhood among Aka Forest Foragers of the Central African Republic: A Comparative Perspective." Unpublished manuscript.

Brown, Judith. 1992. "Lives of Middle-Aged Women," in *In Her Prime, New Views of Middle-Aged Women*, eds. Virginia Kerns and Judith Brown, 17–32. Champaign: University of Illinois Press.

———.1998. "Lives of Middle-Aged Women," in *Women in the Third World: An Encyclopedia of Contemporary Issues*, ed. Nelly Stromquist, 246–51. New York: Garland.

Brown, Paula. 2001. "Colonial New Guinea: The Historical Context," in *Colonial New Guinea: Anthropological Perspectives*, ed. Naomi McPherson, 15–26. Pittsburgh: University of Pittsburgh Press.

Bruel, Georges. 1911. *Notes Ethnographiques sur Quelques Tribus de l'Afrique Equatoriale Française. I: Les Populations de al Moyenne Sanga: Pomo, Boumalu, Babinga*. Leroux: Paris.

Bulmer, M. 1994. *Theoretical Evolutionary Ecology*. Sunderland MA: Sinauer Associates Inc.

Caudill, Mark. 2010. Tuber Foraging Across Tropical Environments. Paper given at the International Conference on Congo Basin Hunter-Gatherers, Montpellier, France, September 22–24.

Cavalli-Sforza, Luca Luigi. 1986. *African Pygmies*. New York: Academic Press.

Cavalli-Sforza, Luca Luigi, and Mark W. Feldman. 1981. *Cultural Transmission and Evolution*. Princeton NJ: Princeton University Press.

Chagnon, Napoleon A.1997. *Yanomamo: The Fierce People*. 5th ed. Holt, Rinehart and Winston, Inc.

Charnov, Eric L. 1993. *Life History Invariants*. Oxford: Oxford University Press.

Chisholm, Jay S. 1993. Death, Hope, and Sex: Life-History Theory and the Development of Reproductive Strategies. *Current Anthropology* 34(1): 1–24.

———.1996. The Evolutionary Ecology of Attachment Organization. *Human Nature* 7:1–38.

CIA (Central Intelligence Agency). 2011. The World Fact Book: Central African Republic. https://www.cia.gov/library/publications/the-world-factbook/geos/ct.html (accessed December 2011).

———. n.d. The World Fact book: Economy—Overview. https://www.cia.gov/library/publications/the-world-factbook/fields/2116.html (accessed December 2011).

Commission for Social Development. 2001. "Way Must be Found to Utilize Vast Contributions of Older Persons, Preparatory Meeting Told." Acting as Preparatory Committee for Second World Assembly on Ageing, 1st Meeting (AM). http://www.un.org/News/Press/docs/2001/soc4570.doc.htm (accessed September 1, 2011).

Csibra, Gergely, and Gyorgy Gergely. 2006. "Social Learning and Social Cognition: The Case for Pedagogy," in *Processes of Change in Brain and Cognitive Development: Attention and Performance*, eds. Y. Munakata and M. H. Johnson, 249–74. Oxford: Oxford University Press.

de Beauvoir, Simone. 1976. *Le deuxième sexe.* Paris: Gallimard. (Orig. pub. 1949.)

Defo, Louis. 2010. Can Forest Certification Help Save Central African Hunter-Gatherers? Paper given at the International Conference on Congo Basin Hunter-Gatherers, Montpellier, France, September 22–24.

Delobeau, Jean-Michael. 1989. *Yamonzombo et Yandenga: Les Relations Entre les Villages Monzombo et les Campements Pygmées Aka dans la Sous-préfecture de Mongoumba (Centraafrique).* Paris: Peeters-Selaf.

Demesse, Lucien.1978. *Changements Techno-Économiques et Sociaux Chez les Pygmées Babinga (Nord Congo et Sub Centralafrique).* Paris: Selaf.

Devin, Luis. 2010. Water Drums of the Baka of Cameroon and Gabon. Paper given at the International Conference on Congo Basin Hunter-Gatherers, Montpellier, France, September 22–24.

Diamond, Jared M. 2005. *Collapse: How Societies Choose to Fail or Survive.* New York: Penguin Group.

———. Forthcoming. *The world Until Yesterday: What can traditional societies teach us.*

Dickerson-Putman, Jeanette and Judith Brown . 1998. *Women among Women: Anthropological Perspectives on Female Age Hierarchies*, eds. Jeanette Dickerson-Putman and Judith Brown. Champaign: University of Illinois Press.

Donahue, Philip. 1985. *The Human Animal.* New York: Simon & Schuster.

Draper, Patricia, and Henry Harpending, 1987. Parent investment and the child's environment. *Journal of Anthropological Research* 38: 255–73.

Draper, Patricia, and Nancy Howell. 2005. "The growth and kinship resources of !Kung children," in *Hunter-Gather Childhoods*, eds. Barry S. Hewlett and Michael Lamb, 262–281. New York: Aldine.

Elfmann, Peggy. 2005. "Women's World's in Dassanetch, Southern Ethiopia," Working Paper No. 53. Munich: Institute of Ethnology and African Studies.

Ellis, Bruce. Forthcoming. "Risky Adolescent Behavior: An Evolutionary Perspective," in *Adolescent Identity: Evolutionary, Developmental and Cultural Perspectives*, ed. Bonnie L. Hewlett.

Ellison, Peter T. 2001a. *On Fertile Ground: A Natural History of Human Reproduction*. Cambridge MA: Harvard University Press.

——, ed. 2001b. *Reproductive Ecology and Human Evolution*. New York: Aldine de Gruyter.

Ember, Carol R., and Melvin Ember. 2000. *Anthropology a Brief Introduction*, 4th ed. Upper Saddle River NJ: Prentice Hall.

Engels, Frederich. 1975. *The Origins of the Family, Private Property and the State*, reprint ed. New York: International Publishers.

Fargeot, Christian, and Pierre-Armand Roulet. 2010. Commercial Camps of Boffi Pygmies. Paper given at the International Conference on Congo Basin Hunter-Gatherers, Montpellier, France, September 22–24.

Farmer, Paul. 2004. An Anthropology of Structural Violence. *Current Anthropology* 45: 305–26.

Fouts, Hillary. 2004. "Social Contexts of Weaning: The Importance of *Cross-Cultural* Studies," in *Childhood and Adolescence: Cross-cultural Perspectives and Applications*, eds. Uwe P. Gielen and Jaipaul L. Roopnarine, 133–48. London: Greenwood Publishing Group.

Fouts, Hillary, Barry S. Hewlett and M. Lamb. 2000. Weaning and the Nature of Early Childhood Interaction Among Bofi Foragers in Central Africa. *Human Nature* 12(1): 27–46.

Fouts, Hillary, and Robin Brookshire. 2009a. Who Feeds Children? A Child'-Eye-View of Caregiver Feeding Patterns among the Aka Foragers in Congo. *Social Science and Medicine* 69: 285–92.

Fouts, Hillary N., and Michael E. Lamb. 2009b. Cultural and Developmental in Toddlers' Interactions with Other Children in Two Small-Scale Societies in Central Africa. *Journal of European Developmental Science* 3: 259–77.

Fouts, H. N., B. S. Hewlett, and M. E. Lamb. Forthcoming. A Bio-Cultural Approach to Breastfeeding Interactions in Central Africa. *American Anthropologist*.

Freedman, D. G., and J. Gorman. 1993. Attachment and the Transmission of Culture: An Evolutionary Perspective. *Journal of Social and Evolutionary Systems* 16(3): 297–329.

Fürniss, Susanne. 2011. "Sexual Education through Singing and Dancing," in *Music, Dance and the Art of Seduction*, eds. Frank Kouwenhoven and James Kippen, 1–12. Delft, The Netherlands: Eburon Academic Publishers.

Fürniss, Susanne, and Daou V. Joiris. 2010. Ritual and Musical Creation in Baka Culture. Paper given at the International Conference on Congo Basin Hunter-Gatherers, Montpellier, France, September 22–24.

Gebru, Bethelem Tekola. 2009. Looking Beyond Poverty: Poor Children's Perspectives and Experiences of Risk, Coping and Resilience in Addis Ababa. PhD diss., University of Bath.

Gergely, Gyorgy, and Csibra Gergely. 2006. "Sylvia's Recipe: The Role of Imitation and Pedagogy in the Transmission of Human Culture," in *Roots of Human Sociality: Culture, Cognition, and Human Interaction*, eds. N. J. Enfield and S. C. Levinson, 229–55. Oxford: Berg.

Gergely, B., K. Egyed, and I. Kiraly. 2007. On pedagogy. *Developmental Science* 10: 139–46.

Ghura, Dhaneshwar, and Benoît Mercereau. 2004. Political Instability and Growth: The Central African Republic. IMF Working Paper. Washington DC: International Monetary Fund.

Giles-Vernick, Tamara. 2002. *Cutting the Vines of the Past: Environmental Histories of the Central African Rainforest*. Charlottesville: University Press of Virginia.

Goody, Jack. 1976. *Production and Reproduction: A Comparative Study of the Domestic Domain*. Cambridge: Cambridge University Press.

Gosden, R. 1985. *The Biology of Menopause: The Causes and Consequences of Ovarian Aging*. London: Academic Press.

Gosso, Y. Otta, E., Morais, M., Riberiro, F.J.L. and Bussab, V.S.R. 2005. "Play in Hunter-Gather Societies," in *The Nature of Play: Great Apes and Humans*, eds. A.D. Pellegrini and P.K. Smith, 213–253. New York: New York, Guilford.

Gray, Sandra J. 1996. Ecology of Weaning among Nomadic Turkana Pastoralists of Kenya: Maternal Thinking, Maternal Behavior, and Human Adaptive Strategies. *Human Biology* 68(3): 437–65.

Grinker, Roy, R. 1994. *Houses in the Rainforest: Ethnicity and Inequality among Farmers and Foragers in Central Africa*. Los Angeles: University of California Press.

Gurven, Michael D., and Kim Hill. 1997. Comment on "Hadza Women's Time Allocation, Offspring Provisioning, and the Evolution of Long Post-Menopausal Life Spans." *Current Anthropology* 38: 551–77.

Gutmann, David. 1992. "Beyond Nurture: Developmental Perspectives on the vital Older Woman," in *In Her Prime: New View of Middle-Aged Women among Women*, eds. David Gutmann and Virginia Kerns, 221–243 Champaign: University of Illinois Press.

Hames, Raymond. 1988. "The Allocation of Parental Care among the Ye'kwana," in *Human Reproductive Behavior: A Darwinian Perspective*, eds. Laura Betzig, Monica Borgerhoff-Mulder, and Pat Turke, 237–251 Cambridge: Cambridge University Press.

Hamilton, William. 1964. The Genetic Evolution of Social Behavior I, II. *Journal of Theoretical Biology* 7: 1–52.

———. 1966. The Molding of Senescence by Natural Selection. *Journal of Theoretical Biology* 12: 12–45.

Hardin Rebecca, Robillard Marine and Bahuchet Serge. 2010. "Social, Spatial, and Sectoral Boundaries in Transborder Conservation of Central African Forests," in *Transborder Gouvernance of Forests, Rivers and Seas*, eds. de Jong, Wil, Denyse Snelder and Noboru Ichikawa 15–30. London: Routledge University Press.

Harkness, Sarah and Super, Charles. M. 1992. The developmental niche: A theoretical framework for analyzing the household production of health. *Social Science and Medicine*, 38(2): 217–226.

Harms, Robert. 1981. *River of Wealth, River of Sorrow: The Central Zaire Basin in the Era of Slave and Ivory Trade, 1500-1891*. New Haven, CN: Yale University Press.

Hawkes, Kim, James F. O'Connell, and Nicholas G. Blurton Jones. 1997. Hadza Women's Time Allocation, Offspring Provisioning, and the Evolution of Post-Menopausal Lifespans. *Current Anthropology* 38: 551–78.

———. 1989. "Hardworking Hadza Grandmothers," in *Comparative Socioecology: The Behavioral Ecology of Humans and Other Mammals*, eds. V. Standen and R.A. Foley, 341–366. London: Basil Blackwell.

Hawkes, Kim, O' Connell James F, Blurton-Jones Nicholas G, and Charnov Eric L . 1998. Grandmothering, Menopause and the Evolution of Human Life Histories. *Proceedings of the National Academy of Sciences USA* 95: 1336–39.

Hawkes, Kim, James F. O'Connell, and Nicholas G. Blurton Jones, Helen Alvarez and Eric L. Charnov . 2003. Grandmothers and the Evolution of Human Longevity. *American Journal of Human Biology* 15: 380–400.

Hayashi, Koji, Taro Yamauchi, and Hiroaki Sato. 2010. Daily Activities among the Baka Hunter-Gatherers of Cameroun from Individual Observations at the Forest Camp and the Settlement. Paper given at the International Conference on Congo Basin Hunter-Gatherers, Montpellier, France, September 22–24.

Headland, Thomas N. 1987. The Wild Yam Question: How Well Could Independent Hunter-Gatherers Live in a Tropical Rain Forest Ecosystem? *Human Ecology* 15: 463–91.

Headland, Thomas N., and Robert C. Bailey. 1991. Introduction: Have Hunter-Gatherers Ever Lived in Tropical Rain Forest Independently of Agriculture?. *Human Ecology* 19: 115–22.

Hewlett, Barry S. 1991. Demography and childcare in preindustrial societies. *Journal of Anthropological Research*, 47.

———.1992. *Intimate Fathers: The Nature and Context of Aka Pygmy Paternal Infant Care*. Ann Arbor: University of Michigan Press.

———. 2001. "The Cultural Nexus of Aka Father-Infant Bonding," in *Gender in Cross-Cultural Perspective*, 3rd ed., eds. Caroline B. Brettell and Carolyn F. Sargent, 45–56. Upper Saddle River, NJ: Prentice Hall.

———. 2007. Why Sleep Alone? An Integrated Evolutionary Approach to Intracultural and Intercultural Variability in Aka, Ngandu, and Euro-American Cosleeping. Paper presented at the annual meeting of the Society for Cross-Cultural Research, San Antonio TX.

———. nd. "Victims of Discrimination: An Anthropological Science Critique of Human Rights and Missionary Narratives of African Pygmy Marginalization." Unpublished manuscript.

Hewlett, Barry S. and Cavalli Sforza, Luigi L. 1986a. Cultural Transmission Among Aka Pygmies, *American Anthropologist*, 88, 922–934.

Hewlett, Barry S., van de Koppel, Jan. M.H., and Maria van de Koppel. 1986b. "Causes of Death Among Aka Pygmies of the Central African Republic", in *African Pygmies*, ed. Luigi L. Cavalli Sforza, 45–63. New York: Academic Press.

Hewlett, Barry S., Michael Lamb, Donald Shannon, Birgit Leyendecker, and Axel Scholmerich. 1998. Culture and Early Infancy among Central African Foragers and Farmers. *Developmental Psychology* 34: 653–51.

Hewlett, Barry S., Michael Lamb, Birgit Leyendecker, and Axel Scholmerick, 2000a. Internal Working Models, Trust, and Sharing among Foragers, *Current Anthropology* 41: 287–297.

———. 2000b. "Parental Investment Strategies among Aka foragers, Ngandu Farmers and Euro-American Urban Industrialists," in *Adaptation and Human Behavior*, eds. Lee Cronk, Napolean Chagnon, and William Irons, 155–77. New York: Aldine de Gruyter.

Hewlett, Barry S., and Andrew Noss. 2001. The Context of Female Hunting in Central Africa. *American Anthropologist* 103(4): 1024–40.

Hewlett, Barry S., and Michael Lamb. 2002a." Integrating Evolution, Culture and Developmental Psychology: Explaining Caregiver-Infant Proximity and Responsiveness in Central Africa and the USA," in *Between Culture and Biology: Perspectives on Ontogenetic Development*, eds. Heidi Keller, Ype H. Poortinga, and Axel Schölmerich, 241–69. Cambridge: Cambridge University Press.

Hewlett, Barry S., A. Silvertri, and C. R. Gugliemino. 2002b. Semes and Genes in Africa. *Current Anthropology* 43: 313–21.

Hewlett, Barry S., Hillary Fouts, Adam Boyette, and Bonnie L. Hewlett. 2011. Social Learning among Congo Basin Hunter-gatherers. *Philosophical Transactions of the Royal Society B (U.K.)* 366: 1168–78.

Hewlett, Barry S., and Jay Fancher. Forthcoming. "Hunter-Gatherer Cultural Traditions," in *Oxford Handbook of the Archaeology and Anthropology of Hunter-Gatherers*, eds. Vicki Cummings, Peter Jordan, and Marek Zvelebil. Oxford: Oxford University Press.

Hewlett, Barry S., and Winn, Steve. n.d. "Allomaternal Nursing among Hunter-Gatherers." Unpublished manuscript.

Hewlett, Bonnie L. 2005. "Vulnerable Lives: Death, Loss and Grief among Aka and Ngandu Adolescents of the Central African Republic," in *Culture and Ecology of Hunter-Gatherer Children*, eds. Barry S. Hewlett and Michael E. Lamb, 322–342 New York: Aldine.

Hewlett, Bonnie L. (ed.). Forthcoming. *Adolescent Identity: Evolutionary, Cultural and Developmental Perspectives.* New York: Routledge, Taylor and Francis.

Hewlett Bonnie L., and Barry S. Hewlett. 2008. "A Biocultural Approach to Sex, Love and Intimacy in Central African Foragers and Farmers," in *Intimacies: Love and Sex Across Cultures*, ed. William Jankowiak, 39–64 Princeton NJ: Princeton University Press.

Hill, Kim, and Magdelena Hurtado.1991. The Evolution of Reproductive
Senescence and Menopause in Human Females. *Human Nature* 2(4): 315–50.
———. 1996. *Ache Life History: The Ecology and Demography of a Foraging People.*
New York: Aldine de Gruyter.
Hill, K.R., R. Walker, M. Mozicevic, J. Eder, T. Headland, B.S. Hewlett, A.M.
Hurtado, F. Marlowe, P. Wiessner and B. Wood 2011. Coresidence patterns in
hunter-gatherer societies show unique human social structure. Science, 331,
1286–1289.
Hrdy, Sarah Blaffer. 1999. *Mother Nature: A History of Mothers, Infants and Natural
Selection.* New York: Pantheon.
———. 2005. "Comes the Child before Man: How Cooperative Breeding and
Prolonged Post-Weaning Dependence Shaped Human Potential," in *Hunter-
Gatherer Childhoods: evolutionary, developmental, & cultural perspectives*
eds. Barry S. Hewlett and Michael Lamb, 65–91. New Brunswick NJ: Aldine
Transactions.
Hurtado, A. Magdalena, M. Anderson Frey, Inés Hurtado, Kim Hill, and Jack
Baker. 2008. "The Role of Helminthes in Human Evolution: Implications
for Global Health in the 21st Century," in *Medicine and Evolution: Current
Applications, Future Prospects*, eds. Sarah Elton and Paul O'Higgins, 151–78.
Boca Raton FL: Taylor & Frances.
Hymas, Olivier. 2010. Recent Migration of Hunter-Gatherers and Bantu-Speaking
Farmers along the Ikoy River Valley (Gabon): Implications for Conservation
and Development in the Area. Paper given at the International Conference on
Congo Basin Hunter-Gatherers, Montpellier, France, September 22–24.
———. 2003. Recent Advances in Central African Hunter-Gatherer Research.
*African Study Monographs*, Suppl. 28: 1–6.
Ichikawa, Mitsuo. 2004. "The Japanese Tradition of Central African Hunter-
gatherer Studies: With Comparative Observation on the French and American
Traditions," in *Hunter-Gatherers in History, Archaeology and Anthropology*, ed.
A. Barnard, 103–114. Oxford: Berg Publishers.
———.2010. Historical Ecology and Contemporary Problems in the Congo Basin.
Paper given at the International Conference on Congo Basin Hunter-Gatherers,
Montpellier, France, September 22–24.
Ichikawa, Mitsuo and Daiji Kimura.1992. Beyond "The Original Affluent Society":
A Culturalist Reformulation [and Comments and Reply]. *Current Anthropology*
33(1): 25–47.
IMF (International Monetary Fund). 2011. Statement at the Conclusion of an IMF
Mission to the Central African Republic, Press Release No. 11/278, July 13.
http://www.imf.org/external/np/sec/pr/2011/pr11278.htm (accessed September
4, 2011).
Ivey, Paula K. 2000. Cooperative Reproduction in Ituri Hunter-Gatherers: Who
Cares for Infants? *Current Anthropology* 41: 856–66.
Jankowiak, William. 1993. *Sex, Death and Hierarchy in a Chinese City: An
Anthropological Account.* New York: Columbia University Press.

Jasienska, G., and Peter Ellison. 2004. Energetic Factors and Seasonal Changes in Ovarian Function in Women From Rural Poland. *American Journal of Human Biology* 16: 563–80.

Jenike, Mark R. 2001. "Nutritional Ecology: Diet, Physical Cctivity and Body Size," in *Hunter-Gatherers, An Interdisciplinary Perspective*, eds. C. Panter-Brick, Robert Layton, and Peter Rowley-Conwy, 224–225. Cambridge: Cambridge University Press.

Joiris, Daou. 2003. The Framework of Central African Hunter-Gatherers and Neighboring Societies. *African Study Monographs*, Suppl. 28: 57–79.

Joiris, Daou, and S. Bahuchet. 1994. "Afrique équatoriale," in *Situation des populations Ingènes des Forêts Denses et Humides,* ed. S. Bahuchet, 387–448. Bruxelles: Commission Européenne.

Kalck, Pierre. 1993. *Central African Republic*, Vol. 152. Oxford: Clio Press.

Kamei, Notuka. 2005. "Play among Baka Children in Cameroon," in *Hunter-Gatherer Childhoods: Evolutionary, Developmental and Cultural Perspectives*, eds. B. S. Hewlett and M. E. Lamb, 343–62. New Brunswick, NJ: Aldine Transaction.

Kaplan, Hillard S. 1997. "The Evolution of the Human Life Course," in *Between Zeus and Salmon: The Biodemography of Aging*, eds. K. Wachter and C. Finch, 175–211. Washington DC: National Academy of Sciences.

Kaplan, Hillard, and Kim Hill. 1985. Food Sharing among Ache Foragers: Tests of Explanatory Hypothesis. *Current Anthropology* 26(2): 223–246.

Kaplan, Hillard, Hill, Kim Lancaster, Jane, Hurtado, Magdalena, A. 2000. A Theory of Human Life History Evolution: Diet, Intelligence, and Longevity. *Evolutionary Anthropology* 9: 156–85.

Kaplan, Hillard and Arthur J. Robson . 2002. The Emergence of Humans: The Coevolution of Intelligence and Longevity with Intergenerational Transfers. *Proceedings of the National Academy of Sciences* 99: 10221–26.

Kaplan, Hillard S., Lancaster, Jane and Robson, Author. 2003. "Embodied capital and the Evolutionary Economics of the Human Life Span," in *Life Span: Evolutionary, Ecological, and Demographic Perspectives*, eds. J. R. Carey and S. Tuljapurkar. Supplement to Population and Developmental Review, 29: 152–182. New York: Population Council.

Kaufert, Patricia. 1982. Anthropology and the Menopause: The Development of a Theoretical Framework. *Maturitas* 4: 181–93.

Kaufert, Patricia A., and Margaret Lock. 1992 "What Are Women for?: Cultural Constructs of Menopausal Women in Japan and Canada," in, *In Her Prime, New Views of Middle-Aged Women among Women*, eds. Virginia Kerns and Judith Brown,187–200 Champaign: University of Illinois Press.

Kazadi, Ntole. 1981. Méprisés et Admirés: L'Ambivalence des Relations entre les Bacwa (Pygmées) et les Bahemba (Bantu). *Africa* 51: 837–47.

Keith, Jennie. 1980. The Best is Yet to Be: Toward an Anthropology of Age. *Annual Review of Anthropology* 9: 339–64.

Kenrick, Justin. 2005. "Equalizing Processes, Processes of Discrimination and the Forest People of Central Africa," in *Property and Equality*, Vol. 2, *Encapsulation,*

*Commercialization, Discrimination*, eds. T. Widlock and W. Tadesse, 104–28. Oxford: Berghahn.

Kerns, Virgina, and Judith Brown. 1992. *In Her Prime: New Views of Middle-Aged Women*. Chicago: University of Illinois Press.

Kisliuk, Michelle. 1991. Confronting the Quintessential: Singing, Dancing and Everyday Life among Biaka Pygmies (Central African Republic). PhD diss., New York University.

Kitanshi, K. 1998. Food Sharing among the Aka Hunter-Gatherers in Northeastern Congo. *African Study Monographs* 17: 35–57.

Konner, Melvin. 1983. *The Tangled Wing: Biological Constraints on the Human Spirit*. New York: Harper and Row.

———. 2005. "Hunter-Gatherer Infancy and Childhood: The !Kung and Others," in *Hunter-Gatherer Childhoods*, eds. Barry S. Hewlett and Michael Lamb, 19–64. New Brunswick, NJ: Transaction Publishers.

Koyama, Tadashi. 2011. Child Development Through Early Symbolic Play. Paper presented at the First Conference on Replacement of Neanderthals by Modern Humans: Testing Evolutionary Models of Learning, Kobe, Japan, February 16.

Lancaster, Jane B., and Chet Lancaster. 1983. "Parental Investment: The Hominid Adaptation," In *How Humans Adapt: A Biocultural Odyssey*, ed. D. Ortner, 33–65. Washington DC: Smithsonian Institute Press.

Lancaster, Jane B., and Barbara J. King. 1985. "An Evolutionary Perspective on Menopause," in *In Her Prime: A New View of Middle Aged Women*, eds. J. Brown and V. Kerns, 7–15 South Hadley MA: Bergin and Garvey.

le Bomin, Sylvie. 2010. The Pygmies of Gabon and their Neighbors: Musical Systematics, Categorization and Phylogeny. Paper given at the International Conference on Congo Basin Hunter-Gatherers, Montpellier, France, September 22–24.

Leclerc, Christian. 2010. Social Evolution and Structural Continuity: The Case of Baka Pygmies with Agriculture. Paper given at the International Conference on Congo Basin Hunter-Gatherers, Montpellier, France, September 22–24.

LeVine, Robert A. 1977. "Child Rearing as Cultural Adaptation," in *Culture and Infancy*, eds. P. Herbert Leiderman, Steve Tulkin, and Anna Rosenfeld, 15–27 New York: Academic.

———. 1988. "Human Parental Care : Universal Goals, Cultural Strategies, Individual Behavior," in *New Directions for Child Development*, 1988, 3–12.

LeVine, Robert, Suzanne Dixon, Sarah Levine, Amy Richman, P. Herbert Leiderman, Constance H. Keefer and T. Berry Brazelton. 1996. Childcare and Culture: Lessons from Africa. Cambridge, UK: Cambridge University Press.

Lewis, Jerome. 2008. Ekila: Blood, Bodies and Egalitarian Societies. *Journal of the Royal Anthropological Institute* 14: 297–315.

———. 2010. Why do the BaYaka Singo so Much? Polyphony and Egalitarianism. Paper given at the International Conference on Congo Basin Hunter-Gatherers, Montpellier, France, September 22–24.

Lock, Margaret, Patricia Kaufert, and Penny Gilbert. 1988. Cultural Construction of the Menopausal Syndrome: The Japanese Case. *Maturitas* 10(4): 317–332.

Lupo, Karen. 2010. Modeling Interrelations of First Forager and Farmers in the Congo Basin. Paper given at the International Conference on Congo Basin Hunter-Gatherers, Montpellier, France, September 22–24.

Markstrom, Carol A. 2008. *Empowerment of North American Indian Girls: Ritual Expressions*. Lincoln: University of Nebraska Press.

Marlowe, Frank. 2000. The Patriarch Hypothesis: An Alternative Explanation of Menopause. *Human Nature* 11(1): 27–42.

Matsuura, Naoki. 2010. Reconsidering Pygmy-Farmer Interethnic Relationships: An "Equal" Relationship between the Babongo Pygmies and the Massango Farmers in Southern Gabon. Paper given at the International Conference on Congo Basin Hunter-Gatherers, Montpellier, France, September 22–24.

Meehan, Courtney. 2005. The Effects of Residential Locality on Parental and Alloparental Care among the Aka Foragers of the Central African Republic. *Human Nature: an interdisciplinary biosocial perspective* 16(1): 58–80

———. 2008. Allomaternal Investment and Relational Uncertainty among Ngandu Farmers of the Central African Republic. *Human Nature* 19: 211–26.

Mercader, Julio. 2002. Forest People: The Role of African Rainforests in Human Evolution and Dispersal. *Evolutionary Anthropology* 11: 117–24.

———. 2003. "Introduction: The Paleolithic Settlement of Rain Forests," in *Under the Canopy: The Archaeology of Tropical Rain Forests*, 1–31. New Brunswick NJ: Rutgers University Press.

Moïse, Robert. 2010. "*Naturvolk* or Entrepreneurs? Toward a History of Political Entrepreneurship among Pygmy Peoples in Equatorial Africa." Unpublished manuscript.

Nardi, Bonnie A. 1985. "Infant Feeding and Women's Work in Western Samoa: A Hypothesis, Some Evidence and Suggestions for Future Research," in *Infant care and Feeding in the South Pacific*, ed. Lorna Marshall, 293–306. New York: Gordon and Breach.

Ndanga, Alfred Jean-Paul. 2010. Central African Forest Paleometallurgy Techniques and Forager-Farmer Interactions. Paper given at the International Conference on Congo Basin Hunter-Gatherers, Montpellier, France, September 22–24.

Noss, Andrew, and Barry S. Hewlett. 2001. The Contexts of Female Hunting in Central Africa. *American Anthropologist* 103: 1024–40.

Ohenjo, Nyang'ori, Ruth Willis, Dorothy Jackson, Clive Nettleson, Kenneth Good, and Benan Mugarura. 2006. Health of Indigenous People in Africa: Indigenous Health 3. *The Lancet* 367: 1937–1946

Oishi, Takanori. 2010. Cash Crop Cultivation and Hunter-Gatherer Society and Their Relationships with Farmers: A Case Study of the Baka Pygmies and the Bakwele of South East Cameroon. Paper given at the International Conference on Congo Basin Hunter-Gatherers, Montpellier, France, September 22–24.

O'Neil, Dennis. 2009. Pattern of Subsistence: Horticulture. Palomar College, August 4. http://anthro.palomar.edu/subsistence/sub_4.htm (accessed March 2010).

O'Toole, Thomas. 1986. *The Central African Republic: The Continent's Hidden Heart.* Boulder CO: Westview Press.

Pakenham, Thomas. 1991. *The Scramble for Africa: The White Man's Conquest of the Dark Continent from 1876 to 1912.* New York: Random House.

Parke, Thomas H. 1891. *My Personal Experiences in Equatorial Africa as the Medical Officer of the Emin Pasha Relief Expedition.* London: Sampson Low, Marston and Co.

Parkes, Colin Murray. 1972. *Bereavement: Studies of Grief in Adult Life.* London: Tavinstock.

Patin, E., G. Laval, L. B. Barreiro, A. Salas, O. Semino, S. Santachiara-Benerecetti, K. K. Kidd, J. R. Kidd, L. van der Veen, J-M. Hombert, A. Gessain, A. Froment, S. Bahuchet, E. Heyer, and L. Quintana-Murci. 2009. Inferring the Demographic History of African Farmers and Pygmy Hunter-Gatherers Using a Multilocus Resequencing Data Set. *PLoS Genetics* 5: e1000448; doi:10.1371/journal.pgen.1000448. http://www.plosgenetics.org/article/info:doi/10.1371/journal.pgen.1000448 (accessed December 2011).

Peccei, Jocelyn S. 2001a. A Critique of the Grandmother Hypotheses: Old and New. *American Journal of Human Biology* 13(4): 434–52.

———. 2001b. Menopause: Adaptation or Epiphenomenon? *Evolutionary Anthropology* 10: 43–57.

Quinlan, Robert J., and Marsha B. Quinlan. 2007. "Parenting and Cultures of Risk: A Comparative Analysis of Infidelity, Aggression, and Witchcraft." *American Anthropologist* 109(1): 164–79.

Quintana-Murci, L., H. Quach, C. Harmant, F. Luca, B. Massonnet, E. Patin, L. Sica, P. Mouguiama-Daouda, D. Comas, S. Tzur, O. Balanovsky, K. K. Kidd, J. R. Kidd, L. van der Veen, J-M. Hombert, A. Gessain, P. Verdu, A. Froment, S. Bahuchet, E. Heyer, J. Dausset, A. Salas, and D. M. Behar. 2008. Maternal Traces of Deep Common Ancestry and Asymmetric Gene Flow Between Pygmy Hunter-Gatherers and Bantu-Speaking Farmers. *Proceedings of the National Academy of Sciences* 105: 1596–1601.

Richerson, Peter J., and Robert Boyd. 2005. *Not by Genes Alone: How Culture Transformed Human Evolution.* Chicago: University of Chicago Press.

Robillard, Marine. 2010. NGO Involvement in Cameroon Southeastern Forests Forest Conservation and Forest Population Advocacy. Paper given at the International Conference on Congo Basin Hunter-Gatherers, Montpellier, France, September 22–24.

Rupp, Stephanie. 2003. Interethnic Relations in Southeastern Cameroon: Challenging the "Hunter-Gatherer"–"Farmer" Dichotomy. *African Study Monographs* Suppl. 28: 37–56.

———. 2011. *Forests of Belonging Identities, Ethnicities and Stereotypes in the Congo River Basin.* Seattle: University of Washington Press.

Sato, Hiroaki, Kyohei Kawamura, Koji Hayashi, Hiroyuki Inai, and Taro Yamauchi. 2010. Observations of the Baka Hunter-Gatherers in Two Controlled Foraging

Trips in the Tropical Rainforest of Southern Cameroun. Paper given at the International Conference on Congo Basin Hunter-Gatherers, Montpellier, France, September 22–24.

Scheper-Hughes, Nancy. 1989. Lifeboat Ethics: Mother Love and Child Death in Northeast Brazil. *Natural History* 98(10): 8–16.

Schweinfurth, Georg. 1874. *The Heart of Africa: Three years' travel and adventures in the unexplored regions of Central Africa from 1868–1871*, Trans. Ellen E. Frewer. New York: Harper and Brothers.

Sear, Rebecca and Ian A. McGregor. 2003. The Effects of Kin on Female Infertility in Rural Gambia. *Evolution and Human Behavior* 24: 25–42.

Shannon, Donald. 1996. *Early Infant Care among the Aka*. MA thesis, Washington State University, Pullman.

Silberschmidt, Margrethe. 1999. *Women Forget That Men Are Their Masters: Gender Antagonism and Socio-economic Change in Kisii District, Kenya.* Stockholm: Elanders Gotab.

Simiti, Bernard. 2010. Organizing NGOs to Assist Aka Pygmies of the Central African Republic: A Case Study of Cooperazione Internationale (COOPI). Paper given at the International Conference on Congo Basin Hunter-Gatherers, Montpellier, France, September 22–24.

Soengas, Beatriz. 2010. Socioeconomic Changes and Evolution of Representations Related to the Practice of Agriculture by the Bakoya Pygmies in Gabon. Paper given at the International Conference on Congo Basin Hunter-Gatherers, Montpellier, France, September 22–24.

Spradley, James P., and David M. McCurdy. 1975. *Anthropology: The Cultural Perspective*. Long Grove IL: Waveland Press.

Stone, Linda, and Caroline James. 2009. "Dowry, Bride Burning and Female Power in India," in *Gender in Cross-Cultural Perspective*, 5th ed, eds. Caroline B. Bretell and Carolyn F. Sargent, 310320– Cranbury NJ: Pearson Education, Inc.

Super, Charles M., and Sarah A. Harkness. 1982. "The Infant's Niche in Rural Kenya and Metropolitan America," in *Cross-Cultural Research at Issue*, ed. L. L. Adler, 247–55. New York: Academic Press.

Takeuchi, Kiyoshi. 1998. Gorillas and Savages: An Ambivalent Relationship between Aka Foragers and Neighboring Farmers. Paper presented at the Eighth International Conference on Hunter-Gatherers Societies, Osaka, Japan.

———. 2001. "He has Become a Gorilla: The Ambivalent Symbiosis between Aka Hunter-Gatherers and Neighboring Farmers," in *The World Where Peoples and Forest Coexist*, eds. M. Ichikawa and H. Sato, 223–53. Kyoto: Kyoto University Press.

———. 2010. Transitions of Social Relationships between Aka Foragers and Neighboring Farmers in Northeastern Region of the Republic of Congo for the Past Twenty Years. Paper given at the International Conference on Congo Basin Hunter-Gatherers, Montpellier, France, September 22–24.

Taylor, Nick. 2010. The Origins of Hunter-Gathering in the Congo Basin: An Archaeological Perspective. Paper given at the International Conference on Congo Basin Hunter-Gatherers, Montpellier, France, September 22–24.

Tegomo, Olivier Njounan. 2010. Mapping of Baka Pygmy Resource Use: Zones Inside and Around Boumba-Bek National Park. Paper given at the International Conference on Congo Basin Hunter-Gatherers, Montpellier, France, September 22–24.

Tomasello, Michael. 1999. *The Cultural Origins of Human Cognition.* Cambridge MA: Harvard University Press.

Trevathan, Wendy, Euclid O. Smith, and James J. McKenna. 1999. *Evolutionary Medicine.* Oxford University Press.

Trivers, Robert L. 1974. Parent-Offspring Conflict. *American Zoology* 14(1): 249–64.

Tronick, Edward Z., Gilda Morelli, and Steve Winn. 1987. Multiple Caregiving of the Efe (Pygmy) Infants. *American Anthropologist* 89(1): 96–106.

Turnbull, Colin M. 1962. *The Forest People.* New York: Simon & Schuster. Quinlan, Robert and Quinlan, Marsha. 2007. Parenting and Cultures of Risk: A Comparative Analysis of Infidelity, Aggression & Witchcraft. *American Anthropologist* 109: 164–179.

U.S. Department of State. 2010. Background Note: Central African Republic, December 28. http://africanhistory.about.com/gi/o.htm?zi=1/XJ&zTi=1&sdn= africanhistory&cdn=education&tm=78&f=00&tt=14&bt=1&bts=1&zu=http% 3A//www.state.gov/r/pa/ei/bgn/4007.htm (accessed January 20, 2011).

Van Donk, Mirjam. 2006. "Positive" Urban Futures in sub-Saharan Africa: HIV/AIDS and the Need for ABC (A Broader Conceptualization). *Environment and Urbanization* 2006 18: 155.

Vansina, Jan. 1990. *Paths in the Rainforests.* Madison, Wisconsin: The University of Wisconsin Press.

Verdu, Paul. 2010. Anthropological Genetics of Central African populations Origins and Genetic Diversity of the "Pygmies." Paper given at the International Conference on Congo Basin Hunter-Gatherers, Montpellier, France, September 22–24.

Verdu, Paul., A. E. Austerlitz, S. Bahuchet, A. Froment, M. Georges, A. Gessain, J-M. Hombert, E.Heyer, S. le Bomin, L. Quintana-Murci, S. Théry, L. van der Veen, and R. Vitalis. 2009. Origins and Genetic Diversity of Pygmy Hunter-Gatherers from Western Central Africa. *Current Biology* 19: 1–7.

Walker, Phil L., and Barry S. Hewlett. 1990. Dental Health, Diet and Social Status among Central African Foragers and Farmers. *American Anthropologist* 91: 270–76.

Wiessner, Pauline W. 1977. (1987). "Socialization and Parenthood in Sibling Care Societies," in *Parenting Across the Lifespan,* eds. J. B. Lancaster, J. Altman, A. S. Rossi, and L. R. Sherrod, 237–70. New York: Aldine.

Woodburn, James. 1982. Egalitarian Societies. *Man* (New Series) 17(3): 431–51.

Wright, Robert. 1994. *The Moral Animal: Evolutionary Psychology and Everyday Life.* New York: Pantheon.

Yasuoka, H. 2006. Long-Term Foraging Expeditions (*Molongo*) among the Baka Hunter-Gatherers in the Northwestern Congo Basin, with Special Reference to the "Wild Yam Question." *Human Ecology* 34: 275–96.

# INDEX

Page numbers followed by an italicized *f* indicate a figure.

CPSIA information can be obtained at www.ICGtesting.com
Printed in the USA
BVOW03s1037080416

443305BV00006B/6/P

9 780199 764235